# TWENTY CENTURIES
OF
# CATHOLIC CHURCH MUSIC

# TWENTY CENTURIES
OF
# CATHOLIC CHURCH MUSIC

By

ERWIN ESSER NEMMERS, MUS.M., A.M., LL.B.
FORMERLY AUSTIN, LEHMAN AND UNIVERSITY FELLOW, HARVARD UNIVERSITY
ASSISTANT PROFESSOR, MARQUETTE UNIVERSITY

GREENWOOD PRESS, PUBLISHERS
WESTPORT, CONNECTICUT

**Library of Congress Cataloging in Publication Data**

Nemmers, Erwin Esser, 1916-
Twenty centuries of Catholic church music.

Reprint of the ed. published by Bruce Pub. Co., Milwaukee.
"Bibliography of bibliographies": p.
Includes index.
1. Church music--Catholic Church--History and criticism. I. Title.
ML3002.N35 1978 783'.026'209 78-17248
ISBN 0-313-20542-6

Nihil Obstat: RAY C. ZEYEN, B.Mus., Censor Deputatus
Imprimatur: ✠ MOYSES E. KILEY, Archiepiscopus Milwaukiensis
Die 20 Iulii, 1948



Reprinted with the permission of Macmillan Publishing Company, Inc.

Reprinted in 1978 by Greenwood Press, Inc.
51 Riverside Avenue, Westport, CT. 06880

Printed in the United States of America

10 9 8 7 6 5 4 3 2 1

Inscribed to the American Line of Descent
of the Nemmers Family,
Contributors to the Cause of
Catholic Church Music,
John Nicholas Nemmers
1783–1870
Michael Nemmers
1822–1883
Michael Ludwig Nemmers
1855–1929
Erwin Plein Nemmers
1879–1944

## *FOREWORD*

To WRITE the history of twenty centuries of Catholic church music, to condense the same within the limits of a single small volume, and to make its contents understandable even to readers who have no particular knowledge of music, would appear to be an almost impossible task to many a musicologist.

The distinguished author of the present volume, however, has succeeded quite well in his undertaking. Thus he deserves credit, first, because of his courage in taking up the challenge; secondly, because of his concise presentation of the development of the various phases and forms of church music (both vocal and instrumental) through the centuries; finally, because of his plain style, devoid of too many technical terms and, therefore, intelligible to any reader with only a college education.

Professional critics, who are apt to scrutinize these pages with the aid of Diogenes' lantern, may find little gaps here and there. They will agree, however, that the author has come through his difficult test with honors.

REV. CARLO ROSSINI
*Master in Gregorian Chant*
*The Pontifical Institute of Sacred Music*

## *PREFACE*

IN A work such as this, the preface is particularly important. It serves to define what is included and what is excluded; it deals with matters of proportion, motives, and objectives.

This volume is principally directed to the educated reader – no particular knowledge of music is necessary to understand it. For this reason, footnotes have been added to give an explanation of the musical terms where that is necessary for the understanding of the text. These definitions are cumulated in Appendix I for the convenience of the reader. Partly because of the bibliographies at the end of each chapter, the book will serve very usefully as a text on college or seminary level. The volume is not primarily a history of Catholic church music; rather, its historical contents are the vehicle for the development of principles – the endeavor is one in synthesis. The principles of liturgical music are now so muddled and the debate about them is so acrimonious that it is necessary for a true study to lean heavily on history. And yet, because the few works on the history of Catholic church music do not have the benefit of the great researches of recent decades and are out of print, this volume is also in the position of being made to serve as a history.

In the field of history (aside from monographs) there are only three works in English and six in German that are of service: Karl Weinmann's *History of Church Music* (Ratisbon: Pustet, 1910) is an anonymous English translation from the German original of 1906. His study is short – in his preface he describes it as ". . . but a compendious exposition, showing the broad lines of development of Church Music.

. . ." The second work is Edward Dickinson's *Music in the History of the Western Church* (New York: Scribner, 1903). Aside from the fact that Dickinson was a Protestant and a good section of the work is devoted to Protestant church music, he had only a very imperfect acquaintance with the liturgy. The third book in English is frequently mentioned in Catholic books on the liturgy: Winfred Douglas, *Church Music in History and Practice,* The Hale Lectures, Northwestern University, 1935 (New York: Scribner, 1937). Although Douglas also was a Protestant, he has a better knowledge of the liturgy than Dickinson but the whole volume is directed to a discussion of the relationship of the history of church music to present *Anglican* ideals. The works of Rene Aigrain; *Religious Music* (New York: Fischer, 1931) and R. R. Terry, *Music of the Roman Rite* (London: Burns, Oates and Washburne, 1931) are rather monographs.

Some readers may wonder that we have not mentioned Gustave Reese, *Music in the Middle Ages* (New York: Norton, 1940). That work is detailed, to be sure, but it is confined almost entirely to a treatment of part of our subject and from the standpoint of the art of music without reference to liturgical ideals. It is strange but nevertheless a fact that Reese does not so much as mention one of the books (except that of Ursprung) which are the only histories of Catholic church music. And this despite a bibliography of 38 pages in fine print (pp. 425–463). Perhaps he would contend that these works want in scholarship.

The six books in German are: Raymond Schlecht's *Geschichte der Geistlichen Musik* (Regensburg: Pustet, 1861); Johannes Katschthaler's *Geschichte der Kirchenmusik* (Salzburg: M. Mittenmuller, 1893); Emil Nikel's *Geschichte der Katholischen Kirchenmusik* (Breslau: F. Goerlich, 1908); Otto Ursprung's "Die Katholische Kirchenmusik," in Bücken's *Handbuch der Musikwissenschaft* (Potsdam: Akademische Verlagsgesellschaft Athenaion, 1931); Andreas

Weissenbach's *Sacra Musica* (Vienna: Klosterneuburg Abbey, 1939); and Karl G. Fellerer's *Geschichte der Katholischen Kirchenmusik* (Dusseldorf: Schwann, 1939). Katschthaler's work is available in Italian under the title *Storia della Musica Sacra.*

The reader will note that two adjectives of the title of the present work are important. Until 1500 there was only *Catholic* church music in Western civilization. The adjective "church," however, separates the materials treated in this volume from a little known but quite definite area which might be called "Catholic secular music." That term does not have much significance in the world today – but of times past it is correct to say that besides Catholic music for the church there was a considerable body of music, definitely Catholic in tone, growing out of the culture of the people. For want of a better term we usually speak of it as "folk music." Religion-outside-the-church-walls is only one of its many subjects; but the Catholic philosophy of life is parcel of its every treatment – whether it sings of love or war, nature or play.

There is considerable dispute, especially in matters of Gregorian chant, and an effort has been made to explain the different positions that can be taken. The subject of American Catholic church music (Chapter VI) is virgin territory, and I am fully aware that years to come will make additions to the bibliography. This chapter was exposed to comment and first printed in *The Catholic Choirmaster,* Vol. XXXII, Nos. 1, 2, and 3, March, June, and September, 1946, and translated into Spanish and printed in the *Schola Cantorum,* Vol. VIII (1946) of Mexico.

In a sense, the title of this book might more correctly be *Nineteen Centuries, etc.,* since by deliberate decision I have avoided any discussion of contemporary church music composers, being content to list them.

I have assumed no greater knowledge of the liturgy on the part of the reader than the "average" Catholic has. And since only a limited knowledge of music – and more particularly, of church music – is assumed, the bibliographies at the end of each chapter will serve as an introduction to the literature. The bibliographies are not complete but selective, and therefore I have added a bibliography of bibliographies as Appendix II. I am not aware that a similar list is available elsewhere in English, and therefore I have added a compilation of the leading Catholic church music periodicals in the several languages as Appendix III. This list does not include periodicals devoted generally to the liturgical arts (of which music is only one), nor does it include general music periodicals which have sections devoted to church music. As Appendix IV, I have added an English translation of the *Motu Proprio* of Pope Pius X, the most important document on church music.

The acknowledgments I must make cannot include all who have contributed to this work. First of all, I am immeasurably indebted to the more than fifty libraries and their custodians, scattered from Massachusetts to California, from Texas to Wisconsin, who furnished their assistance. In a backhanded sort of way, I must pay my respects to the army air corps which unwittingly, perhaps, also contributed by transporting me around the country for three years. For their aid in criticizing the manuscript my thanks go to two members of the faculty of Marquette University, Rev. Cyril P. Donohue, S.J., and Rev. Charles T. Corcoran, S.J., and to Mr. J. V. Higginson. A greater debt is due, however, to one whose counsel and instruction have aided me through the years, the Rev. L. A. Dobbelsteen, O.Praem., formerly Dean of Music, St. Norbert's College, and a friend to three generations of the Nemmers family. If Palestrina is recorded as *Princeps Musicae,* then certainly Father Dobbelsteen will be labeled in history as *Princeps Musicae Sacrae Americanae.* But the greatest gratitude I owe to two scholars whose learning was deeper than mine shall ever be, my grandfather, Michael

Ludwig Nemmers, and my father, Erwin Plein Nemmers. Much, perhaps most, of what is here set down was spilled by them to me, amid the clouds from their pipefuls.

I am indebted to W. W. Norton, Desclee & Cie, and The Catholic Education Press for permission to use certain copyrighted materials.

## CONTENTS

## *LIST OF ILLUSTRATIONS*



## *LIST OF TABLES*

# CHAPTER I

## *EARLY CHURCH MUSIC – TO* A.D. *400*

### GREEK AND OTHER INFLUENCES

MUCH investigation has been done by musicologists in attempting to reconstruct the music of the early Church. However, the earliest manuscripts of any length in the field of church music are the ninth-century codices of St. Gall Library, Switzerland, 359, Roman Vallicellian Library, B 50; and National Library, Paris, Latin 909.[1] For a knowledge of church music prior to that time, we are reduced to an examination of writers who treat of music, to some fragments of music, and to studies of the liturgy itself. This necessarily involves a certain amount of speculation and inference. In that process it is necessary to have some knowledge (of the same type, to be sure) of the antecedents of church music: the Greek and Roman music and Hebrew music, in particular.

Our knowledge of Greek music comes primarily from writings *about* music, as we have stated, and not from manuscripts of music. There were two systems in Greek music: the Greater Perfect System, consisting of a two octave scale, and the Lesser Perfect System, consisting of eleven notes. The basis of both systems was a tetrachord.[2] Nothing like the

[1] There are also the eighth-century codices of Monza and of Zurich-Rheinau 33, which give the text of the chant but no notes. The texts, however, are apparently grouped in some order with regard to modes. In addition there are partial manuscripts of the eighth century which contain music. The whole question of Gregorian chant manuscripts is considered in greater detail in Chapter II.

[2] The tetrachord is a series of four steps within the interval of a fourth. Within the tetrachord it is possible to place a half tone between steps 1–2, 2–3, and 3–4 (the other intervals being whole tones) yielding respectively the Dorian, Phrygian, and Lydian tetrachords.

modern notation or the medieval system of neums for notation was used by the Greeks. Rather, an alphabetical system was employed. By placing the letters of the alphabet above or below the syllables of the text and assigning to each letter a different tone, the Greeks had a system of intervals between notes which was accurate. During the early Christian centuries, the Greek alphabetical notation was used, as is seen in the third-century *Oxyrhynchos* hymn to be mentioned later. The Greeks employed the same diatonic system of intervals used in music today (consisting of whole-tone and half-tone intervals), but they also employed other intervals. They developed seven different modes: Dorian, Phrygian, Lydian, Hypodorian, Hypophrygian, Hypolydian, and Mixolydian. Each mode was determined by the location of the half tones and whole tones in the series of eight steps constituting the octave.[3] Each mode was considered as having a different emotional coloring. The Greek music was monodic[4] except

[3] In modern music, the location of the half tone between the third and fourth steps and again between the seventh and eighth steps (the other steps being whole tones) determines the major mode. Similarly, the location of the half tone between the second and third steps and again between the fifth and sixth steps (the other steps being whole tones) determines the minor modes.

The Dorian mode had the half tones between steps 1–2 and 5–6; the Phrygian mode – 2–3 and 6–7; the Lydian mode – 3–4 and 7–8; the Hypodorian mode – 2–3 and 5–6; the Hypophrygian mode – 3–4 and 6–7; the Hypolydian mode – 4–5 and 7–8; the Mixolydian mode – 1–2 and 4–5.

Thus the modern major is the counterpart of the Lydian mode of the Greeks, and the modern minor mode of the Greek Hypodorian.

While the ecclesiastical modes to be discussed in the next chapter have the same names as the Greek modes and some relationship to the Greek modes, they do not have the same name for the same mode (nor is the mode itself the same, being dependent for determination on factors in addition to the location of the half steps).

The reason that the Greeks did not use more than the above seven modes is that they did not think in terms of the whole-tone and half-tone structure but rather in terms of combining *two* tetrachords with an added step to complete the octave in three different ways depending on the position of the added step. See Gustave Reese: *Music in Middle Ages* (New York: Norton, 1940), p. 28.

[4] Monody distinguishes music as "one voiced," i.e., without an accompaniment or harmony of other voices. The term *chant* is used in general to describe monody, it does not refer to the manner of performance. The term

for a type of singing in octaves. In fact, all music continues as monodic down to the ninth century.

Such was the technical apparatus of the Greeks, but we are more interested in the function of their music. Music was an integral part of the dance and of poetry. Music as such did not exist. That in itself is sufficient reason why musical notation was not developed. This is further borne out by the fact that the system of notation used in the Middle Ages (called neums) derives from the symbols used to express poetic meter (the dactyl, spondee, iambus, trochee, etc.) and from the accent marks of the Greek language. This development is shown in Plate IX of Chapter II (page 58).

That Greek music was bound to influence early Christian music is clear from the fact that for the first three centuries the language of the Church was Greek. But actual evidence for the influence is thin. The scale and modes were taken from the Greeks — but this may be more likely a process of later Christians reading Greek influence into the Christian music. For example, Boethius' (*c.* 480–524) *De Institutione Musicae* was for the Christian mind, in the several centuries after him, a prime source for knowlege of Greek civilization. As is indicated in the next chapter, the confusion of names of the Church modes with the same names of *different* Greek modes comes partly through misreadings of Boethius' statements about Greek music.

The music of Rome was the music of Greece and under Rome, Greek music retrogressed. It can be stated as simply as that. This, however, is not to pass over the important influence of the Latin language and literature on Gregorian music — that will be considered later.

The bond between Greek music and the beginnings of

---

*Plain* or *Gregorian* added to "chant" is, however, not redundant since it further denotes the particular rhythm that such music has, namely, *free* rhythm, i.e., there are no regularly recurring "beats," or "bars" as in modern music.

church music lies in the fact that the liturgy of the Church is poetical. The union of music and poetry in Greece was taken over by the Church as an idiom suited to divine service. And just as there was no fixity of music throughout Greek lands (such as the fixity we find in the modern major and minor modes and the music of the eighteenth and nineteenth centuries) so the music of the early Church varied from city to city. This was the more inevitable because the liturgy itself varied from city to city.

The Hebrew influence on early church music is at least as great as the Greek influence. The psalmody of the Church comes chiefly from the temple and synagogue. The temple music centered around the Jewish *Credo,* the *Shema* (Hear, O Israel), with the singing of the psalm for the day. The Jews employed an instrument of the organ family, the magraphah, and trumpets in the temple. One important fact is that the singing was congregational. Further, the first verse of the psalm was repeated after each succeeding verse. Here are the seeds of the Christian form of the antiphon and responsory to be discussed later. The *Mishnah* or book of tradition which the Rabbi Jehuda compiled in the second century describes the antiphonal use of *Hallelujah* in the singing of the Hallel psalms. Recent research[5] has uncovered more information about the synagogue and its liturgy. There we find the singing of Scriptural readings, of the *Shema,* of prayers which included the *Kedushah* or Jewish precursor of the *Sanctus,* of the psalms for each day of the week and special psalms for certain feasts. A work by the Rabbi Akiba of the first century describes the use of cheironomy – the use of the hand for leading the singing and for showing the meaning of the text. This directly carried over in church music to the Gregorian chant and from there to modern music.

[5] See particularly Oesterly, W. O. E., *The Jewish Background of the Christian Liturgy* (London: Oxford University Press, 1925); Idelsohn, A. Z., *Jewish Music* (New York: Holt, 1929); Saminsky, Lazare, *Music of the Ghetto and the Bible* (New York: Bloch, 1934).

There are recent researches arguing that the chanting employed by the Georgian, Persian, Babylonian, and Yemenite Jews of the twentieth century is an essential tradition from ancient times remaining uncontaminated through the centuries. Strong evidence exists for the argument: it can be shown that these groups have been quite isolated since as early as the sixth century. The liturgical music of the separated groups still is strongly similar. But the fact remains that except for some fragments from the twelfth century, the earliest extant manuscripts of Jewish music date from the sixteenth century.

However, we can conclude that Jewish sources made available to Christianity many principles of music: the monodic system of chanting with cadences, the congregational song with the use of repetition in the manner of the antiphon and responsory, the relationship of music to the rhetoric of the text (as shown by cheironomy, and involving a "free" — in the sense of nonmensural — rhythm) and elaborate melodies on a single vowel (the principle involved in the Christian *Alleluia*). While certain Christian chants bear a remarkable similarity to certain Jewish chants, a more important contribution was the fact that the Jews kept liturgical music separate from secular music and developed a rhetorical style for liturgical music.

There are some other influences besides the Greek and Jewish that are important for early church music, particularly for the Eastern Church, from which music descended to the Western Church. Chief of these are the Egyptian music and the Babylonian influences on the Jewish music and perhaps directly on the Christian music.

## DOCUMENTARY TESTIMONY

The New Testament vouches that music was employed in the Church from the very beginning. We also know that the position was immediately taken that music in the Church must be subordinate to the purposes of the liturgy. Perhaps it would be better said to be co-ordinate with the liturgy, and not an end in itself. Since the liturgy itself was in a state of flux, church music could hardly be otherwise. The dance had no place in church music but poetry did. Likewise the introduction of instruments into the church was resisted. The voice being wedded to words and instruments lacking this unity, instruments would more easily tend to become ends in themselves. Further, they carried an association from pagan life.[6] Such associations have always been an important factor to the Church in the matter of music. The instruments then in use were mainly harps and flutes; their association with the dance was obvious.

The oldest manuscript extant of Catholic church music is a hymn in a third-century manuscript found at Oxyrhynchos[7] in Egypt. The musical notation is alphabetical and Greek, the music structure is Greek, and the text is Greek, ending with a reference to the Father, Son, and Holy Ghost. Anthropologists may be able to reconstruct the entire animal from a jawbone but musicians would not venture such reconstruction of the music of the early centuries of the Church on the basis of a single hymn. This does not mean we will pass over the writings on church music — though they are not always clear and are certainly not analytical. Greek music in the secular world did not, of course, cease with the advent of Christianity but continued side by side with church music for at least four centuries. The secular authors of the Christian era who wrote on music are primarily known as philosophers, e.g., the neo-Platonists, Plotinus (205–270), Porphyry (233–

[6] The suitability of the organ for church music arises from several reasons. First, the organ was of later origin and had no extraecclesiastical associations. Second, the organ is musically the instrument most resembling the human voice with its sustained tone and peculiar coloring. Theoretically, perhaps, a choir of woodwinds could serve as an imitation of an organ for church music purposes.

[7] Grengelt, B. P., and Hunt, A., *The Oxyrhynchos Papyri Edited and Translated* (London: Egypt Exploration Society, 1922).

304), and Proclus (412–485), all centered around Alexandria; Iamblichos (d.*c.* 330), the neo-Pythagorean; the Syrian, Nichomachos (second century A.D.); and the Jew, Philo of Alexandria (*c.* 20 B.C.–*c.* A.D. 45). Philo in his *On the Contemplative Life* describes the Therapeutae, early Christian ascetics, as singing in antiphonal fashion. Antiphony is of two kinds: (*a*) between two or more choral groups, and (*b*) between a soloist and a chorus. The former is usually given the name of antiphon while the latter is called responsory. Philo describes the former type. Pliny the Younger also testifies to the use of two choral groups by the Christians in the year 115. Philo tells us another significant fact, namely that the members of the Therapeutae composed their own music.

The writings of the early Christian fathers say something of the relation of music to the liturgy but do not speak in analytical terms. St. Justin (*c.* 100–*c.* 165) describes the early Mass as comprised of readings from the Old and New Testaments, followed by a sermon, the offering of bread and wine, the prayer of the faithful, the kiss of peace, the consecration, and finally Communion. While the outline of the Mass is there represented, it appears that singing was more usually employed in the Office. Pliny the Younger observed the singing of the Office, that is of psalms and canticles. The psalmody down to that time probably represented the whole of church music.

Clement of Alexandria (*c.* 150–*c.* 220) admits the lyra and kithara to church music because King David used them. But he excludes other instruments for reasons already given. What is thought to be the oldest hymn text, the *Hymn of the Saviour,* is attributed to Clement though it may be of even older date. Origen (*c.* 185–*c.* 250), also at Alexandria, notes that each branch of the early Church sings in its own tongue. When we come to Eusebius (*c.* 260–*c.* 340), bishop of Caesarea in Palestine, we find that he clearly states the voice is preferable to instruments in the church. He refers to the widespread practice of singing psalms and hymns. St. Athanasius (*c.* 298–373), patriach of Alexandria, objects to overelaborate music for the psalms. St. Basil (*c.* 330–379), bishop of Caesarea, in one of his letters defends the singing of psalms and notes the budding antiphonal singing in both the senses pointed out above.

With St. Jerome (*c.* 340–420) we come to an important point. St. Jerome translated the Bible to give us the standard Vulgate Latin edition. He also counseled Pope Damasus, during whose pontificate from 366 to 384 the Roman liturgy took on more definite organization. While there are extant copies or copies of copies of the music book, *Antiphonarium Gregorianum,* compiled under Pope Gregory I (pontificate: 590–604) that date from several centuries later, it seems well enough established that the music there collected is not the work of any one man.[8] The only likely source would be the Roman *Schola Cantorum,* a musical organization established at Rome during the reign of Pope Sylvester (314–336). It should not be forgotten that until the Edict of Galerius on April 30, 311, and its confirmation by the Edict of Milan two years later, in 313, by Constantine, the Christians had been continuously persecuted. We find the Benedictine monk, Gerbert, in 1774 mentioning[9] that although during Pope Sylvester's time there were several basilicas in Rome they did not have sufficient income to support schools for singers and as a result a *schola cantorum* was established for all the churches in Rome. Under Pope Hilary (pontificate: 461–467), a group of seven singers with the rank of subdeacon was established and they alone were to be called the *Schola Cantorum.* They were responsible for the music wherever the bishop of Rome celebrated. The *Schola* continued without interruption until the fourteenth century. In 595, Pope Gregory I

[8] Perhaps no point in church music is more disputed through the centuries than the relationship of Gregory to the Gregorian chant.

[9] Gerbert, Martin, *De Cantu et Musica Sacra* (St. Blasien, 1774), I, 36.

issued the decree expanding the two schools then existing (the other being the one opened about 580 by the Benedictines who had just removed from Monte Cassino after the destruction of their abbey by the Lombards) and establishing two more of a different type. Until then the *Schola* served several functions: first and most important, it developed degree by degree the system of Gregorian chant; secondly, it served for all papal functions; and thirdly, it trained the perpetuating members. The two schools set up by Gregory were called *Orphanotrophia,* one at the Lateran Church and the other at St. Peter's, and they took over the function of teaching new singers for the various churches of Rome. From the Roman schools music spread throughout the Western Church. Roman music went to England with St. Augustine of Canterbury (?–604) and a continuous tradition was established between England and Rome in music. Pope Agatho (pontificate: 678–681) sent the leader of the *Schola* to establish a school at Wearmouth Abbey in 678. Under Charlemagne's father, the famous *Schola* at Metz was established about 760, and from there a branch went to St. Gall, Switzerland.

But we have been getting ahead of the story by tracing the *Schola.* Shortly before the time of St. Jerome, the Council of Laodicea (343–381) in its thirteenth canon decreed: "Besides the appointed singers who mount the *ambo* and sing from the book, others shall not sing in the church." In the fifty-ninth canon, the Council forbade what it termed *"psalmi idiotici"* which were hymns of non-Biblical origin or hymns not already established and set to music. They amounted to folk song and included even hand clapping and dancing.

St. Jerome strongly approves, as does St. Augustine (354–430), of the use of the *jubilus* (a long-extended melody on one syllable, usually the last vowel of *alleluia*) when he says,[10] "By the term *jubilus* we mean that which neither words nor

[10] Migne, *P.L.,* XXVI, 970.

syllables nor letters nor speech can express or explain as to how much man ought to praise God."

### EASTERN CHURCH INFLUENCE

At this point we leave the Roman liturgy to return a little later with St. Ambrose (*c.* 340–397). The Eastern Church prospered at least as well as the Roman Church in the earlier centuries. In the case of the Eastern Church no manuscripts are available but some important conclusions can be drawn. Jeannin, Gastoué, and Wellesz, leading scholars of the subject, on the basis of elaborate research sufficiently establish the proposition that chants were developed earlier in the Eastern Church. For example, the Syrian chant in modern times differs from the Arabian, which means that although the Syrians adopted the Arabian language and civilization after invasion, they were probably preserving an earlier chant system. Further, the older Gregorian melodies have a definite similarity to the Syrian chant. Much of the thesis rests upon the fact that the development of the early liturgy came from the Eastern Churches. There psalmody[11] was found too rigorous and prosody was introduced. Some of the older hymn texts of the Church still in use come from the Syrian, St. Ephraim (?–373). There is evidence that his purpose in hymn writing was to give the liturgy greater appeal by means of existing popular melodies. This process of trimming existing melodies and fitting them to verses of hymns gives rise to a product called *ris-qole* which is met with later in church music history. An effort was made by Hilary of Poitiers (?–366) to introduce Syrian hymnology to the Western Church but he was unsuccessful. Where he failed, St. Ambrose suc-

[11] We use the term "psalmody" to describe a musical form in which an intonation is made on one tone (or a short melodic figure) and then the psalm recited on another tone and the conclusion is a short melodic figure. The figures at beginning and end follow established routines or formulae; the reciting tone may shift in a long psalm or be broken in the middle by a short figure. This is essentially the musical form used in the Church today for the singing of the Epistle and Gospel in a High Mass, for example.

ceeded. As St. Augustine says:[12] "At this time it was first instituted here after the Eastern Churches that hymns and psalms should be sung, lest the people become faint with sorrow; and the custom was retained from that day to this and is still imitated by different, yea, almost by all the congregations throughout other parts of the world."

But Byzantium made another important contribution, the development of a notation independent of the classical Greek (alphabetical) notation. The notation has two species, one designed for psalmody and the other for hymn singing. The Byzantine notation endeavors to trace graphically the design and development of the melody – but it does not give exact pitch. Here lies the origin possibly of the neum.[13]

Byzantine notation has three periods of development. The first runs up to the tenth century and is as yet undecipherable. The second, from the tenth to the twelfth centuries, can be interpreted by parallelism with the next notation. The third system which runs from the twelfth to the fourteenth centuries, overlapping with the first, includes many new signs which enable a complete notation of the rendition of the music. The reason for the abrupt change in the twelfth century is still unknown. One can speak of a fourth period in which the cheironomic signs were revised. Byzantine chant of this kind still endures in the Eastern Church. The final form is melismatic.[14] The unearthing of Byzantine music has

[12] *Confessions* (book IX, chap. vii). St. Augustine wrote *De Musica* in six books, intending to write a more elaborate work. His treatise, however, deals more with poetry than music, or more correctly we should say it deals with the classical concept of music-poetry. St. Augustine introduced singing into the North African Church.

[13] The term "neum" is from the Greek νεῦμα meaning "sign." It is a generic term used to separate medieval notation from the classical Greek (alphabetical) notation and the modern or mensural notation (the term "mensural" is used to denote music divided into "bars," i.e., following a set rhythmical pattern with arsis and thesis recurring regularly, at the same interval of time).

[14] Melisma is the term applied to an elaborate melody in the chant. Thus the *jubilus* (on the final vowel of the word *alleluia*) of the Gregorian chant is always melismatic.

taken place largely in the twentieth century and now the theory of development of the neums from the Greek metric and accentual signs is being challenged by a theory that the Gregorian neums come from the Byzantine.[15] How far back the origin of the notation runs in the Byzantine chant is as yet unknown though it has now been traced to the ninth century and at this time it was so well developed as to indicate an origin several centuries earlier. The Byzantine chant also developed a system called *echoi* involving tetrachords and the whole called the *Oktoechos* (eight *echoi*).[16] There is a dispute as to whether the *echoi* involve a modal system such as the Greeks had.[17]

Now to return to the Western Church and St. Ambrose, bishop of Milan (*c.* 340–347). We have already mentioned that St. Ambrose introduced much of the music of the Eastern Churches to the Western Church, particularly the hymns. How much of the Ambrosian music can be attributed to St. Ambrose himself is a question. No satisfactory answer is yet possible though the tradition is strong and was early developed that St. Ambrose is to be credited with composition of some chants. We do know that the Ambrosian chant (distinguished from the Gregorian chant) originated about his time, although the earliest manuscripts containing Ambrosian music date from the twelfth century, whereas the

[15] Plate IX of Chapter II, after the monks of Solesmes, shows another avenue of derivation for Gregorian neums, namely, from the Greek accents. The missing links in that development may be the neums of the Byzantine chant although the Byzantine neums themselves seem to have originated as independent, "ecphonetic" notation not related to the accents.

[16] This aspect of Byzantine music appears in a treatise entitled *Hagiopolites* (unavailable in a complete edition) which attributes the development of the *echoi* to St. John of Damascus (*c.* 676–*c.* 770) and in the *Papadike* (one can be found in Fleischer, Oskar, *Neumen-Studien* [Leipzig: Fleischer, 1895–1904] 3 vols., Vol. III, part 3, 18) which are instruction books in Byzantine chant used from the fourteenth century.

[17] Mention should be made of the existence of early chant in the Armenian, Coptic, and Ethiopian churches. Practically all of these chants are not decipherable. The modern chants of these churches cannot be verified for more than the last few centuries.

earliest Gregorian manuscripts date from the ninth century. St. Augustine attributes four hymns to St. Ambrose: *Aeterne Rerum Conditor, Deus Creator Omnium, Jam Surgit Tertia Hora,* and *Veni Redemptor Gentium.*[18] The hymns were intended to be sung by the congregation. They are simple in style, being eight stanzas of four lines with iambic dimeters. St. Ambrose emphasized especially the use of hymns: *"Hymnus specialiter Deo dicitur."* Rome did not adopt hymns until the ninth century but Gaul and Spain followed the lead of St. Ambrose immediately.

The Church was by this time in a crucial position. The persecutions had been alleviated in 313, St. Jerome had translated the Bible into Latin, Greek as the language of the Church was being replaced by Latin, the liturgy was developing rapidly from the East, and the increasing pressure of the heresies made it necessary that codification take place. This was a gradual process and with it the influence of the Eastern Church upon the Western Church began to decline. The supremacy of the Roman liturgy in the Western Church, however, was not easily established. The Ambrosian liturgy of Milan continued, the Celtic liturgy was not replaced by the Roman until the seventh century, the Gallic continued until the time of Charlemagne and even later in some areas, the Mozarabic (Christians-in-Moslem-Spain) was not supplanted until the twelfth century on the whole. The Greek, Syriac, and Byzantine liturgies began to follow a separate course.[19]

18 The *Te Deum* is traditionally credited to St. Ambrose at the time of the baptism of St. Augustine. This has in modern times been doubted and Niceta of Remesiana (*c.* 335–414) credited with authorship. The *Te Deum* was widely used by the sixth century and in the Middle Ages was called *Hymnus Ambrosianus.* The music we have for the *Te Deum* seems to be partly pre-Gregorian and partly Gregorian.

19 We pass over the Russian chant (after the separation of the Greek Orthodox Church, in 1054, there was not much intercourse between the Churches). The earliest manuscripts in Russia date from the eleventh century. The Russian Church took its music mainly from the Byzantine Church. Then

With this brief survey of the liturgical scene we can see that St. Ambrose occupied a strategic position in the history of church music. Besides giving impetus to the use of hymns, he brought antiphonal singing to the foreground and during the pontificate of Celestine I (422–432) the practice was officially adopted for a while in Rome.

### A BRIEF STATEMENT FOR MUSICAL PURPOSES OF THE DEVELOPMENT OF THE PARTS OF THE LITURGY

From the time of Pope Gregory I (pontificate: 590–604) the Roman liturgy was unified; the liturgical book *Sacramentarium Gregorianum* is found side by side with the musical volume *Antiphonarium Gregorianum*. The function of Gregory with regard to both was primarily that of compilation although there was some innovation. It is difficult in this connection to separate history and legend since no copy of the *Antiphonarium* from Gregory's time survives. Music was cut to fit the pattern of the liturgy. The process of adapting the chant then in existence to the codified liturgy can no longer be traced in detail, although much can be done in reestablishing the details of the development of the liturgy. However, the general statement can be made that the Roman chant derives even more from the Eastern Church than the Roman liturgy does. The codification performed by Gregory was not cataclysmic; in Milan the Church retained a separate liturgy and music, in Spain the Roman liturgy and chant did not become general until the twelfth century, and in some parts still has not supplanted the Mozarabic.

At that time singers performed a more essential function in the Church than now. Hence the derivation of certain liturgical ideals of today – the preference that the choir consist of men only because they were in older times more

---

the Russians modified and added to it until a truly Russian chant developed. The Russians devised a system of notation with its beginnings in the eleventh century and in use until the fourteenth century, consisting of two lines of notation which are as yet undecipherable.

directly participants in the liturgy, and similarly the ideal that the choir be vested.

At High Mass there were the celebrant, the lectors, and the singers, giving rise to three books respectively: the sacramentary, the lectionary, and the antiphonary. The priest has since acquired part of the singers' portions of the text of the liturgy so that today the priest recites certain texts whether they are sung by the choir or not. In the eleventh century all the parts of the Mass — prayers, readings, and music — were gathered to form the *Missale Plenarium* from which it is but one step to the Missal of today.

The parts of the Mass that are sung are divided into three groups, musically speaking: (1) the prayers and invocations of the priest, the readings from Scripture, and the responses of the congregation; (2) the *Proprium,* or Proper of the Mass; and (3) the *Ordinarium,* or Ordinary of the Mass. The *Proprium* and the *Ordinarium* are distinguished by the fact that the former varies in text and music from day to day (except in the Requiem Mass), and the latter is constant in text although the music may vary.

The first group, the prayers and invocations of the priest, the Scriptural readings, and the responses of the congregation, have always been simple and sung in a reciting tone with short but routine melodic figures for intermediate and final cadences except for the Preface and *Pater Noster*. Prior to the sixteenth century they were sung more elaborately, particularly on festal days. Such elaborations were known as *Toni* and *Accentus* and survive today in the liturgy of a few of the older orders.

The skeleton of the Mass is the dialogue between the priest and the congregation. All of the dialogue is dignified, but, with the exception of the Preface (including the *Sursum Corda*) and the *Pater Noster,* the melodies are simple. The *Sursum Corda* is found in the Canons of Hippolytus (220–230) and in St. Cyprian's (?–258) *De Oratione*. The music of the *Sursum Corda* probably antedates the fifth century. The Preface was developed very early. The *Leonine Sacramentary* of the middle sixth century contains 267 different kinds of Preface. The Preface is first referred to by Pope Clement I (pontificate: 90–99). From the time of Pope Gregory I, the number of Prefaces was reduced and the literary *cursus* (to be discussed later) had great effects on the music.

The *Pater Noster* in early times followed the *Communio*. Pope Gregory I moved it to its present position after the Consecration. Benedictine research shows the relation of the music of the *Pater Noster* to that of the *Te Deum* and *Gloria* and further shows the Jewish inheritance involved in the music of all three. The *ekphonesis*[20] introducing both the *Sursum Corda* and the *Pater Noster* derives from the Greek Church.

## THE PROPRIUM

The second group, the *Proprium*, has a more complicated history. From the end of the Middle Ages, the *Proprium* of the Mass has been divided into the *Proprium de Tempore* and the *Proprium de Sanctis*, the former including the *Proprium* for Sundays, ember days, ferial days in Lent and certain vigils and the latter for the saints' days. The *Proprium* is today made up of the *Introitus, Graduale, Alleluia, Tractus, Sequentia, Offertorium*, and *Communio* in that order, with the *Tractus* serving as substitute for the *Alleluia* in certain cases. All these parts are essentially psalmodic chants. From earliest traditions they consisted of solos (*Graduale*,[21] *Alle-*

[20] In music, the term *ekphonesis* has acquired a different meaning than that shown in most dictionaries. The original derivation is "to say in a loud voice" but as a rhetorical figure it means an ejaculation or interjection. In music, however, it refers to (*a*) primitive musical notation as derived from grammatical signs, or (*b*) melodic formulae at the beginning or ending of a song. We have used it in the latter meaning.

[21] There are, unfortunately, a number of equivocal terms in church music. The term *Graduale* may be used to mean either (*a*) the collection of the music for the Mass (*Proprium* and *Ordinarium*) in contradistinction to the *Antiphonale* containing the Office, or (*b*) the part of the *Proprium* between

*luia, Tractus,* and *Sequentia*) and choruses (*Introitus, Offertorium,* and *Communio*).[22] The texts of the solos were in themselves liturgical ends; but the choruses or antiphonal parts were embellishments of the Mass. The *Introitus* served as the music for entrance of the celebrant and could be melismatic without distracting the congregation from the ceremony. Similarly the *Offertorium* accompanied the ceremonies of the Offertory and the *Communio* the administration of Holy Communion.

The *Introitus* and *Communio* are more fully termed the *Antiphonae ad Introitum* and *ad Communionem.* In the

---

the Epistle and the Gospel readings. Their context is commonly enough to keep the meanings separate. Another such term is "sequence" which may refer: (*a*) to the part of the *Proprium* following the *Alleluia* or *Tractus* – for this the Latin form *Sequentia* will always be used in this volume or (*b*) the musical form in which a section of music is repeated, for example, a tone higher or a tone lower than the preceding section – for this the English word "sequence" will always be used in this volume.

22 The codification process of the liturgy also affected the *Proprium.* The different saints are easily enough grouped together by reason of characteristics, e.g., martyrdom, the episcopacy, virginity, etc. Accordingly from the twelfth century on the various texts of the *Proprium* which were suitable for each class of saints were grouped together to form the *Commune.* Hence developed the *Commune Apostolorum, Commune Confessorum, Commune Martyrum, Commune Virginum,* etc. This has been carried on today until there are such groups as the *Commune Unius aut Plurimum Summorum Pontificum* added in 1941. This is, of course, primarily a process of arrangement and not of the introduction of new texts. However, additions are made from time to time by the Church when new feasts are established, *e.g.,* the feast of Christ, the King.

Similar grouping occurred in the case of the Ordinarium from the twelfth century on. As a result, a particular *Kyrie,* for example, became associated with a particular *Gloria* or *Sanctus* or *Agnus Dei.* Such grouping has crystallized today on the basis of the particular feast or season for which the Mass is used. This grouping is arbitrary and not based on any musical connection between the parts, as is shown by the fact that the *Credo* even today is listed separately from the arbitrary groupings of the other parts of the *Ordinarium,* and by the fact that the Church permits the selection of the music for the various parts of the *Ordinarium* without regard to the grouping employed in their publication. The parts of the *Ordinarium* as arbitrarily grouped are referred to as an entire Mass by name, *e.g.,* the Gregorian chant Mass *Cunctipotens* (a trope deriving its name from the first word of a phrase interspersed in the *Kyrie* during the days of decay to give syllables under each series of notes). All other Gregorian Masses similarly draw their names from the first words of phrases added to their *Kyries.*

earlier days the two had similar structures: the opening was an antiphon (*antiphona,* returning song) which was followed by a verse and then the antiphon repeated and followed by another verse and so on, with the antiphon and verse being sung by alternating choirs. The books of the Middle Ages show a process of abbreviation until the present *Introitus* consists of the antiphon and one verse followed by the lesser doxology, the *Gloria Patri.* In the case of the *Communio* the psalm has not survived and hence the antiphonal singing has vanished.

The *Introitus* was a part of the liturgy of the Mass from an early date but is mentioned for the first time in the *Liber Pontificalis*[23] referring to the time of Pope Celestine I (pontificate: 422–432). The whole psalm was sung after the antiphon up to the ninth century from which time the psalm verse, only, was used. This is indicated even today by the abbreviation *PS* (*psalmus*) as well as *V* (*versus*). The lesser doxology was added after the verse except for the period from Passion Sunday to Easter and in the Requiem.

The *Offertorium* can be traced to the time of St. Augustine (354–430). Since the *Offertorium* is termed from the earliest times as an antiphon it probably began like the *Introitus* and *Communio.* The oldest extant music of the *Offertorium* shows a melismatic solo of verses with the preceding antiphon in responsory fashion. The verses were dropped in the Middle Ages and only in the Requiem does something of the original form remain.

The *Communio* is one of the most ancient chants of the Church. It was originally sung with a psalm, usually the thirty-third psalm. By adding the required number of versicles alternating with the antiphon, the time could be adjusted to that required for the administration of Holy Communion. There is a remnant of this in the Requiem. The antiphon was dropped about the twelfth century.

23 *Liber Pontificalis,* ed. Duchesne (Paris: Thorin, 1886).

In the case of the choral chants (the *Introitus, Offertorium,* and the *Communio*) the celebrant originally cut off the choirs at the end of the ceremony by a signal. In the case of the solo chants, however, even the celebrant from the earliest times waited until they were finished. Thus there was no liturgical objection to their length.

The *Graduale* after the reading of the Epistle derives from the Jewish synagogue. The term comes from the steps (*gradus*) of the platform from which the soloist sang. The *Graduale* has undergone much change. In the earliest times it was the musical climax of the Mass. About the sixth century the *Responsorium* (the sentence in the *Graduale* alternating with the verse) was sung by the choir and the choral part had developed the fullness of the solo on the verse so that the whole chant was uniform in this regard. By Gregory's time it had been cut down so that there remained the introductory sentence (the *Responsorium*) and only one verse. The *Responsorium* was repeated after the verse until the thirteenth century when another abbreviation occurred and the repetition was dropped. Thus it was no longer a true responsory.

The *Alleluia* is definitely of Eastern origin and was considered of even more importance in the East than in the Roman liturgy. It was brought into the Roman liturgy during the time of Pope Damasus I (pontificate: 366–382). Gregory required it for Sundays and holydays. The *Alleluia* is the most melismatic chant, consisting of the opening melody and the *jubilus* (an extended melodic figure on the last vowel of *alleluia,* followed by a verse). Prior to the Missal of Trent (1590) it contained not only the *Alleluia* followed by the verse it now has, but sometimes had additional verses if the melismata were of that length. The opening part, the *Alleluia* with the *jubilus,* was repeated after each verse. The *Alleluia* follows the *Graduale* except from Septuagesima to Good Friday, inclusive, on certain penitential days and in the

Requiem. In those cases the *Tractus* is substituted for the *Alleluia* except for the ember days of Advent which have no *Tractus* or *Alleluia.*

The *Tractus* (from *tractim,* uninterruptedly, without interpolation) is an extended musical form.[24] It consists of several verses of a psalm or even a whole psalm (except in the Requiem) and is not interrupted by an antiphon repetition. Some hold that this represents the original form of the *Graduale* (before the *Responsorium* was added). The melodies appear to scholars to be the oldest of the Mass.

The *Sequentia* (*sequi,* to follow) is a late development and will be dealt with in detail in the next chapter in its musical aspects. It is a musical form that originated as a melody (*jubilus*) following the *Alleluia* with many repetitions. Its real home is France. The melodies became so long that words were added to the *Alleluia* and the result was called *Sequentia cum prosa.* Thus an entirely new form developed. From the tenth century, strophes with carefully measured verse, structure, and rhyme were fitted to the melodies. Notker *Balbulus* (the Stammerer) (?–912) is clearly associated with its development and Adam of St. Victor (*c.* 1110–1192) brought the form to highest development. Finally the Council of Trent eliminated all *Sequentiae* except four, those for: (*a*) Easter (the *Victimae Paschali* by Wipo [?–1048]); (*b*) Pentecost (the *Veni Sancte Spiritus* by Pope Innocent III [pontificate: 1198–1216], or Hermannus *Contractus* [the Lame] [1013–1054]); (*c*) *Corpus Christi* (the *Lauda Sion* of St. Thomas Aquinas [1125–1274]); and (*d*) the *Requiem* (the *Dies Irae* by Thomas of Celano [?–1250]). The fifth *Sequentia* (the *Stabat Mater* by Jacopone da Todi [?–1306]; Innocent III [pontificate: 1198–1216]; or St. Bonaventure [1225–1274]) was not added to the liturgy until 1727 and its melody is of

[24] For another explanation of the *Tractus,* see: Wagner, Peter, *Einführung in die Gregorianischen Melodien* (Leipzig: Breitkopf & Härtel, 1901–1921), Vol. I, p. 102 f.

uncertain date. In addition, a few of the older orders which have their own *Graduale* are permitted to retain special *Sequentiae,* e.g., the *Laetabundus,* the Christmas *Sequentia* in the Praemonstratensian *Graduale.*

## THE ORDINARIUM

While the *Ordinarium* (consisting of the *Kyrie, Gloria, Credo, Sanctus,* and *Agnus Dei* in that order) is listed as the third group of the chants of the Mass, it originally did not involve the choir but belonged to the priest and the congregation. Herein lies the liturgical and traditional origin of the present preference for congregational singing of the *Ordinarium* of the Mass. Shortly after the time of Pope Gregory I, the congregational singing embraced the *Kyrie, Sanctus,* and *Agnus Dei,* the parts of the *Ordinarium* then common. Not until the fourteenth century, as we shall see, was the *Ordinarium* of the Mass developed as a unified musical form in which the parts of a Mass were grouped together musically. Until that time the chant books gathered the melodies of the *Kyrie* together as a unit, the melodies of the *Gloria* together, etc. The modern practice of grouping the melodies, for example, of the *Missa de Angelis* together is arbitrary. The various parts of what are now presented as individual Masses derive from different centuries. Even today, chant books handle the melodies of the *Credo* as a unit and not as a part of a particular Mass. It was not until the eleventh century that the choir took over the singing of the *Ordinarium.* This fact is important in explaining why the chants from that time forward grow more and more complicated with the exception of the *Credo.* It is further evidence that all the chants are functional: not only geared to the capacity and skill of the particular group that was to sing them, but designed to serve the particular part of the liturgical text, as we have seen.

The parts of the *Ordinarium* are derived from the Eastern

Church. Tracing the original parts of the *Ordinarium,* the *Kyrie, Gloria,* and *Sanctus,* we find that the use of the phrase *Kyrie eleison* as an important part of the song of the Church can be traced to the first century in the East, but it did not become prominent in the West until the time of Pope Gregory I. While the original Greek words are still retained in the *Kyrie,* the introduction of the *Christe eleison* occurred under Pope Gregory, and the pattern of three *Kyries,* three *Christes,* and three *Kyries* came during the ninth century. For the church musician it is interesting to note the unity of form involved in the use of the melodies of the *Kyrie* which is at the beginning of the Mass, again at the end of the Mass in the *Ite Missa Est* or *Benedicamus Domino* of the priest and the response *Deo Gratias* by the congregation or choir.

The *Gloria*[25] continued for a while in the original Greek even when it was brought into the Roman liturgy in the fifth century. From about the second century the *Gloria* in Greek was used in the East not as a part of the Mass but as belonging to the Office. Benedictine research concludes that the translation of the *Gloria* into Latin was done by St. Athanasius (298–373). It first came into the Mass for Christmas and then Pope Symmachus (pontificate: 498–514) directed its use in the Mass on Sundays and the feasts of martyrs but only in the pope's Mass. Until the ninth century, priests could sing it only at Easter and its general use dates from the eleventh century. The earliest melody of the *Gloria* is related to the melody of the *Pater Noster* and of the *Te Deum* and there probably was a common melody from which the three were derived. All three melodies being old, such a common original melody would date from very early.

The *Sanctus* was originally a musical projection by the people of the Preface. This characteristic still survives in the *Sanctus* of the Requiem. The *Sanctus* derives from Jewish

25 The *Gloria* is the greater doxology as distinguished from the *Gloria Patri,* the lesser doxology, used after psalms.

sources, particularly the *Kedushah* which antedates Christianity. There are references to it from the first century. Although the chant seems to have been sung by the people from earliest times, the *Ordo Romanus I* instructs that it is to be sung by the deacons. While the use of the *Sanctus* as a continuation of the Preface has been dated from the second century, some scholars think that was not the original location of the *Sanctus.* The singing of the *Benedictus* after the Consecration was not officially sanctioned until 1921. Prior to that it was a part of the *Sanctus,* although during the polyphonic period the separation had been practiced.

The *Agnus Dei* did not enter the Roman liturgy until the direction of Pope Sergius I (pontificate: 687–701), in 687, that the priest and the people sing the *Agnus Dei* together at the breaking of the Host. The *Agnus Dei* derives its text from the central part of the *Gloria.* Musically it was also a projection by the people of the *Pater Noster* by the priest. In the eleventh century the *"dona nobis pacem"* was substituted for the third *"miserere nobis."* The oldest melody of the *Agnus Dei* is related to the melody of the old litany.

The *Credo* has a history separate from the other parts of the *Ordinarium.* In the fifth century it was introduced at Antioch, in the sixth century (589) the Council of Toledo added it for the Church in Spain before the *Pater Noster* where it still stands today in the Mozarabic rite. It was not added to the Roman liturgy until the eleventh century by Pope Benedict VIII (pontificate: 1012–1024) as a substitute for the sermon. While the melodies of the other parts of the *Ordinarium* became more elaborate, the *Credo* retained its simple monodic form of one note for each syllable in all except a few instances. The liturgical function of the *Credo* is a profession of faith; this is clearly shown by the uniform steadfastness conveyed by the Gregorian melodies for the *Credo.* It is without liturgical foundation to portray the several articles in music, *e.g.,* sorrowful music at the *"crucifixus,"* joyful music at the *"resurrexit,"* etc. although there is no objection to singing the *"et incarnatus"* more softly than the other parts of the *Credo.*

### THE OFFICIUM

By comparison with the Mass, the musical forms of the Office experienced little change, the liturgy as well as the music of the Office being early settled. The responses, antiphons, and hymns underwent some development, however. As in the Mass, the Responsory experienced the greatest change: the number of verses was cut down. Also today only the latter part of the *Responsorium* is repeated after the verse whereas in the older times the entire *Responsorium* was repeated.

The antiphon in the Office has also seen some changes. Originally the antiphon was repeated only before and after the lesser doxology and now it is sung only before and after the psalm and sometimes only the first words of the antiphon are used before the psalm. The modern compositions called "antiphons" (e.g., of the Blessed Virgin Mary) are a further abbreviation since there is nothing of the psalm left to constitute the antiphonal form. The antiphon of the Office, being sung by the choir, is simple chant except on feast days and in the *Benedictus* of Lauds and the *Magnificat* of Vespers.

### HYMNS

Until about the twelfth century, there was a perpetual struggle between two groups in the Church with regard to hymns. The point of contention was whether the liturgy should be limited to Biblical texts or not. In the fourteenth, fifteenth, and sixteenth centuries a similar contest was to take place, as we shall see, about the admittance of hymns in the vernacular (and their attendant music) to use during the Mass since they were admitted without much opposition to processions, pilgrimages, and benediction. As we have already seen, St. Ambrose was particularly influential in gaining admittance for hymns. Whereas the hymns of the time of St. Ambrose followed the classical meters (particularly the iambic dimeter, but also the trochaic dimeter, hexameter, sapphic, asclepiadic, and others), the shift was made as in secular poetry from quantitative meter to accentual meter. While hymns originally were, as a matter of musical form, syllabic and followed the meter closely, the musical differences of the hymn from other musical forms disappeared when the shift was made from quantitative meter to accentual and rhyme. Musical forms closely related to the meter of the poetry are grouped under the term *cantus doctus* (or *cantus accuratus*). Such musical forms existed principally during the time of quantitative meter. When the shift was made to accent meter, the musical form shifted also to the *cantus planus,* a "free" rhythm in the music following a "free" rhythm in the language. The *cantus doctus* was revived in the *musica mensurata* (mensural music) which came to the fore starting with the twelfth century and supplanted the *cantus planus,* thus completing the cycle.

An important corollary of the shift from the quantitative meter to the accent meter was the development of the *cursus.*[26] In English the accent is familiar; the primary accent of a word tends to raise the voice on that syllable and thus to have a melodic emphasis. The grouping of words makes certain accents even more important because one word is more important than others. The *cursus*[27] was a system by

26 An extended discussion of the *cursus* will be found in Mocquereau, Andre, *Paleographie Musicale,* IV (see bibliography end of Chapter II); also Ferretti, Paul, *Il Cursus Metrico e Il Ritmo Della Melodia Gregoriana* (Rome: Desclee, 1913).

27 The *cursus* was not so named until the eleventh century. While it was greatly used in the fourth to seventh centuries, it vanished then until the eleventh century. The *cursus* is one of the classical arguments for establishing Gregorian chant as dating from prior to the seventh century and for establishing the connection of Pope Gregory I with the chant. Other arguments are: (*a*) the text used by the old Gregorian melodies is from the *Itala,* the oldest Latin translation of the Bible. Since St. Jerome (340–420) made his translation of the

which patterns were established at the endings of sentences. Classicial Latin knew the *cursus* in poetry (though there it was based on quantity); but from the time of the shift of the language of the Church from Greek to Latin at the end of the third century, the *cursus* is important in ecclesiastical Latin. It involves using an extended metrical foot and a *caesura* after the second syllable of each different type of *cursus.* There are three principal types of *cursus:* the *cursus planus* of five syllables, the *cursus tardus* of six syllables, and the *cursus velox* of seven syllables. The *cursus* was employed not only in the Roman Church but in all the various churches using Latin. Similarly, its effect on the chant is common to all the churches. That effect is the establishment of a musical cadence every time there is a *cursus,* with higher notes set to the accented syllables. The *cursus* was observed whether the chant was simple or elaborate; it establishes a unity of text and music that is rhetorical. The *cursus* added greatly to the structural strength of the hymn, both its literary and musical structure.

The music of the Mass and Office does not exhaust the music of the liturgy though it does constitute the great bulk of the music. There remains special music for episcopal and papal functions, the special music for Paschal time and Holy Week and other miscellaneous music. But that music is only a particular aspect of either the Mass or the Office.

## BIBLIOGRAPHY FOR CHAPTER I

Douglas, Winfred, *Church Music in History and Practice* (New York: Scribner's, 1937), pp. 12–63.

Dreves, Guido M., *Aurelius Ambrosius "der Vater des Kirchengesanges"* (Freiburg: Herder, 1893).

---

Bible in the early fifth century, and it immediately supplanted the *Itala* translation, there would be no reason for using the *Itala* in the chant unless the chant antedated the St. Jerome translation. (*b*) The texts for Masses dated after 600 do not use original melodies but rather adaptations of the preexisting Mass melodies.

Gastoué, Amedee, *Les Origines du Chant Romain* (Paris: Picard, 1907).

Gerbert, Martin, O.S.B., *De Cantu et Musica Sacra* (See end of Chapter II, bibliography).

——— *Scriptores Ecclesiastici de Musica* (See end of Chapter II, bibliography).

Gevaert, Francois A., *Les Origines du Chant Liturgique de l'Eglise Latine* (Ghent: Hoste, 1890).

Idelsohn, Abraham Z., *Jewish Music* (New York: Holt, 1929).

Johner, Dominic, O.S.B., *A New School of Gregorian Chant* (New York: Pustet, 1925), 3 English ed. from the 5 German ed., pp. 179–227.

Leitner, Franz, *Der Gottesdienstliche Volksgesang im Judischen und Christlichen Altertum* (Freiburg: Herder, 1903).

Mocquereau, Andre, O.S.B., "Chant Ambrosien," *Paleographie Musicale,* IX (See end of Chapter II, bibliography).

Morin, Germain, O.S.B., *Les Veritables Origines du Chant Gregorien* (Maredsous: Bureau de la Revue Benedictine, 1890; 3 ed., 1912).

Oesterley, W. O. E., *The Jewish Background of the Christian Liturgy* (London: Oxford, 1925).

Prado, German, O.S.B., "Mozarabic Melodies," *Speculum,* III, 218 (1928).

Quasten, Johannes, *Musik und Gesang in den Kulten der Heidnischen Antike und Christlichen Fruhzeit* (Munster i. W.: Aschendorff, 1930).

Reese, Gustave, *Music in the Middle Ages* (New York: Norton, 1940), pp. 1–114.

Saminsky, Lazare, *Music of the Ghetto and the Bible* (New York: Bloch, 1934).

Thibaut, Jan B., *Origine Byzantine de la Notation Neumatique* (Paris: Picard, 1903).

Wagner, Peter (See end of Chapter II, bibliography).

Wellesz, Egon, *Eastern Elements in Western Chants: Studies in the Early History of Ecclesiastical Music* (Oxford: University Press, 1947).

——— *A History of Byzantine Music and Hymnography* (Oxford: University Press, 1948).

Weinmann, Karl, *History of Church Music* (New York: Pustet, 1925), pp. 1–21.

NOTE: The work by Reese above is encyclopedic and from the musical viewpoint alone, with few observations of the liturgy. It contains a few errors, e.g., in note 23, p. 191, the author refers to the *Ars Musice* of St. Thomas Aquinas. This is a spurious work, see V. J. Bourke, *Thomistic Bibliography, 1920–1940* (St. Louis: The Modern Schoolman, 1940), p. 41, item 1328.

# CHAPTER II

## *THE GREGORIAN CHANT*

IT MAY be well to begin this chapter with an explanation of the chant as presently reconstructed and then to trace its history from the time of St. Ambrose. While the chant begins with the fifth or sixth century and runs to the sixteenth century, the period of maximum development is generally considered to be in the eleventh or twelfth century. From the sixteenth to the nineteenth century the true chant was by and large buried. It must be remembered that chant does not constitute the whole of church music. The polyphonic school was significant for church music from the thirteenth to the seventeenth centuries. From the last part of the seventeenth century to the nineteenth century, true church music was dead. The destruction of Gregorian chant was the last event of the Reformation. Music was the last aspect of the Church to suffer from that religious upheaval. It has also been the last aspect of the Church to be brought back from oblivion.

### GREGORIAN CHANT AT PRESENT

The restoration or renaissance of the chant began in the mid-nineteenth century under the Benedictine monks at the Abbey of Solesmes in France shortly after the lifting of the clerical restrictions in that country. The renaissance in music was only part of the general resurrection of the liturgical arts begun at that abbey. The guiding light was Dom Prosper Gueranger (1805–1875), succeeded by his pupil, Dom Joseph Pothier (1835–1923), who worked mainly in the restoration of the melodies of the chant. Then followed

Dom Andre Mocquereau (1849–1930), a pupil of Pothier,[1] whose main contribution has been the attempt to restore the rhythm of the chant and the editing of the monument of Gregorian music, the *Paléographie Musicale,* of which 16 volumes have appeared since its inauguration in 1889. It contains facsimiles of Gregorian manuscripts from various countries and centuries, the translation into modern notation of many of them, and many critical studies. Also issued at Solesmes is *Monographies Gregoriennes,* of which 13 volumes have appeared since 1910. It contains critical studies.

As a result of the researches of the Benedictines of Solesmes, the Vatican has published the official chant books of the Church. The first to be published was the *Graduale Sacrosanctae Romanae Ecclesiae* in 1908, containing the *Ordinarium*[2] and the *Proprium* of the Mass. Then followed the *Officium Defunctorum* in 1909, containing the Requiem and Office of the Dead, and the *Cantorinus Romanus, seu*

1 We do not mean to pass over the other important contributors at Solesmes, such as Dom Germain Morin; Dom Jules C. Jeannin; Dom Paul Jausions; Dom Jean Desroquettes; Dom Joseph Gajard; Dom Lucien David; nor the Benedictines at other locations such as Dom Gregory Sunol, until his death in 1946 president of the Pontifical Institute of Music at Rome; Dom Paul Ferretti of Italy; Dom Gregory Hügle, Dom Ermin Vitry, and Dom Adelard Bouvilliers in the United States; Dom Gregory Murray in England; Dom Dominic Johner, Dom Ambrose Kienle; Dom Benedict Sauter, Doms Raphael and Gregory Molitor in Germany. Nor do we mean to pass over the Jesuit scholars, Antoine Dechevrens, Louis Lambillotte, and Guido Dreves in France; Angelo deSanti in Italy; Gerhard Gietmann in Germany; and Ludwig Bonvin in the United States; nor the lay scholars, Peter Wagner in Switzerland and Amedee Gastoué and Francois Gevaert in France and Justine Ward in the United States. Mention should also be made of Vincent Donovan in restoring the Dominican *Graduale.*

In stating that the restoration "began" with Solesmes, no slight is intended for previous efforts by the Jesuit Lambillotte or others as discussed later in this chapter and in Chapter IV.

2 The Gregorian chants for the *Ordinarium* of the Mass are sometimes published separately as *Kyriale.* The *Kyriale* contains 29 melodies for the *Kyrie,* 22 for the *Gloria,* 6 for the *Credo,* 21 for the *Sanctus,* and 20 for the *Agnus Dei.* The Gregorian chants for the Vespers (of the *Antiphonale*) are sometimes printed separately as the *Vesperale.*

The *Liber Usualis* is a comprehensive edition of music from the *Graduale* and the *Antiphonale.*

*Toni Communes Officii et Missae* in 1911, containing the psalm tones and intonations. In 1912 appeared the *Liber Antiphonarius pro Diurnis Horis,* containing most of the Office, and in 1922 the *Officium Majoris Hebdomadae,* containing the full services of Holy Week.

The restored Gregorian chant appears in the "chant" notation in the official books of the Church but transcriptions of the melodies are available in modern notation for common use. There is no dispute as to the translation of the intervals of the melodies. Thus Plate I shows the "chant" notation and its modern equivalent in the Solesmes notation. The figures of the original "chant" are known as neums.

This plate is based on Dom Sunol's *Introduction à la Paléographie Musicale Gregorienne* and shows the modern chant notation with the equivalent in modern music. Four categories of neums are recognized: simple, compound, strophici, and liquescent. Of the simple neums, the virga is distinguished from the punctum in that the former indicates a relatively higher tone and the latter a relatively lower one. The distinction probably dates from the period before the adoption of the staff. The scandicus differs from the salicus in that the first note of the scandicus receives the ictus, or rhythmical distinction, while the second note of the salicus receives the ictus.

The apostropha, distropha, tristropha, and oriscus are sometimes printed today as the simple punctum but their differences are as follows. The apostropha originally added a vocal nuance to the neum and today the distropha and tristropha are sung with a slight vibrato and diminuendo. The oriscus appears at the end of a neum and is sung more lightly than the notes of that neum. In the pressus, the two notes of the same pitch are sung as one sustained tone with the ictus.

Liquescent neums, as the term indicates, appear where there are two or more consonants together or a *g* or *m* be-

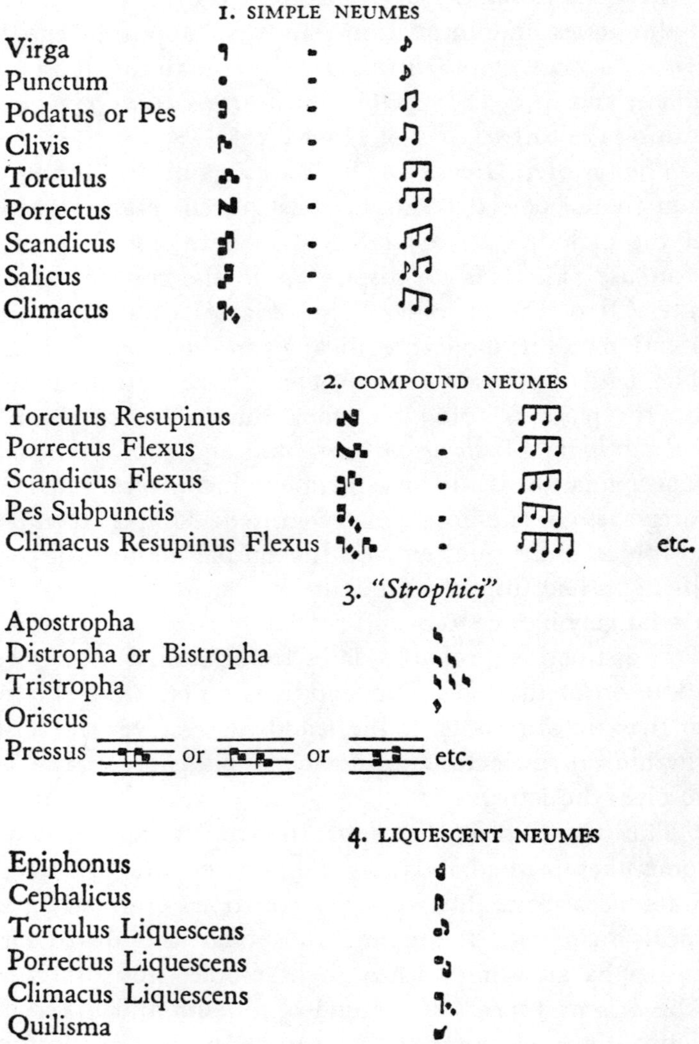


Plate I. Chant Notation and Modern Equivalent.

With permission, from Reese, Gustave: *Music in the Middle Ages* (New York: Norton, 1940) at p. 130 f.

tween two vowels in order to make a smooth passage. The notes are sung in legato manner the smaller note or notes sung softer. The quilisma is used between notes forming the interval of a third or fourth (usually minor third) and requires that the preceding note be retarded and the quilisma sung lightly.

To complete modern chant notation, a four-line staff is used with either the C clef  or F clef . Four bars are used 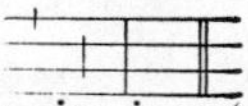: the bar through the top line marks the end of an incise (the smallest melodic unit), the bar through the second and third lines for the end of the member of a phrase, the bar through four lines for the end of a phrase and the double bar for the end of a selection or the changing of choirs. In addition, the custos  is the small note at the end of a line of music which indicates to the singer the pitch of the first note of the next line of music.

The dispute arises as to the rhythm employed in such neums (and accordingly in their translation). There are three schools of thought on the subject of rhythm: the accentualist, the Solesmes, and the mensural. The Solesmes school is followed in almost all translations in common use, largely because of the authority accruing to Solesmes as a result of the initial work done there in restoring the traditional melodies of the chant, and because of the role of Solesmes in preparing the official edition in the original "chant" notation.

The accentualist school (headed by Dom Pothier in his *Les Mélodies Grégoriennes*) argues that about the time Gregorian chant began in the fifth century, the change took place in the meter of Latin from measuring syllables in terms of quantity (long and short) to a system of equal time value for all syllables, with the rhythm established by the accent (or stress) given to a particular syllable. Gregorian chant, therefore, the accentualists argue, also assumed *equal* time values for the notes and therefore the accent became the principal determinant of the melodic rhythm. (Some members of the school hold that accent is the *sole* determinant.) The rhythm, in this view, is free, however, in the sense that in a long melisma on one syllable, the first note of each group of notes replaces the word accent.

The Solesmes school of rhythm under the leadership of Dom Mocquereau in his *Le Nombre Musical Gregorien* agrees with the accentualist principle that all the notes of the neums are basically of equal duration and that the rhythm is free, but rejects the principle that accent of the word dominates the rhythm of the music. The accent of the word need not receive the stress in rhythm but can be "spot-lighted" by the direction of the melodic intervals or by contrast such as the frequently found single note on an accented syllable where the bulk of the syllables have melismas. The Solesmes rhythmical theory is complex and is found in Dom Mocquereau's work just cited. The single indivisible time unit is the *punctum* or *virga* in the chant notation or the eighth note in modern translation. These units are grouped in twos and threes and then the groups are freely combined into the larger rhythmic groups: incises, members, phrases, and periods. Each group of two or three has its arsis (rise) and thesis (fall). In a binary group there is one arsis and thesis and in a ternary group one arsis and two theses or two arses and one thesis. The first of each group of two or three notes has an *ictus,* which marks out the groups. The *ictus* may be arsic or thetic depending on the nature of the group. The critics of Solesmes rhythm sharply attack the vagueness of the *ictus,* and not without reason, as can be seen from the following passage in which Dom Sunol offers a definition:[3]

[3] Sunol, Gregory, *Metodo Completo de Canto Gregoriano,* English tr. by G. M. Dunford, *Text Book of Gregorian Chant* (Tournai: Desclee, 1930), p. 73.

> The rhythmical ictus is simply a "dip" of the voice, an alighting place sought by the rhythm at intervals of every two or three notes in order to renew or sustain its flight until it reaches its final resting place. The ictus must be divorced from any idea of force or lengthening out. It is a common fault to assimilate it to the accent of the words and give it their value. In itself it may be strong or weak; it only gains its dynamic or quantitative value from the note which happens to correspond to it. If the ictus chances to be strong by its position, it does not appropriate the intensity thus bestowed upon it; its stress extends to the whole of the compound time which it commands, and it keeps only the function of an alighting or resting place. It can be readily understood that this must be so in order to safeguard the unity of the compound beat.

What *physical* measure is used to denote the *ictus* is thus in doubt. It has recently been admitted that the *ictus* may take the form of a slight prolongation.[4] There is a sign (the episema – ) in the manuscripts that is carried over to modern transcriptions to indicate a prolongation. There are other rhythmic indications in the manuscripts called Romanian letters.[5] The Solesmes rhythmical signs are: (1) the *ictus* (a vertical line, ı); (2) the episema (a horizontal line over the note or group of notes affected –); (3) the dot (.) after a note to almost double or triple its time value; and (4) the comma (,) for guiding the breathing. Except for the *ictus,* little exception is taken to the signs or their location.

[4] Murray, Gregory, "Gregorian Rhythm: A Pilgrim's Progress," *The Catholic Choirmaster,* XXI, 55 at 56 (1935).

[5] The Romanian letters are named after Romanus who introduced them when he established the chant at St. Gall, according to tradition. They are: *c* (*celeriter,* quickly); *t* (*trahere,* to drag or *tenere,* to hold); *p* (*pressio,* holding); and *x* (*exspectare,* to retard), all with reference to *tempo.* With reference to stress, they are: *f* (*fragere,* to diminish); *k* (*klange,* hard); *g* (gutteral), *h* (aspiration), *r* (crispness), and *o* (emphasis); but the modern edition brought out by Solesmes does not carry these signs. The Solesmes school recognizes gradual *crescendos* and *diminuendos* over phrases, however. Particularly in view of Dom Murray's concession about the *ictus* (see preceding footnote) it seems that a revamping of the attitude on intensity is in order. The above has been a brief survey of that aspect of the Solesmes school that has produced the greatest diversity of opinion.

The mensuralist school rests on the principle that the notes are not of equal length but made up of longs and shorts. Different views are expressed by the Jesuits Antoine Dechevrens, Ludwig Bonvin, Gerhard Gietmann, and Dom Jules Jeannin[6] who belong to this school. The last named – viewed as a dissenter from the Solesmes school – has produced some unity in the mensural school by arguing that the longs are twice as long as the shorts. The notes are then combined to produce groups of two to eight beats and the groups make up measures of irregular length. The Syrian chant is today so organized and it is claimed the Gregorian chant has Eastern origins. The mensuralists agree that in the twelfth century with the development of the staff and the *organum* (a form of polyphony to be discussed later) the notes were assessed equal values but that prior to that time different values existed. (All admit that the chant prior to the twelfth century is the "pure" chant.) This the Solesmes school cannot refute easily since the absence of the staff prior to the twelfth century makes it necessary to decipher the pre-twelfth-century manuscripts in the light of the post-twelfth-century manuscripts, on the assumption of no intervening change in the system or theory of rhythmical notation. The mensuralists can find considerable support in different writings of the period from the fourth to the twelfth centuries. Jerome of Moravia, the author of a work written in the latter part of the thirteenth century, gives rather definite rules for chant rhythm and he specifies that the notes have equal time value. But because of the late date, the other two schools find no inconsistency in admitting his statement.

What conclusions do we have? *All* the schools agree that the chant has free rhythm, i.e., that there is no regularly recurring rhythm as in modern music. They disagree as to

6 Other mensuralists include: Oskar Fleischer, Alexandre Fleury, Georges Houdard, Ewald Jammers, and Eduard Bernouilli. They all differ on important points.

the particular "rules" governing the freedom. The accentualists and the Solesmes schools agree that the notes are of equal value but disagree on word accent as the key to stress. The Solesmes and mensuralist schools agree that word accent is unimportant in rhythm but disagree as to the equality of note values in terms of time. Each of the schools brings forward credible and weighty evidence for its own system of rhythm. Particularly, among the works of the Solesmes Abbey who have made very thorough and lifelong studies, we find representatives of all three schools. All this suggests that perhaps the three schools are searching for a unity which did not exist. In short, the various theories advanced could very easily have each been true in different times and places. This is borne out by the disparity in the liturgy — in different times and places. Such musical disparity could easily be limited to matters of rhythm and yet have an entire agreement as to the melody (in terms of its intervals). To top it off, not until the twelfth century did the staff develop and with it the possibility of time measurement and regularly recurring rhythms — and more particularly, the *accurate* measurement of rhythm. The most reasonable conclusion seems to be that just suggested — that the true chant rhythm varied from time to time and from place to place.

Plate II shows a section of Gregorian chant in the transcriptions by three schools of rhythm. The transcriptions appear to differ widely and yet in actual performance it might be doubted whether expert exponents of the three schools could distinguish one performance from another.[7]

There is another important conclusion. All admit that the Solesmes performance (and rhythmic theory) results in a fine piece of artistry. Hence, even if it should develop that the Solesmes theory is without sufficient historical basis and one

[7] To be sure, a difference in rhythmic notation *should* be apparent in the performance. What is meant here is the suggestion that each school does not adhere in performance to its own rhythmic notation but all three tend to the same result in performance.

of the other two is correct, there could be no objection to a continuation of the Solesmes rhythmic method.

The discussion of the problems of rhythm of Gregorian chant at such length is justified because the chant rhythm separates Gregorian chant from modern music just as effectively as do the Gregorian modes.

The Gregorian modes (see Plate III) are usually termed church or ecclesiastical modes because they are also employed in polyphonic music.[8] For purposes of Gregorian chant, the first eight are mainly employed. The last four are first found in a treatise by Galrean in 1547, though they are attributed to Charlemagne in the ninth century. The table shows that the names are not parallel to the Greek names, but that is not the important difference. The "character" of the mode is determined in church music by three factors: (1) the location of the half tones – in this respect the modes are similar to Greek modes, (2) by the location of the final (except for a few cases this is the tone on which the melody ends) and the dominant[9] (which is the tone around which the melody revolves) – and here is a difference from the Greek modes, and (3) the initial figure with which the melody begins. In later times rules were established governing the melodic figures to be used in opening a chant in a given mode. The exception with regard to the "final" note of the melody is that the

[8] To abbreviate we simply refer to them hereafter as "modes," using the term "Greek modes" to refer to the modal system of classical Greece already explained in Chapter I.

In chant editions today, the mode is usually indicated by a Roman numeral at the beginning of a melody. Also the Roman numeral with the word "century" indicates the century in which the melody is found in that form (or merely that form where editing has occurred). A few chants (e.g., the *Preface* and *Pater Noster* have no indicated mode because they antedate the use of modes by the chant or can be fitted to several modes).

[9] Here is another equivocal word. The "dominant" of the mode does not carry the meaning that the word "dominant" has in modern music. A better term would be "tenor" (although that, too, is equivocal since it applies also to the high male voice), that tone which "holds" (*tenere*) the melody together. Another term used instead of "dominant" is "tuba" (but that, too, is equivocal since it applies also to a particular instrument).

# Plate II Different Rhythmical Transcriptions of Antiphon, *Videntibus illis*

## 1. Mensuralist School Transcription

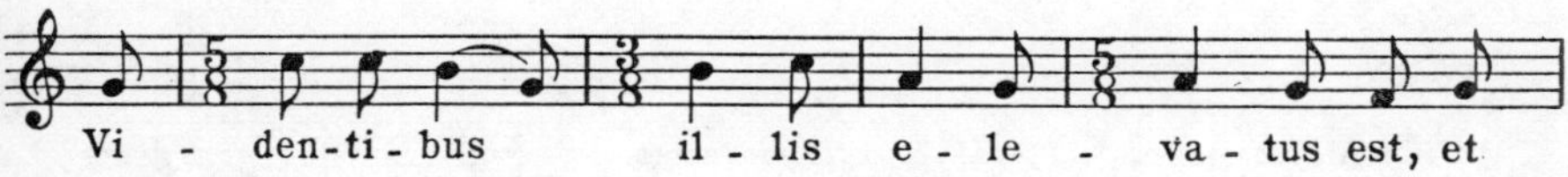


By Jules Cecilien Jeannin, O.S.B.
*Mélodies Liturgiques Syriennes et Chaldéenes*
(Paris: Leroux, 1924) Vol. I, p. 170.

## 2. Mensuralist School Transcription

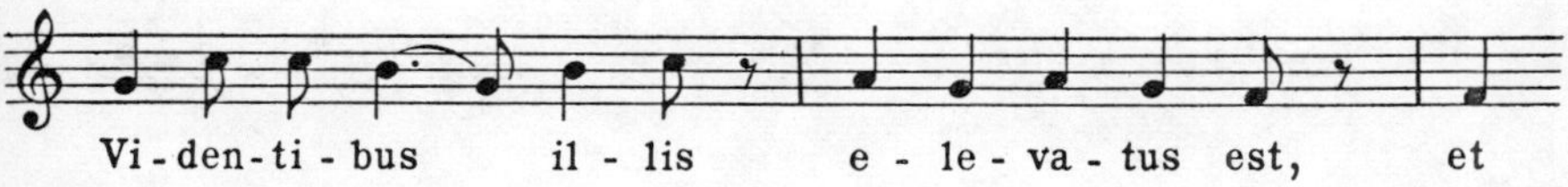


By Antoine Dechevrens, S. J:
*Les Vraies Mélodies Gregoriennes*
(Paris: Beauchesne, 1902) Part II, p. 31.

## 3. Solesmes School Transcription

*Compendium Gradualis et Antiphonalis Romani*
(Rome: Desclee, 1924) p. 656.

# The Ecclesiastical Modes

**Plate III**

| No. | Ecclesiastical Name | Authentic or Plagal | Greek name for same mode | Modern transcription |
|---|---|---|---|---|
| I | Dorian | Authentic | Phrygian |  |
| II | Hypodorian | Plagal | Hypodorian |  |
| III | Phrygian | Authentic | Dorian |  |
| IV | Hypophrygian | Plagal | Mixolydian |  |
| V | Lydian | Authentic | Hypolydian |  |
| VI | Hypolydian | Plagal | Lydian |  |

★ NOTE : The slur indicates the half-tone. The bar separates the diapente (range of five tones) and the diatesseron (range of four tones). The hollow note indicates the final and the star indicates the dominant.

Modes (XI) and (XII) do not appear in the usual schema of ecclesiastical modes. They were seldom used. Mode IX was seldom used because it extends beyond the Gregorian range which extended to G above the staff.

The Gregorian chant is limited to Modes I to VIII included.

| No. | Ecclesiastical Name | Authentic or Plagal | Greek name for same mode | Modern transcription |
|---|---|---|---|---|
| VII | Mixolydian | Authentic | Hypophrygian or. Iastian |  |
| VIII | Hypomixolydian | Plagal | Phrygian |  |
| IX | Aeolian | Authentic | Aeolian |  |
| X | Hypoaeolian | Plagal | |  |
| (XI) | Hyperaeolian (also Locrian) | Authentic | |  |
| (XII) | Hyperphrygian (also Hypolocrian) | Plagal | |  |
| (XIII) XI | Ionian | Authentic | |  |
| (XIV) XII | Hypoionian | Plagal | |  |

"final" may be a fifth higher than the "normal final" in which case the note is known as the *cofinalis* or *affinalis* or *socialis*. The modes are obviously related in pairs, as the table shows, having the same final tone. This relationship is that of authentic mode to plagal mode. Not only are the scales begun a fourth lower for the plagal modes, their half steps located between different intervals, and their dominant notes different, but there are differences in the melodic uses of the modes. The melody in an authentic mode seldom descends more than one note below the final and continually rises and falls above the final. The melody in a plagal, on the other hand, often descends more than one note below the final. Further, the final for the pair (authentic and its related plagal) is the same but the dominant is different.

It would seem that what has already been said would constitute the definition of Gregorian chant. But we have missed the quintessence so far. That is the wedding of music and text. It is this quality which has caused the Church to emphasize that Gregorian chant is the most appropriate form of church music; and it is this that is passed over in ignorance by most "standard" treatises on music in their description of Gregorian chant. It is this quality which is the test employed by the Church in deciding whether music is liturgical (and therefore acceptable) or unliturgical (and therefore objectionable).[10] How this ideal is achieved in Gregorian chant will be one of the objectives of the balance of this chapter. Now that we have examined some of the technical features

10 To make the point more clear, there is nothing *per se* unliturgical about music written in three-quarter time or with the dominant seventh chord or in the use of chromatics. Likewise music is not *per se* liturgical because it is written in chant rhythm or in chant notation or in the contrapuntal style. The test is not formal; the test is rather in the effect and impression created by the music. If it is vocal music, does it correctly express the feeling of the text? The test is not different in the case of the *liturgical* standard from that of the *artistic* standard. The test is the same: truly liturgical music is true art. But not all art is contained in or is proper to the liturgy. For example, the love of man for woman as such does not belong in the liturgy which treats of man's relation to God. Thus we can easily understand why Wagner's

of the chant, we will again pick up the threads of history that we momentarily set aside after tracing church music down to the time of St. Ambrose.

### THE HISTORY OF CHANT — AMBROSIAN CHANT

The history of the rise and perfection of the Gregorian chant runs from the fifth to the twelfth centuries. The twelfth century is crucial for it marks the discovery of the perfected staff and the beginning of mensural music (i.e., the use of notes of unequal time value or with regularly recurring rhythm). From the twelfth to the fifteenth centuries, Gregorian chant underwent gradual corruption and deterioration in the same proportion as polyphonic music achieved progress and finally perfection in the sixteenth century. In this chapter we shall trace Gregorian chant to its virtual extinction in the seventeenth century and in the next chapter shall begin the tracing of polyphony, starting with the ninth century.

In tracing the first four centuries of church music one finds that there is a lack of musical manuscripts and that the treatises on music are not analytical and furnish aid only in correlating musical development with liturgical development. This lack of musical manuscripts continues for the period down to the eighth century when we find the first extant manuscripts (incomplete) of Gregorian chant with neums, Brussels Codex, 10127–10144, Zurich-Rheinau, 33, Monza, etc.[11] Manuscripts continued to use the original notation shown in the plates until the perfection of the staff sys-

---

"Wedding March" from the opera *Lohengrin* is unliturgical — Wagner never intended it to express the relation of man to God that is found in the Christian sacrament of marriage. Yet that in no way reflects on Wagner's work as a piece of art.

[11] Sunol, Gregory, *Introduction á la Paléographie Musicale Gregorienne* (Paris: Desclee, 1935), at p. 33 gives facsimiles. Sunol refers at p. 480 to the sixth-century Codex 912 of St. Gall, a palimpsest (document in which one layer of writing has been erased and another added — or, indeed, several

tem by Guido D'Arezzo in the twelfth century, and even for several centuries beyond that.

The Ambrosian chant was in existence as early as the year 400, and there are extant three manuscripts[12] which are thought to preserve the chant in use before the time of Gregory the Great (pontificate: 590–604). These indicate a continuity of Ambrosian chant.[13] Analytically we can hazard a few statements about the chant in use at the time of St. Ambrose. The chant then employed the four authentic modes, although as we shall see, the best conclusion with regard to modes is that practice anticipated theory. Thus it appears more likely that the four authentic modes (Dorian, Phrygian, Lydian, and Mixolydian) were not developed consciously during the time of St. Ambrose. Rather the melodies stay within the range of five notes (except for later interpolations). The five notes constitute the diapente of later modal theory. Perhaps at this point the Greek theory of music with its tetrachord (the diatesseron or range of four notes) came

---

layers erased and added) containing a layer thought to belong to an even earlier period. The layer contains notation resembling neums and was brought out by a secret chemical process.

12 *Graduale* F 22 and *Antiphonale* F 79 in St. Peter's Archives and *Graduale* 5319 in the Vatican Library. The earliest Ambrosian chant manuscript extant is Codex Add 34209 of the British Museum. This is from the twelfth century and facsimiles and transcriptions appear in volumes V and VI of *Paleographie Musicale*. This manuscript has many examples of musical rhyme, i.e., many of the phrases of a melody end with the same melodic figure. This would indicate the influence of the hymn and metric structure. The Ambrosian chant survives today in the *Antiphonale Missarum Juxta Ritum Sanctae Ecclesiae Mediolanesis* (Rome: Desclee, 1935), more commonly referred to as the Ambrosian Antiphonale.

13 There are evidences of a continuous fostering of the chant by the popes. About the time of St. Ambrose a school for chant seems to have been established at Rome. Then Pope Celestine I (pontificate: 422–432) introduced the antiphonal singing already used in the Office into the Mass. In the pontificate of Pope Leo the Great (440–467) a monastery established in Rome devoted its full time to chanting. Under Pope Boniface (pontificate: 530–532) a complete chant for the whole year was developed. During the pontificate of Pelagius II (578–580) the Benedictines abandoned Monte Cassino to the Lombards, settled in Rome, and devoted themselves to the Office. These developments can be found traced in an anonymous Latin work. Migne, *P.L.*, CXXXVII, 1347.

to Christian attention, probably *via* Boethius. The addition of the four plagal modes, which are attained by adding the diatesseron below the diapente of the authentic modes, is often attributed to Gregory because it is known that he added four new psalm tones, and about his time the range downward in the melodies brought the plagal modes into existence. The octave is achieved by adding the diatesseron above the diapente of the Ambrosian range in the case of the authentic modes, with the fifth of the scale being common to the diapente and the diatesseron. This process of development would seem likely since the related authentic and plagal modes in each case have the same final tone. Herein also is an explanation why the Gregorian melodies in the authentic modes seldom run below one note lower than the final, and the Gregorian melodies in the plagal modes frequently descend lower than that range.

Beyond this, we know the psalmody of the Ambrosian chant is even simpler (the melodic figures at the cadences and at the intonation being simpler) than the psalmody of the Gregorian, and that the antiphonal music of the Ambrosian chant is more elaborate than that of the Gregorian. It is clear that the Ambrosian chant and the Gregorian interacted upon each other and borrowed melodies from each other. The Ambrosian chant was never widely used, however, and did not receive the benefit of continuous development as did the Gregorian. There is something of a tradition in the Ambrosian chant in the Cistercian order, and it has been generally retained particularly in northern Italy. Monte Cassino employed it exclusively until Pope Stephen IX (pontificate: 1057–1058) directed that the Gregorian be used there.

### GREGORY THE GREAT AND THE CHANT

There is a strong tradition beginning with John the Deacon's *Life of St. Gregory the Great* (*c.* 870), although there are earlier references to the fact that Gregory the Great undertook the reform and codification of the chant. This tradition remained unchallenged until 1675.[14] John the Deacon has been suspect as an historian but his work shows that it is accurate in a number of particulars by corresponding with earlier statements on various matters. Charlemagne was at least as important a factor in the success of this program as Gregory the Great. He strove hard for unity not only politically (being crowned Emperor of the West by Pope Leo III in Rome in 800) but also culturally. Pope Adrian I (pontificate: 772–795) responded in 790 to Charlemagne's requests for trained musicians and sent two monks north, according to tradition, with copies of the authoritative *Antiphonale*[15] of Gregory. One went to Metz and the other to St. Gall. Whatever the truth of the tale, we know these two schools flourished from about this time. Charlemagne followed his practice in cultural matters[16] by ordering all the Ambrosian chant books burned in favor of the new *Antiphonale*.[17] No copy of the original *Antiphonale* of Gregory is extant but manuscripts of the ninth century have led scholars to conclude that such a "master" *Antiphonale* did exist from which come the variants of the ninth century[18] with perhaps

14 When the tradition was challenged by Pierre Gussanville. This and later objections argue that the reform came somewhat later and point to Gregory II's pontificate (715–731) and Gregory III's (731–741).

15 It is important to remember that the word *antiphonale* was not restricted in the time of Gregory to the modern meaning of that term (set out earlier in this chapter) in which a distinction is taken from the *Graduale*. Rather, in the time of Gregory the *Antiphonale* included *all* the music.

16 Reference can be made to his handling of the Rule of St. Benedict and the other rules of monastic life. Given an "official" rule, he knew how to bring it about that there would be no other rules.

17 Pepin, the father of Charlemagne, cut down the Gallican chant (to be discussed later in this chapter) in favor of Gregorian chant by securing the proper edict in the dioceses of Rouen and Metz.

18 The evidence linking Gregory I (pontificate: 590–604) with Gregorian chant can be briefly summarized. The internal evidence is strong. Much of the text of the older Gregorian melodies is set to texts taken from the *Itala*, the oldest Latin translation of the Bible. The *Itala* was replaced by the Vulgate translation of St. Jerome in the early seventh century. Thus the chants antedate the seventh century. Further, new Mass texts added after 600

Leading American Composers of Catholic Church Music

John B. Singenberger 1848–1924

Michael L. Nemmers 1855–1929

Leading American Composers of Catholic Church Music

Rev. Carlo Rossini
1890–

Rev. Lambert A. Dobbelsteen, O.Praem.
1878–1947

another copy intervening in the chain of transcription. The variation was not great until the twelfth century as is shown by the uniformity in the collection of facsimiles of the *Justus ut palma* melodies from 219 manuscripts of the ninth to the eleventh centuries from widely scattered parts of Europe gathered in Volumes II and III of *Paléographie Musicale*. The scholar Gastoué[19] recognizes the following chants of the Mass as dating back to the early seventh century at the least:

1) *Kyrie* and *Gloria* XV, Mass XVIII, *Credo* I;
2) *Proprium de Tempore;*
3) *Commune Sanctorum;*
4) *Proprium Sanctorum* of at least forty-seven feasts;
5) Requiem Mass (except *Kyrie, Dies Israe,* and *Libera*).

## NEUMS AND CHANT NOTATION

The history of neums had an important effect on Gregorian chant. We have already seen what Gregorian notation is today and Plates IV to VII show the equivalent before the time of Guido D'Arezzo and the staff. How did this notation develop? Greek music employed an alphabetical notation. The difficulty with such notation lies in indicating whether the interval is a whole or a half tone. The establishment of modes

did not employ original Gregorian melodies but arrangements of older chants. A third internal evidence is the use of the *cursus* (discussed at the end of Chapter I) and its observance in the melodies. By the seventh century, knowledge of the *cursus* had lapsed.

External evidence also supports the connection of Gregory I with the chant. There are numerous references in English writings to Gregory I and his *Antiphonale* (e.g., by Egbert, Bishop of York, 732–766, in his *De Institutione Catholica,* Migne, *P.L.,* LXXXIX, 441; by the second council of Glasgow in 747; by Acca, Bishop of Hexham, 740, in Bede's *Historica Ecclesiastica,* Migne, *P.L.,* LXXXXV, 270; by Putta, Bishop of Rochester, 669, in *Littera,* Migne, *P.L.,* LXXXXV, 175; and others). Pope Adrian I (pontificate: 772–795) directly states Gregory "composed this book of chants." Similarly, Walafrid Strabo (807–849), in his *De Rebus Ecclesiasticis,* Migne, *P.L.,* CXIV, 948; and Pope Leo IV (pontificate: 847–855) in his *Littera, Neues Archiv,* 1880, 389; and finally John the Deacon (*c.* 870) in his *Vita Sancti Gregorii,* Migne, *P.L.,* LXXV, 90.

[19] Gastoué, Amedee, *L'Art Gregorien* (Paris: Alcan, 1911) and *Le Graduel et L'Antiphonaire Romains, Histoire et Description* (Lyon: Janin, 1913).

in which the half-tone intervals are fixed solves this problem to some extent. Greek music, however, had largely been forgotten by the fifth century and what was retained was misunderstood.[20] There is no direct evidence as to how the neums originated; several hypotheses have been advanced, however. In recent years the influence of Byzantium on both early liturgy and early church music has received greater attention.[21] The Western Church may have taken over the Byzantine notation. The editors of *Paléographie Musicale,* however, follow the hypothesis that the neums developed from the accent signs of the Greek. On this assumption, Rousseau[22] gives the derivation shown in Plates IV to VII based on St. Gall manuscripts. The two primary accents: the *acute* (ʹ) which became the *virga* or rising note and the *grave* (ˋ) which became the *punctum* or falling note, together with the apostrophe form the core of development. All further neums came from the various combinations of these three, which were primarily designed, as they meet the eye, to demonstrate the movement of the hands of orators in ancient times. Thus both neums and cheironomy stem from this process.

This development could account for all the neums except the quilisma (the liquescent neums being merely a refinement of the liquescent syllables). The quilisma as a special neum for musical purposes would be a natural invention. The difficulty is that the first neums extant are rather fully developed.[23] Sunol quotes[24] a decree of the Council of Glas-

20 A specific instance of this misunderstanding will be considered a little later in this chapter: the mistake of the modes in Boethius.

21 This may even extend to Gregory the Great himself since he visited St. Leander in Constantinople.

22 Rousseau, Norbert, *L'Ecole Gregorienne De Solesmes* (Tournai: Desclee, 1910), pp. 91–98.

23 An intermediate system between the staffless and staff neums is suggested by Hermannus *Contractus* in the eleventh-century *Opuscula Musica* (whose authorship is doubted). This manual develops the daseian notation which specifies the interval of each note relative to its predecessor (but not abso-

gow, in 747, referring to the method of chanting which requires the Church in Scotland to follow "the sample we received in writing from the Roman Church." However much of an improvement the neums in manuscripts of the eighth and ninth centuries may be over the alphabetical notation, they do not have staff lines. Thus while the neums show the exact number of notes and exactly how they are grouped, there is no accurate indication of the intervals between the notes. Sunol[25] is more correct than earlier chant zealots in recognizing that the process probably was such that one who knew the neums could use them as memory guides so that "usage, context, the liturgical text, as well as the contours of the neums, their peculiar combinations, the place they occupy and the melodic formula formed, immediately suggest the exact interval." That this is true is shown by the fact that the system endured in practical use even after the exactness of the staff system was made available in the twelfth century. In Germany, the neums continued as late as the fourteenth century. However, the defect of inaccurate intervallic notation was early a source of complaint by Hucbald in the late ninth or early tenth century and by Cotton in the eleventh century, for example.

There are at least three distinct systems of neums prior to the perfection of the staff by Guido D'Arezzo, and various names have been given to the three groups. The first is the rhetorical or accent or cheironomic notation used especially in northern France, northern Italy, Germany, and Switzer-

---

lutely). Obviously a mistake anywhere in the composition by the copyist will raise havoc.

24 Sunol, Gregory, *Introduction á la Paléographie Musicale Gregorienne* (Paris: Desclee, 1935), gives at p. 34 a facsimile of the eighth-century Brussels Codex 10127–10144. Sunol also refers at p. 480 to the sixth-century Codex 912, St. Gall, a palimpsest (document on which one layer of writing has been erased and another added — or there may be several layers) containing a layer thought to belong to an even earlier period. This layer contains notation resembling neums.

25 Sunol, Gregory, *ibid.,* p. 45.

# GREGORIAN NEUMS

(St. Gall Manuscripts)

## I. — Simple Neums

| | Name | Origin |
|---|---|---|
| Simple Neum | The square and diamond shaped punctum | grave accent (hereafter abbrev g) |
| Simple Neum | Virga *or* Bivirga. | acute accent (hereafter abbrev g) |
| Simple Neum | Apostropha. | apostropha. |
| Neums of two | Pes *or* Podatus. | g. a. |
| Neums of two | Clivis. | a. g. |
| Neums of three notes | Scandicus. | g. g. a. |
| Neums of three notes | Salicus. | g. g. a. |
| Neums of three notes | Climacus. | a. g. g. |
| Neums of three notes | Torculus. | g. a. g. |
| Neums of three notes | Porrectus. | a. g. a. |

Notation

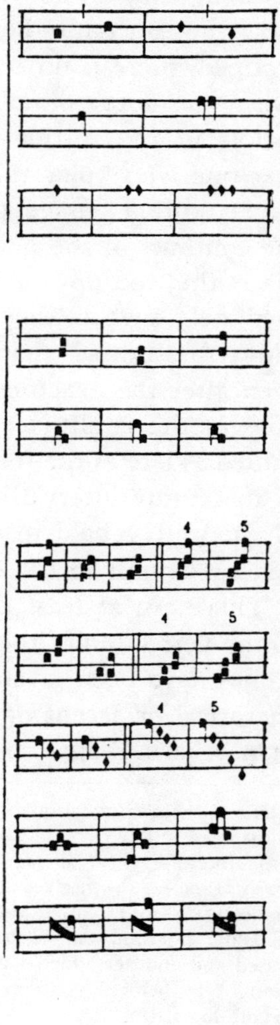


Plate IV.

## II. — Neums of more than three notes

| | | Name | Origin | | Notation |
|---|---|---|---|---|---|
| flexi | | Scandicus *flexus* | | g.g.a.g. | |
| | | Salicus *flexus* | | g.g.a.g. | |
| | | Porrectus *flexus* | | a.g.a.g. | |
| resupini | | Torculus *resupinus* | | g.a.g.a. | |
| | | Climacus *resupinus* | | a.g.g.a. | |
| subpunctes | Subbipunctis | Pes *subbipunctis* | | g.a.g.g. | |
| | | Porrectus *subbipunctis* | | a.g.a.g.g. | |
| | | Scandicus *subbipunctis* | | g.g.a.g.g. | |
| | Subtripunctis | Pes *subtripunctis* | | g.a.g.g.g. | |
| | | Porrectus *subtripunctis* | | a.g.a.g.g.g. | |
| | Subdiatesseris | Pes *subdiatesseris* | | g.a.g.g.g.g. | |
| | | Scandicus *subdiatesseris* | | g.g.a.g.g.g.g. | |
| | Subdiapentis | Virga *subdiapentis* | | a.g.g.g.g.g. | |
| | | Pes *subdiapentis* | | g.a.g.g.g.g.g. | |

Nota — When the simple neum is preceded by a *punctum*, it is called *praepunctis*. Example: *porrectus-praepunctis:*

Plate V.

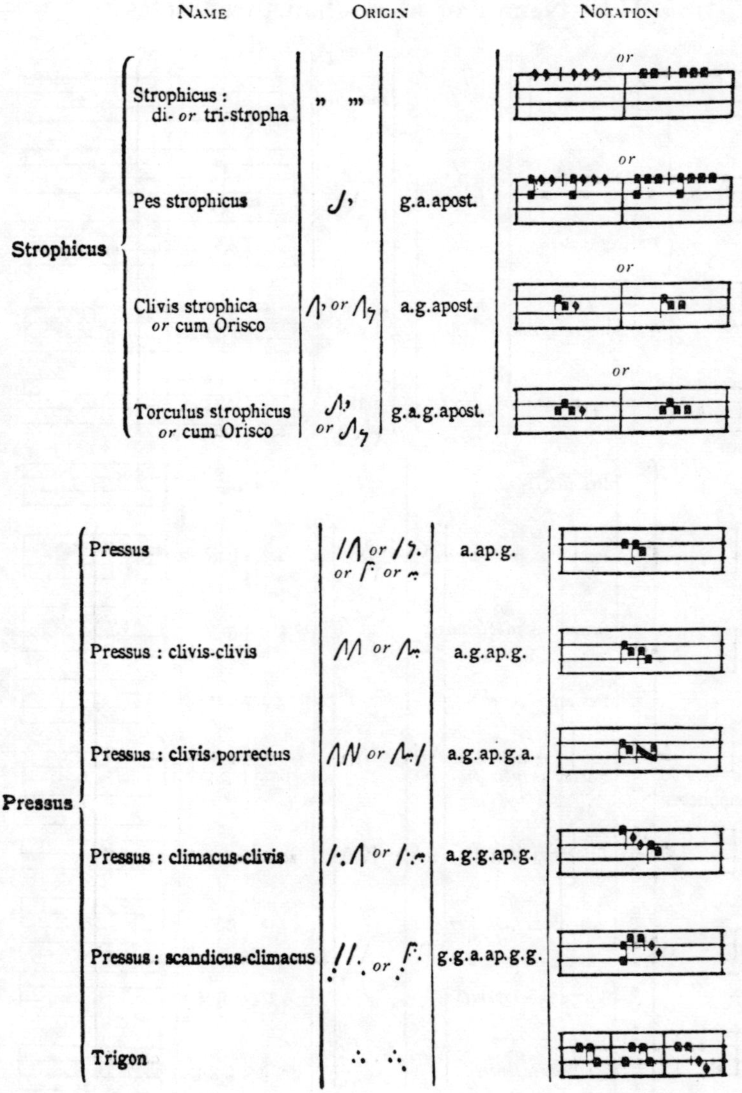
NAME
ORIGIN
NOTATION
Strophicus
Strophicus :
di- or tri-stropha
Pes strophicus
g.a.apost.
Clivis strophica
or cum Orisco
a.g.apost.
Torculus strophicus
or cum Orisco
g.a.g.apost.
or
Pressus
Pressus
a.ap.g.
Pressus : clivis-clivis
a.g.ap.g.
Pressus : clivis-porrectus
a.g.ap.g.a.
Pressus : climacus-clivis
a.g.g.ap.g.
Pressus : scandicus-climacus
g.g.a.ap.g.g.
Trigon

Plate VI.

| | | Name | Origin | | Notation |
|---|---|---|---|---|---|
| Quilisma | Preceded by a punctum | Punctum & quilisma podatus |  | g.q.a. |  |
| | | Punctum & quilisma torculus |  | g.q.a.g. |  |
| | | Punctum & quilisma pes subbipunctis | 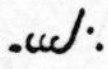 | g.q.a.g.g. |  |
| | Preceded by a group | Clivis & quilisma torculus | 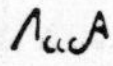 | a.g.q.a.g. |  |
| | | Torculus & quilisma torculus | 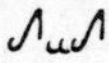 | g.a.g.q.a.g. |  |
| | | Climacus & quilisma pes subbipunctis | 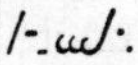 | a.g.g.q.a.g.g. | 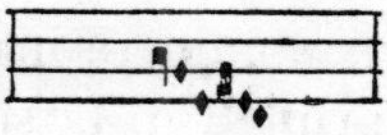 |

## III. — Liquescent Neums

| | Name | Origin | | Notation |
|---|---|---|---|---|
| Liquescent Neums | Epiphonus *or* Podatus liquescent | 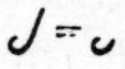 | g.a. | 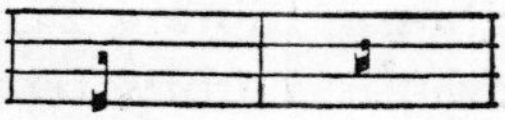 |
| | Cephalicus *or* Clivis liquescente | 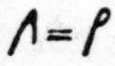 | a.g. | 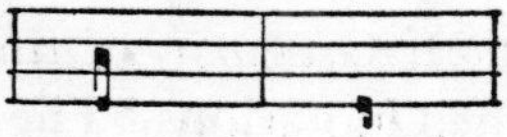 |
| | Ancus *or* Climacus liquescent | 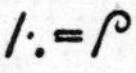 | a.g.g. | 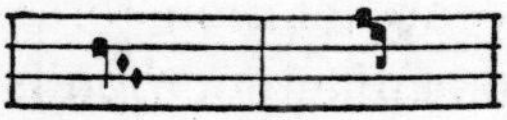 |
| | Porrectus liquescent | 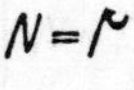 | a.g.a. | 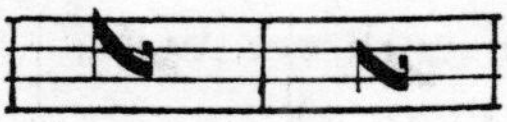 |
| | Scandicus liquescent | 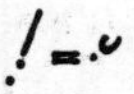 | g.g.a. | 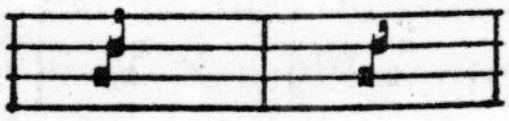 |
| | Torculus liquescent | 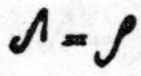 | g.a.g. | 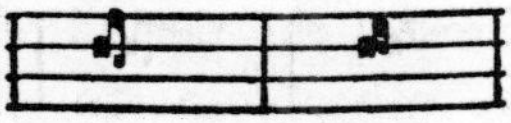 |

Plate VII.

land. The early manuscripts of St. Gall employed this notation heavily. The system is horizontal and not accurate for intervals. Accordingly the Romanian notation (already referred to) of letters to assist the neums for particular expressions was employed. The second system is the Aquitanian or dot or diastematic notation used primarily in southern France, Spain, and Aquitania from the tenth century. It is from the dot system that the square notes of Gregorian notation developed (or lozenges of the German notation because of the angle at which the pen was held). This is more accurate as to intervals since the dots are carefully spaced. The third system is a combination of the two preceding systems. The combination is found principally in the manuscripts of Metz and Chartres.

A complete manuscript of each type of neum notation is reprinted in facsimile in the volumes of *Paleographie Musicale:* (1) in Volume I is Codex 339, St. Gall, the *Antiphonale Missarum Sancti Gregorii,* of the tenth century, representing the first or accent notation; (2) in Volume XIII is Codex 903, National Library Paris, the *Graduale of St. Yrieix,* of the eleventh century, representing the dot notation; and (3) in Volume XI is Codex 47, Chartres, the *Antiphonale Missarum Sancti Gregorii,* of the tenth century, representing the combined notations. The Romanian letters were added to the accent notation for greater certainty. The best example of Romanian notation is in Volume IV, Codex 121, Einsiedeln, the *Antiphonale Missarum Sancti Gregorii,* of the tenth and eleventh centuries.

Plate IX is reproduced from Volume I of *Paléographie Musicale* and shows by centuries the development of the neums. Plate XIII is based on Rousseau and is derived from the manuscripts of St. Gall which are more complete in terms of the period of time covered than the manuscripts of any other location. It brings out the matter of rhythmic notation in particular, which is our next topic.

## GREGORIAN CHANT RHYTHM

As stated earlier in this chapter, the subject of rhythm in Gregorian chant is sharply disputed. There are almost as many views as there are students of the subject. Nevertheless, the rudiments of the matter can be stated.[26]

The following translation from pages 96 and 97 of Rousseau[27] is a reasonable summary of the Solesmes theory when related to Plate VIII:

> *The rhythmic signs proper* (i.e., as distinguished from Romanian letters)
> "We distinguish two classes: 1) the rhythmic signs which affect the original neums by modifying them and 2) the signs which affect the original neums by being added to them." (A quotation from Andre Mocquereau's *Le Nombre Musical.*)
>
> The first, which we call modifying signs, lengthen, color or accent the integral lines of the neums and thus enter into the graphic representation of the group; the second, which we call supplementary signs, consist simply in additions of a small line, the episema, which sometimes is placed at the top of the *virga* and sometimes is added to the *punctum.*
>
> It is here that a fundamental proposition asserts itself: that whether they be modifying or supplementary signs, both indicate a lengthening of the neums, an emphasis, a more or less pronounced retard, but never a shortening: there are no rhythmic signs for shortening. Thus, in the beginning, all the notes were equal when they were not affected by a rhythmic sign, or in other words a lengthening. All that remains is to present the different signs with their transcription in the Solesmes edition. (See Plate VIII.)

Shortly after this passage, at page 99, in discussing the Romanian letters, Rousseau treats of the *c* (*celeriter,* quickly)

[26] The bibliography at the end of the chapter gives an introduction to the voluminous literature in Gregorian chant rhythm.

[27] Rousseau, Norbert, *L'Ecole Gregorienne de Solesmes* (Tournai: Desclee, 1910), pp. 96, 97. This and the following translation from Rousseau are mine.

## I. — Modifying Signs

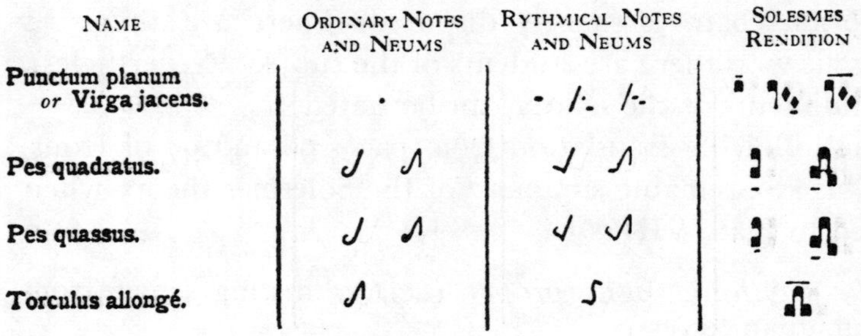


## II. — Additional Signs

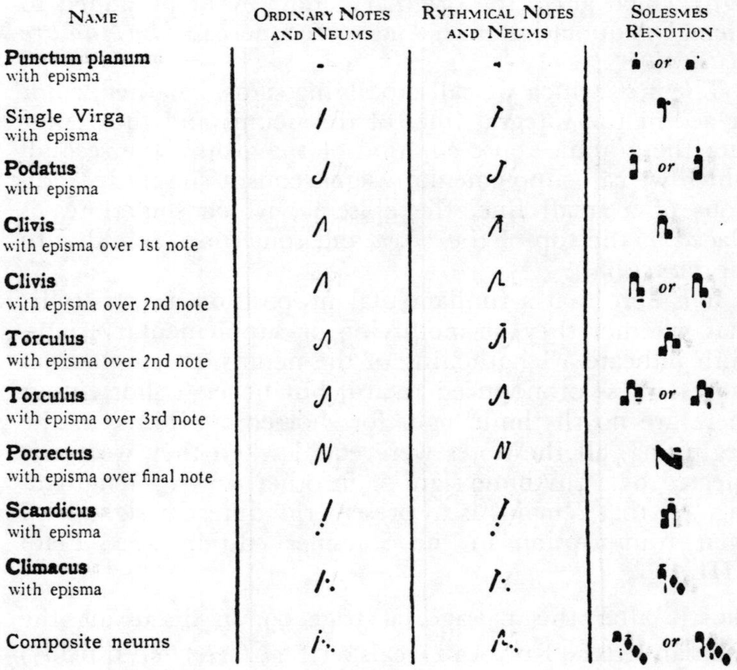


Plate VIII. Rhythmic Signs of Chant.

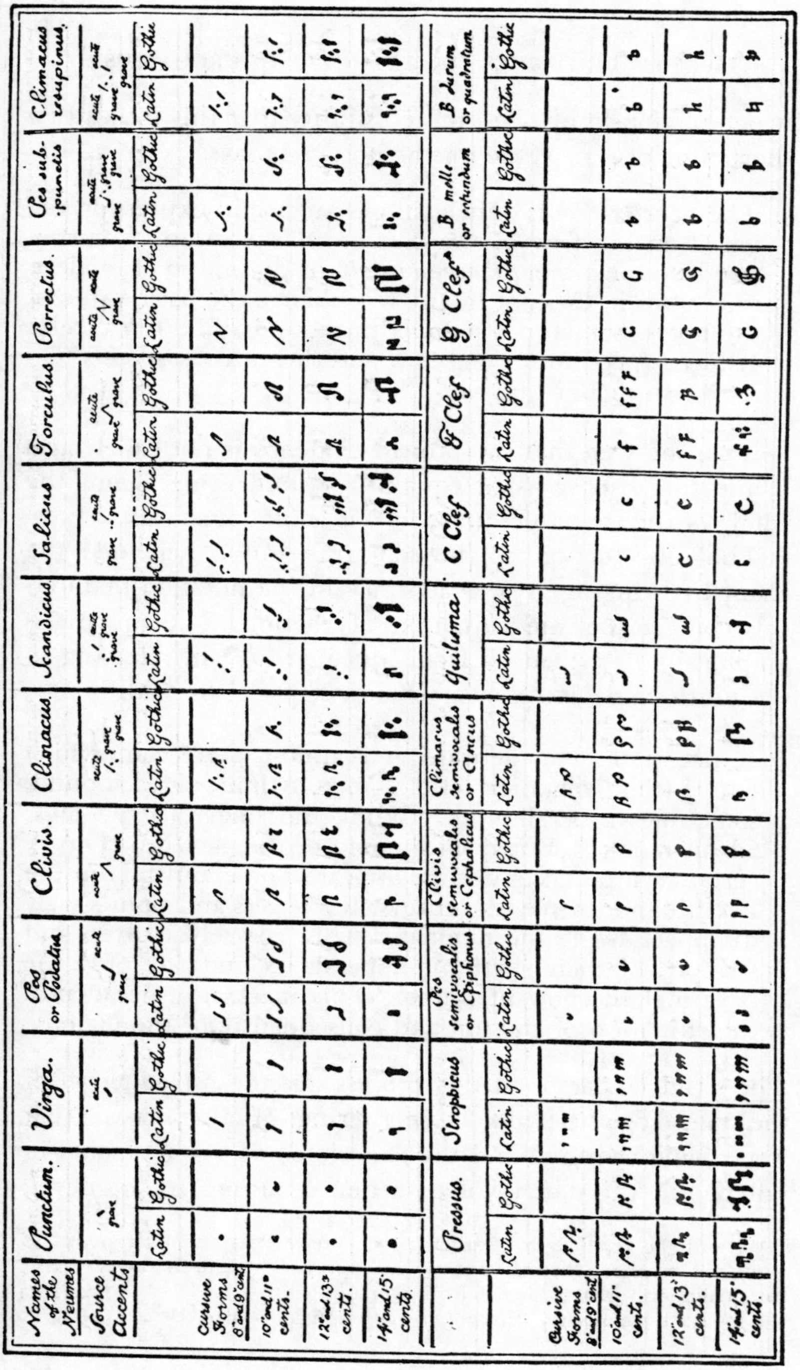


Plate IX. Development of Chant Notation.

which obviously involves the possibility that this indicates a shortening of time value for the notes. He says:

> The *c* (*celeriter*) is only a simple nuance in expression imposed on the flow of the passage in execution; it corresponds to the *animato, accelerando* or *piu mosso* of modern music but it does not in any way change the basic value of the notes. Sometimes its only purpose may be to cancel a reduced speed in normal flow and thus it corresponds to *a tempo* in modern music.

It can be seen that the present evidence is not conclusive. While the dispute as to equality of note value is not the whole of the rhythmic question,[28] it is fundamental.

The introduction of the staff into music benefited the chant by bringing greater accuracy in the notation of intervals, but it was the ruination of rhythm. The process is graphically described by Dom Mocquereau[29] in referring to the ninth- and tenth-century manuscripts of St. Gall:

> a nice notation — delicate and almost perfect in which letters (the Romanian letters) and rhythmic signs abound, sometimes superabound, guiding the singer to the most adroit nuances. But from the end of the eleventh century certain symptoms of decline appear. These multiply in the twelfth and thirteenth century, the letters and signs slowly disappear while the neumatic signs, coarsely written and stripped of their rhythmic appendages, indicate only the bare melodic flow of sounds. This marks the decadence, the ruination of rhythm and consequently of the melody.

The strongest factor in this process was the introduction of the staff. Together with the smatterings of Greek music that were being acquired and the experimental developments in polyphony, the staff involved a new notation. In the devel-

[28] It will be recalled that earlier in the present chapter other points of dispute about chant rhythm were briefly discussed, particularly the matter of the significance of word accent in Gregorian chant.

[29] Mocquereau, Andre, *Paléographie Musicale* (Tournai: Desclee, 1889).

opment of that notation, the chant rhythmic signs were eliminated.

The summary of what has been said about neums so far is found in three important characteristics of Gregorian chant: (1) Gregorian chant is monodic and not accompanied, (2) Gregorian chant employs melodic formulae, and (3) Gregorian chant has a "free" rhythm paralleling the rhythm of the prose text. More than one voice (vocal or instrumental) would have been impossible, or at least very difficult with staffless neums. Secondly, to ease the difficulty in memorizing hundreds of chants, it was necessary to employ frequently repeated melodic figures — not merely compound neums but patterns for groups of neums. This forced a higher order of originality (creativeness) than is needed when the staff is available to permit greater freedom.

## THE DEVELOPMENT OF THE STAFF AND ITS SIGNIFICANCE

We have already shown the role of the staff in the matter of neums and rhythm. It remains to recount briefly the historical facts of its development. Guido D'Arezzo (*c.* 995–1050), a Benedictine monk, is often called the most important figure in the history of music from the theoretical point of view. And not without reason. Not only did he perfect the staff system and rediscover solmization (to be discussed later) but his *Micrologus* is the most important theoretical treatise of the Middle Ages, particularly on such matters as modes and *organum* (early polyphony). The seeds of a staff system appear in tenth-century manuscripts. The notes seem to have been placed with reference to a single, "imaginary," horizontal line. By the end of that century the line actually appeared and later in the eleventh century two lines appeared. Perhaps the most important foundation for Guido's work with the staff was the *Musica Enchiriadis* of the ninth century whose author was once thought to be Hucbald. That author developed a system known as *dasiean* notation in which each symbol represents a given tone. To be doubly sure, he added a staff of five or more lines (in which he used the spaces and not the lines) and the syllables of the text were distributed in the staff spaces. He further added a symbol for each space at the beginning of each staff to indicate the tone for all the syllables in that space. Guido drew upon these sources to develop a four-lined staff in which he used both the lines and the spaces and marks on the staff for notes. He further employed the *F* and *C* as clefs at the beginning of each staff to indicate the tone assigned to a given line. The *F* line was in red, the *C* line in yellow and the other two lines in black. The first staff thus consisted of four lines, and Gregorian chant to this day continues to employ the four-lined staff.

The results of the introduction of the staff were great and immediate. First, it encouraged the composition of more chants since the load on the memory of the choir was greatly relieved. But more unfortunately, it also made possible great elaboration of the original chants — as well as their corruption by acquiescing to the whims of a particular soloist who sought suitable vehicles for displaying his voice. Second, the way was now open for polyphonic vocal composition, and this was not long in coming. Third, or rather a corollary of the second result, the chant could now be accompanied.

## THE MODAL SYSTEM AND SOLMIZATION

Also important to an understanding of chant history is a knowledge of the history of the modal system.[30] If anything, the history of medieval modal development is more complicated than the problems of the history of rhythm in the chant! The saving feature, however, is that there is agreement on the modal system of the chant whereas there is no such agreement in the case of the rhythm.

30 A knowledge of the modal system is necessary to an understanding of the liturgical problems of polyphonic church music to be discussed in Chapter III.

The Greeks had solmization.[31] Guido D'Arezzo, besides perfecting the staff system, is credited with the rediscovery of solmization. Medieval solmization consists of the six syllables *ut, re, mi, fa, sol,* and *la* – bringing out the hexachord as the basis of medieval music. When the octave was later developed as the basis of theory, the syllable *si* was added for the seventh tone. In the seventeenth century the syllable *do* was substituted for *ut* in Italy thus completing the solmization used today. The solmization *ut, re, mi, fa, sol,* and *la* invariably represented the five intervals: whole tone, whole tone, half tone, whole tone, and whole tone. Odo of Cluny (?–947) is credited with a work in which the range, in modern equivalents, is from *G* below middle *C* to *a* above the staff. This was later expanded to reach *e* above the staff. The complete hexachordal system for this range is set out in Plate X. Guido's revival of solmization reflecting the hexachordal nature of the Gregorian range of six tones sufficed for most Gregorian melodies. It is sometimes said[32] that the hexachordal system has no modal significance. That might be true if it could be said that the matter of using *B flat* and *B*

31 Solmization may be defined as the assigning of syllables to notes for scale purposes in a manner similar to the assignment of letters to notes in the scales of modern music. Thus the Greeks assigned the syllables *tah, ta, toh,* and *teh* to the tunes of the tetrachord. The medieval solmization derives from the first syllables of the first words of each of the phrases of a hymn to St. John the Baptist, in which the melodic figure for each successive line begins a note higher than the previous line began:

*Ut* queant laxis
*Re*sonare vibris
*Mi*ra gestorum
*Fa*muli tuorum
*Sol*ve polluti
*La*bii reatum
Sancte Joannes

When the seventh syllable *si* was later added to solmization, it came from the two initial letters of *S*ancte *J*oannes

32 E.g., Reese, Gustave, *Music in the Middle Ages* (New York: Norton, 1940), p. 150. This is an apparent contradiction of a later statement by Reese at p. 161 ". . . the substitution of b flat for b natural changed the character of a mode – in fact, changed it into another mode. . . ."

*natural* is without modal significance. From as early as the ninth century the interval of an augmented fourth (or diminished fifth) also known in medieval books as the tritone was barred as too discordant. In the later Middle Ages the interval became known as the *diabolus in musica* (the devil in music). To avoid the augmented fourth, it was necessary to introduce *B flat*. The succession of *B flat* and *B natural* was not used – no chromatics being admitted to the chant.[33] It is clear from the modes (see Plate III) that the augmented fourth will arise most frequently in the Lydian and Hypolydian modes, and it is there that *B flat* most often is used.

It is generally conceded that Gregorian chant in its pure form is the chant antedating the twelfth century. It is clear that no elaborate theoretical system supported that structure. Guido's solmization is an effort to fit a theoretical system to an existing set of melodies.

By using the hexachord as his unit, Guido was able to erect a series of five hexachords which covered the range of Gregorian chant at that time – later two or more hexachords covered the addition to the range. (See Plate X.) The hexachords were named *durum* if they contained *B naturale, molle* if they contained *B flat,* and *naturale* if they contained neither. The important point of the hexachordal system was the preservation of the *mi-fa* step for the half-tone progression. Thus if a melody extended beyond a range of six notes, it was necessary to shift from one hexachord to another. This Guido did by changing the hexachord at a point that would preserve the *mi–fa* for the half-tone step in the new hexachord. Guido developed a mnemonic tool – the famous Guidonian hand found in any musical dictionary – to teach the hexachordal system, and it became popular. This is significant because it

[33] This is made more clear by the matter of notation. For *B natural* the Middle Ages used a square note (the b *durum* or *quadratum,* from which modern music gets its natural sign) but for *B flat* a rounded note was used (the b *molle* or *rotundum,* from which modern music gets its sign for the flat).

shows clearly that the theory of the Gregorian modes as sometimes represented today by simply defining the location of the half tones in the scales was not known to the Middle Ages as modal theory but as solmization.

The confusion in theoretical work is illustrated in the mixing of Greek names for modes and the names of the church modes (shown in Plate III). Boethius (*c.* 480–524) was an author well known and respected throughout the Middle Ages. It was largely through him that the Middle Ages down to the twelfth century got its knowledge of Greek music. The tenth-century anonymous *Alia Musica* shows the confusion in the Middle Ages that caused the mix-up of mode names. Boethius describes the modes as running from the Mixolydian as the highest to the Hypodorian as the lowest. The author of the *Alia Musica* took this to refer to the octaves whereas Boethius meant the *tonoi* (which constituted the Greek series of "keys" and not of "modes"). The mix-up thus came about by a misunderstanding of what the Greeks meant by *tonoi*.[34]

This is not to deny that there was a discussion of modes prior to the time of Guido. As far back as Alcuin (753–804) there is mention of eight melodic formulae and also in Cassiodorus (485–580), Isidore of Seville (570–636), Aurelian of Réomé (*c.* 850), and others but until the discussion in the *Alia Musica* just referred to, there was no modal theory — though in practice the modes were there.

The next real contribution to modal theory was made by Hermannus Contractus (the Lame) (1013–1054) in his *Opuscula Musica* when he added the Hypomixolydian mode, which is the plagal mode needed to fill the symmetry of the eight modes. Until this time the Middle Ages had recognized only seven modes because the Greeks (and Boethius) had only seven. In the time of St. Ambrose it is said there were only

[34] And not as some musical texts say, simply due to the fact that the Greeks read their scales downward whereas the Middle Ages read the scale upward.

| | | | | | | | | | | | | | | | | | | | | |
|---|---|---|---|---|---|---|---|---|---|---|---|---|---|---|---|---|---|---|---|---|
| 7. Durum | | | | | | | | | | | | | | | ut | re | mi | fa | sol | la |
| 6. Molle | | | | | | | | | | | | | | ut | re | mi | fa | sol | la | |
| 5. Naturale | | | | | | | | | | | ut | re | mi | fa | sol | la | | | | |
| 4. Durum | | | | | | | | ut | re | mi | fa | sol | la | | | | | | | |
| 3. Molle | | | | | | | ut | re | mi | fa | sol | la | | | | | | | | |
| 2. Naturale | | | | ut | re | mi | fa | sol | la | | | | | | | | | | | |
| 1. Durum | ut | re | mi | fa | sol | la | | | | | | | | | | | | | | |
| Modern scale tone | Γ | A | B ♮ | C | D | E | F | G | a | b | c | d | e | f | g | a a | b b | c c | d d | e e |

♮—for durum modes—♮
♭—for molle modes—♭

The hexachords numbered 6 and 7 were added after Guido D'Arezzo's (c. 995–1050) time. In Guido's time the Gregorian range ceased at a a.

Plate X. The Hexachordal System of Guido D'Arezzo. Adapted, with permission, from Reese, Gustave: *Music in the Middle Ages* (New York: Norton, 1940), p. 151.

the four authentic modes; it is usually stated that at the time of St. Gregory the four plagal modes were added. It would be more correct, however, on the basis of the evidence to say that the *range* of the melodies was expanded and the number of melodic formulae increased – since the modes were not theoretically recognized as such.

That this analysis is valid can be seen from the phenomenon of the *Tonalia.* When neums were used without lines, it was difficult to recognize a mode. As a teaching aid and to keep understanding of the organization of music for the liturgy, books called *Tonalia* were developed. In these volumes the melodies were grouped by the modes to which they belonged and, at the beginning of each category the typical melodies of the modes were placed, set to arbitrary syllables. Thus the grouping further developed a knowledge of the different parts of the liturgy from the point of view of musical forms.

About the time that modal theory began, the role of the final and dominant notes came to be examined. Not only could the existing melodies be grouped, on the basis of the formulae they employed, into modes but likewise each particular group *ended* on the same final note and was *dominated* by another note that was the same in each group.

Much dispute and technical discussion has evolved among the scholars as to whether "modulation" (shifting from one mode to another in the same melody) occurred. In modern music, modulation is used to describe a transition from one *key* to another. Thus to speak of modulation in the chant as referring to a shift from one *mode* to another, is to use the term analogously. In this sense, modulation does occur in the chant. A cursory examination of Plate III will show how easily this could be achieved because of (1) the identity of the final tone in both the authentic and its related plagal mode, and (2) the identity of the dominant tone in several modes. However, it must be remembered that this view is an afterthought.

The melodies existed before the modal theory; difficulties are due to the fact that the modal theory later developed is not a perfect fit to the melodies.

Plate III shows the fourteen possible modes, all of which can be said to be employed here or there in Gregorian chant. However only twelve occur with any frequency and these are the twelve commonly referred to as the ecclesiastical modes. The chant itself, in the modern editions, recognizes only the "original" eight modes.

Throughout the literature of the Middle Ages we find a discussion of the "characteristics" (or "coloring," *ethos*) of the different modes. In fact such discussion constitutes most of the "theoretical" discussion of the modes by the Middle Ages. This was also the practice of the Greeks. Thus Guido, for example, gives the character of each mode in a famous verse recorded by Adam of Fulda (*c.* 1450–*c.* 1500):[35]

*Omnibus est primus, sed alter est tristibus aptus;*
*Tertius iratus, quartus dicitur fieri blandus;*
*Quintum de laetis, sextum pietate probatis;*
*Septimus est iuvenum, sed postremus sapientum.*
For every mood the first will be good; the second so tender to grief;
If anger the third one provoke, then the fourth will bring the relief;
The fifth be the mode for the joyous; the sixth one the pious will prize;
The seventh is pleasing to youth, but the last is the mood of the wise.

The modern view, in which the Solesmes school concurs, is to decry this situation. As Kienle says: "We ought not give

[35] Johner, Dominic, *A New School of Gregorian Chant* (New York: Pustet, 1925), p. 214.

Another frequent reference is: *Primus gravis, secundus tristis, tertius mysticus, quartus harmonicus, quintus laetus, sextus devotus, septimus angelicus, octavus perfectus.* — The first is serious, the second sad, the third mystic, the fourth melodious, the fifth joyful, the sixth devout, the seventh angelic, and the eighth perfect.

one ecclesiastical mode a joyful character and another a sad one because we find in each bright and jubilant sections, and likewise in the same one sad and mournful parts. Rather, each mode achieves these results in its own way."[36]

## THE PSALM TONES

A logical outgrowth of a discussion of modal theory is a treatment of the psalm tones.[37] The history of the psalm tones with their many variations in melodic figures is further evidence of the development of modal theory as just outlined. The psalm tones derived from the Jewish synagogue, and the antiphonal singing they involve was introduced in early centuries, being already fully recognized at the time of St. Ambrose. The psalms are made up of several verses, sung alternately by two choirs. In modern editions an asterisk is used to indicate the division of the verse. From the standpoint of musical form, the canticles (or hymns of praise) *Magnificat, Benedictus, Nunc Dimittis,* and others follow the rules for psalms.

There are eight psalm tones together with the famous *tonus peregrinus* and a few exceptional tones. These are related to the eight modes and in modern editions a Roman numeral indicating the mode of the psalm tone appears at the beginning together with a letter indicating the note on which the psalm ends.[38]

The psalm tone has a definite musical form. First comes the intonation consisting of two or three notes in a melodic

36 Kienle, Ambrose, *Choralschule* (Freiburg: Herder, 1890), 2 ed., p. 140. Translation mine.

37 The liturgical book for the psalm tones is the *Cantorinus Romanus, seu Toni Communes Officii et Missae,* 1911. A good English treatment will be found in Dominic Johner, *A New School of Gregorian Chant* (New York: Pustet, 1925), pp. 65–93.

38 The letter (A, B, C, D, E, F, or G corresponding to modern notation) is capital if the final note of the psalm and the final of the mode for that tone are the same. In some cases the letter is followed by an arabic numeral indicating the melodic formula to be used from the group of several available endings on that letter of that mode.

figure (except that tone 7 has four notes). There is an exception to beginning with a melodic figure; this is the *tonus in directum* which begins immediately on the dominant of the mode without any introduction (whence the name). After the intonation the psalm continues as a recitative on the dominant tone of the mode. Then, the *flexa,* which is a melodic figure at the middle of both halves of the verse, sometimes follows. It serves, musically, to bring the choir into synchronization again and involves stepping down a whole note (in tones 1, 4, 6, 7, and *tonus peregrinus*) or a minor third (in tones 2, 3, 5, 8, and the *tonus in directum*) for one or two syllables depending on whether the word at that point is a monosyllable or polysyllable. After this the melody returns to the dominant and the first part of the verse ends with the melodic figure of the *mediatio* or middle cadence. In the second part of the psalm verse, the recitative continues on the dominant except that the *tonus peregrinus* changes its dominant. The second part concludes with the melodic figure of the *terminatio* or final cadence. The *flexa, mediatio,* and *terminatio* are each equipped with accessory notes (the *syllaba superveniens)* to permit adjustment of the cadence to the number of syllables in the word at that point.[39]

The psalm tones are grouped into three categories. In Group I are the psalm tones with one accented note or neum in the middle and final cadence: tones 2, 4, 6, and 8 and the *tonus peregrinus, tonus in directum,* and *tonus* of Easter week. In Group II are the psalm tones with two accented notes or neums in one or two cadences: tones 1, 3, and 5. In Group III is the tone with two accented notes in both cadences: tone 7. The tones of each group differ in that each tone has its own different figure at intonation and at the cadence (and, of course, the dominants are different). Further,

39 At the *mediatio* only, the so-called *mediatio corrupta* may also be used where there is one accented note in the *middle* cadence only (i.e., where there is a monosyllable or indeclinable Hebrew word), the last note of the cadence being omitted.

several psalm tones have several different forms for the final cadence.

In the Office, the intonation is used only for the first verse of psalms and for the canticles of the Old Testament. In the canticles of the New Testament, such as the *Benedictus, Magnificat,* and *Nunc Dimittis,* however, it is used for every verse. There is also a solemn melody which is more elaborate for the *Magnificat* and *Benedictus* used on the more important feasts.

Thus even in psalm tones, the simplest group of musical forms employed by the chant (except the short dialogues between the celebrant and the congregation), there are a symmetry and variation that indicate true art. But the beauty of this chant must be brought out in adequate execution and this was early recognized. St. Isidore of Seville (*c.* 570–636) long ago laid down sound rules.[40]

> The cantor must in his voice and rendition, apply himself in a correct way so he will move the hearts of those who attend by a quiet and smooth delivery. His voice should not sound rough, brash or disquieting but should be melodious, mellifluous, flexible, precise and clear, in the pattern of the sacred text. There should be none of the pathos of the theater but, even when modulating, he should bring out the simplicity of Christian doctrine. He should not be guilty of the coloring of worldly music or of the drama but should move his audience to contrition.

## TROPES AND SEQUENTIAE

With the greatness and splendor of church music as it stood in the eleventh and twelfth centuries, it is difficult to conceive the disintegration that took place in the centuries that followed. And yet the phenomena of decadence are no more startling than, for example, those in the field of philosophy following upon the achievements of Thomas Aquinas.

[40] *De Ecclesiasticis Officiis,* II, c. xii (Migne, *P.L.,* LXXXIII, 792). Translation mine.

The processes were not exactly alike, however. With church music, the disintegration of chant was accompanied by the rise and perfection of polyphony – a music rivaling the chant in its adequacy for the liturgy. The processes of decadence stem from the development of the trope as early as the ninth century. The trope consists of adding syllables to the text of the chant where the melismas of the chant over one syllable are long. The adding of texts in this fashion definitely aids the memory which we have seen was heavily taxed before the perfection of the staff.

The invention of the trope is usually attributed to Tutilo (?–915), a monk of St. Gall. Notker *Balbulus* (The Stammerer), (?–912), another monk of St. Gall, has left us a statement, however, on the subject[41] in which he describes the difficulty he had in his youth with learning long melodies on one syllable. A monk of Jumieges Abbey near Rouen while fleeing from the Normans came to St. Gall with his music books. These contained tropes and Notker introduced the practice at St. Gall. As things developed, however, not only was the liturgical text abused by the introduction of extraneous matter but new music was added or interpolated.[42] Not all of these additions were corruptions. Some rank as artistic enlargements. But the corrupt introductions got the upper hand. The process of "troping" afflicted all parts of the Mass except the *Credo* which was already a syllabic chant. The deathblow was struck at tropes by the Council of Trent (1562) which eliminated them all from the liturgy. They never had appeared in official books and their introduction

[41] In the preface to a collection of sequences. The preface is in Migne, *P.L.*, CXXXI, 1003.

[42] It is from the tropes thus introduced that the Gregorian *Kyries* derive their names (e.g., in *Kyrie Fons Bonitatis,* the words *Fons bonitatis, pater ingenite, a quo bona cuncta procedunt,* were inserted between the words *Kyrie* and *eleison* to give a syllabic treatment to the extended melody) and from trope-named *Kyries* come the names of the Gregorian Masses in modern editions of the chant, e.g., *Missa, Fons Bonitatis,* in which other parts of the Mass *Ordinarium* are grouped by custom with a given *Kyrie.*

into many churches was long resisted. Troping had perhaps reached its zenith in the tenth century as the principal outlet for inventiveness but as the *Sequentia* came into prominence, troping gave way.

It is often said[43] that the *Sequentia* is a form of trope. While there is a relationship, this is not an accurate statement and only serves to confuse. The *Sequentia (sequentia,* following)[44] grew out of the *jubilus* of the *Alleluia* chant. Groups of melismas were built up in repetitious *(sequentia)* form without words. To what extent this must be attributed to Oriental sources is not clear but since the *Alleluia* chant was supplied with a text from St. Gregory's time, the new melodic material was distinctly an addition.[45] Thus the *Sequentia* served, in common, with the trope, as an outlet for invention, but, in contrast with the trope, the *Sequentia* did not consist in essence in adding words to melodies. Later, but prior to the tenth century, words were added to the *Sequentiae* to form the *sequentia cum prosa,* or melodies with prose text. The words were fitted in strophic (hymnlike) form. From the tenth century on, the *Sequentia* stood on its own feet as an independent form. Melodies were composed to new texts as an integral process. As far as records go, Notker is usually credited with being the father of the *Sequentia.* Im-

43 E.g., in Reese, Gustave, *Music in the Middle Ages* (New York: Norton, 1940), p. 187, he says "The kind of trope that most nearly crystallized into a definite form is the *sequence.*"

44 Refer to the liturgical discussion at the end of Chapter I, p. 14 ff.

45 Weinmann, Karl, *History of Church Music* (New York: Pustet, 1910), says on p. 36: "The Oriental origin of the new form is shown indisputably by the increased length of the vocalization (for which there was no place in the Gregorian liturgy, since Gregory the Great had supplied the Alleluja-chant with verses) and by the peculiar Semitic notation of these chants, from right to left, which is found in the oldest existing manuscripts (Cod. 484 of St. Gall). It must also be added that the oldest sequences of Notker, as well as those of his first German successors, belong, in the arrangement of the verses, entirely to the Middle Greek (or Byzantine) hymnody, while no single analogue is to be found for their structure in any of the Latin hymns since the time of St. Ambrose. The musical style of the oldest sequences finally shows many pecularities foreign to Latin music, but found in Byzantine."

mediately following him in the tenth century two great centers for *Sequentia* composition developed at St. Gall and at St. Martial in Limoges. The perfection of the form is often attributed to Adam of St. Victor (*c.* 1110–1192) at Paris although the composing of *Sequentiae* was practiced throughout Europe at this time. The variation in forms is great but certain general characteristics can be observed: (1) *Sequentiae* tended to be syllabic in musical style, (2) *Sequentiae* were in strophic form and usually the melody was repeated with a different verse of text the second time, and (3) *Sequentiae* formed the springboard for the development of hymns in the vernacular in most countries.

While the *Sequentia* was fertile ground for invention, it was just as fertile for abuse. As a result, the Council of Trent (1562) struck down all except the four sequences mentioned in Chapter 1, p. 20.

## CHANT ACCOMPANIMENT

There is no question that the chant was developed as unaccompanied monody. Not until the introduction of *organum,* the beginning of polyphony, did the matter of accompaniment receive attention. Accompaniment came as part of the era of invention (and decadence of the chant) that received its principal impetus from the perfection of the staff. It would serve no useful purpose to give a detailed history of chant accompaniment since it is not possible to speak of a "traditional" or artistically correct chant accompaniment by organ until the nineteenth century.

Chant accompaniment by the organ is permitted with the justification that the pitch of the choir can thus be maintained or the choir in a sense "supported" (e.g., rough voices, or singing out of tune with each other can be corrected). The very statement that a choir needs "support" from the organ indicates the choir is not giving a skillful performance and the question then is mainly one of preventing a bad execution from becoming worse. This in itself, however, is a worthy end.

Such accompaniment as the chant receives from the organ must, for historical reasons as well as from principles of musical form, be entirely unobtrusive and subordinate to the chant itself. This immediately suggests a number of rules. The most important principle is to preserve the rhythm of the chant in the accompaniment. Despite the dispute as to chant rhythm, all scholars agree that wherever the accents (or rhythmic divisions) are placed, those accents must be observed by the accompaniment. This immediately excludes such an accompaniment as a change of chord for every note. Rather chords must be changed only at the accents to preserve the unity of rhythm. Modal unity also must be preserved in the accompaniment. The chant melody is written in one of the eight chant modes. The accompaniment can employ only the chords proper to the mode of the melody; to use others would hinder the choir rather than aid it for the singer would hear notes he should *not* sing.

The unity of rhythm and the modal unity combine to place further restrictions on an artistic accompaniment. Since the number of chords proper to a given mode is very limited (for it must be remembered that in modern music there are more chords available in a given "key," to say nothing of the freedom to modulate into other "keys" and thus make hundreds of chords available), true art would prevent an accompaniment with monotonous repetition of these chords. Rather, the accompaniment must rely on the sustaining of chords (by common notes interlocking one chord with its predecessor or successor). As a result while the melody moves freely, the chords do not change frequency and, in most cases, only one voice of the accompaniment besides the melody moves at any one time, except at cadences.

No chant accompaniment is permitted, of course, during the time when the liturgy requires the organ to be silent.

Beyond these few rules of artistic unity of chant and accompaniment, the composer is free. There can be no dispute as to the fact that an excellent accompaniment makes a finer artistic and liturgical achievement than the same chant without accompaniment. But tradition favors the unaccompanied chant.

### MOZARABIC AND GALLICAN CHANT

Within the Catholic Church – and in the Western World – there have been four great traditions of chant: the Ambrosian, the Gallican, the Mozarabic, and the Roman or Gregorian. We have thus far discussed the Ambrosian and Roman, the only two that survive except that the Mozarabic can still be claimed to exist in isolated parts of Spain.

Most of the history of Mozarabic[46] chant is as yet unexplored. The Mozarabic developed in Spain (excluding Catalonia, the northern part of that country) and in early days it was called the Visigothic liturgy. It survived longer than the Gallican – until the fifteenth century for a good part of Spain. St. Isidore of Seville (*c.* 570–636)[47] mentions that St. Leander, Archbishop of Seville (?–599) who had traveled to Constantinople, "has composed many selections to sweet sounds." Tradition credits him with the same role in the Mozarabic chant that Gregory had in the Roman. And St. Isidore himself, in his encyclopedia that missed little of the learning then known, gives some descriptions of music. The earliest manuscript fragments are from the end of the ninth century and the earliest reasonably complete manuscript is the eleventh-century Antiphonary of Leon. The development of a separate liturgy apparently involved abuse, and the

46 The term derives from those who remained Christians in Spain after the Moslem invasion of the eighth century.

47 *De Ecclesiasticis Officiis,* Migne, *P.L.* LXXXIII, 1104. The principal work with the sources on the Mozarabic chant is by Casiano, Rojo, and Prado, R. P. German, *El Canto Mozarabe, Estudio Historico-critico de su Antiguedad y Estado Actual* (Barcelona: Diputacion provincial, 1929), and by Peter Wagner in the *Spanische Forschungen der Gorresgesellschaft.*

Roman liturgy was ordered substituted, in 1071, by the Vatican and, in 1085, by King Alfonso VI upon his reconquest of part of Spain from the Moslems. Thereafter the Mozarabic continued in only six churches of Toledo and in that part of Spain still held by the Moors. The Mozarabic employed a notation which is still undecipherable[48] except for the eleventh-century manuscript of St. Millan de la Cogolla in which sixteen melodies were transcribed in the twelfth-century Aquitanian notation above the Mozarabic notation.

In 1500, Francisco Cardinal Ximenez de Cisneros printed his version of the Mozarabic chant which he attempted to revive. This printing is in mensural notation and undoubtedly is a corruption. Three chant books also were written about this time in Mozarabic. Whether these were based on earlier manuscripts then existing is not known. They also contain some Gregorian texts and music, however.[49]

From the few Mozarabic melodies available that are known to be genuine, the chant is simple and seems to be more closely related to the Ambrosian than the Gregorian, employing the authentic modes for the most part. The theory has been brilliantly advanced by Dom Mocquereau[50] that the four Western chants, the Ambrosian, Gallican, Mozarabic, and Gregorian, are but four dialects, musically speaking, of a common language. This must not be understood to mean that a perfected language later developed dialects, but rather that there was a certain interchange of three elements in the premanuscript days. These elements are: (1) the Eastern influence, (2) the Greco-Roman influence, and (3) a certain folk or native element. As the chants developed, the native element may have come more to the fore and separated the four chants.

48 See Sunol, Gregory, *Introduction à la Paléographie Musicale Grégorienne* (Paris: Desclee, 1935), Chapter XIII.

49 Care must be taken with printed materials purporting to be Mozarabic; sometimes only the text is Mozarabic.

50 In *Paléographie Musicale*, I,. 33 ff.

Mention has already been made of the suppression of the Gallican chant by Pepin and Charlemagne in the late eighth century. It is doubtful that neums existed at this early date. Despite the efforts at suppression, the chant continued in some places and fortunately a manuscript of Fleury dated 877 and two eleventh-century manuscripts, one of Albi Cathedral, Paris National Library, and the other of St. Yrieix, Codex 903, Paris National Library,[51] survive. Three of the Good Friday chants in use today in the Roman liturgy are incorporations from the Gallican.[52]

## THE HISTORY OF LATER GREGORIAN CHANT TO ITS EXTINCTION

The history of later Gregorian chant to its virtual extinction in the seventeenth century is a dismal story whose value is mostly negative. It will, therefore, be short.

The gradual decadence and disuse of the chant can be traced to a number of factors. Most important of all was the growth of polyphony. Step by step, first this part of the Mass and then that was replaced with the "new art." This process was related to the humanism prevalent during the period. The reintroduction of Greek and Roman learning without adequate understanding of those civilizations by the smaller minds caused much criticism of the chant. We have already seen that the loss of the rhythmic notation peculiar to the chant and the development of the staff caused an imperfect chant to be presented from at least the thirteenth century on. With the new learning, esthetic criticism was launched against the chant on three main fronts.

The first criticism was directed against the undue length

[51] The St. Yrieix manuscript is printed in facsimile in *Paléographie Musicale,* XIII.

[52] The *Improperia,* the *Crux Fidelis,* and the *Pange Lingua . . . certaminis.* Amedee Gastoué published the leading work on Gallican chant in 1939, including transcriptions from the three manuscripts mentioned above. The volume is a reprint of a series of articles in *Revue du Chant Gregorien,* XLI to XLIII incl., 1937–1939, incl.

of certain of the melodies. These were the melodies of the soloists. The critics failed to perceive that the liturgy was constructed functionally: the melodies of the various chants being adjusted to the technical abilities of the particular performer or performers expected to execute them. For the liturgy to have cut all melodies to the same length whether for soloist, choir, or congregation would have been artistically false. The Church could only have met this objection by transferring the parts entrusted to soloists to the choir, both liturgically and musically. The primary reason for the criticism was that the standards of the new art – polyphony – were applied to a different art – monody. In short, the criticism would have been valid if chant were a form of polyphony.

The second criticism was directed against the treatment of the text by the chant. The critics spoke of the "barbarisms" of the chant because it did not conform to the *quantity* of the syllables of the text. Essentially, this was a criticism of Church Latin as against classical Latin. Given the structure of Church Latin with its accentual measure of syllables, there can be no criticism of the chant. In the discussion of the *cursus* at the end of Chapter I, it was pointed out that while the Church made great use of the *cursus* from the fourth to the seventh centuries, it went into disuse until at least the eleventh century. Thus some of the early chants conformed in part to the laws of classical Latin. The critics accordingly undertook to shave or embellish the chant here and there to force it to conform to the rules of classical Latin at those points where it did not already do so. Rather, by their own standards, the critics should have fought for the conforming of Church Latin to classical Latin. This was a task that was too great for them and their "improvements" of the chant only added a false current to the other false currents then already obscuring the true chant.

The third criticism embraced many details. For example,

the modal system of the chant was attacked. The chant names for modes did not correspond to the Greek names for the same modes. In fact, the Church modes were not the same as the Greek modes. The critics did not recognize that the Church modes have their own theoretical structure and are in no sense merely an imperfect imitation of Greek modes. Much less did they understand that the Gregorian melodies had grown up without the theoretical structure of modes — that Church modes were a later effort to fit theory to an already existing body of melodies.

The remarkable thing about the whole process of decadence and criticism is that throughout it all the Church authorities never lost sight of the original ideals of the chant, but clung to tradition though they did recognize that the tradition was by now distorted. There were frequent efforts at reform. Thus in the twelfth and thirteenth centuries the Cistercians and Dominicans undoubtedly brought things back into line for a while by their reforms — they were still close enough in point of time to know what the true chant had been. But later "reformers" traveled in just as much fog as the critics. The powerful Council of Trent (1545–1563) brought matters to a head. There was a strong movement in the Council to ban all music except Gregorian chant from the liturgy. At this point we must anticipate the next chapter. Giovanni Pierluigi Palestrina (1526–1594), justly termed *Musicae Princeps* (the Prince of Music), was then the leading man in polyphony — and as has since developed, the leading contrapuntist of all time. He held a number of posts under several popes and was, in effect, the head of Vatican music. He perceived the seriousness of the situation and embarked on two great projects: (1) the justification of polyphony in the Church by eliminating its defects and bringing it to perfection,[53] and (2) the revision of the chant books with which he was entrusted by Pope Gregory XIII (pontificate:

[53] This process is the story of Chapter III.

Leading American Composers of Catholic Church Music

Rev. Mathias J.
Vanden Elsen, O.Praem.
1870–

Rev. Ludwig J.
Bonvin, S.J.
1849–1939

Pietro A. Yon
1886–1943

Philip G. Kreckel
1893–

LEADING AMERICAN COMPOSERS OF CATHOLIC CHURCH MUSIC

Nicola A. Montani
1880–1948

Joseph J. McGrath
1889–

J. Vincent Higginson
(Pen name: Cyr de Brant)
1896–

Richard K. Biggs
1886–

1572–1585). The first he achieved brilliantly so that never again was non-Gregorian music in danger of exclusion from the liturgy. The second achievement, in which Zoilo participated, he began diligently, but death balked its realization. There are very serious doubts whether even Palestrina, great musician though he was, could have resurrected the true chant. That would have been possible only if he had returned to the manuscripts of the ninth to eleventh centuries or to even earlier manuscripts which may then have existed.[54]

The death of Palestrina did not bring an end to the movement, however, and in 1614 and 1615, Francesco Suriano (1549–1620) and Felice Anerio (*c.* 1560–1614) prepared the famous *Graduale Medicaenum.* It was not an official edition but a private enterprise of the publisher, Raimondi, with the *Stamperia Orientale* of Cardinal Medici. This edition was to be revived in the nineteenth century as we shall see in Chapter IV. Whether the two editors employed manuscripts left by Palestrina cannot be determined although for a long time the edition was ascribed to him. The edition was necessitated by a new and official revision of the Breviary and Missal. A comparison of the *Graduale Medicaenum* with the Vatican edition of 1907 or with the manuscripts of the ninth to eleventh centuries shows how the chant was mutilated. The melodies are abbreviated, with some melismas cut out entirely and others combined into unnatural groups and shifted to the accented syllables. The length to which the mutilation was carried is illustrated by the endeavor to adjust syllables in view of solmization. If the text read *sola,* then the melody was changed to the interval *sol–la,* or if it read *quare faciem,* then *re–fa* was sung over those syllables. The scholar Müller succinctly summarizes things when he says,

[54] After Palestrina's death one of the interesting frauds of history was perpetrated by his son, who sold the alleged Palestrina manuscripts of the revised chant to a publisher — but the fraud was uncovered in time.

"In the Medicaean edition the chant bleeds at a thousand places."[55]

In speaking of chant as dead by 1600, we do not mean to imply that efforts parading under the name of Gregorian chant came to a halt. The Medicaean edition had little influence outside Italy until the nineteenth century, but there it was the basis for all further editions. In France, Guillaume Nivers (1617–1701) issued his *Graduale* and *Antiphonale* in 1658 under the privilege of the king and the approval of the Belgian, Henri Dumont (1610–1684), a chant composer. This served as the basis for future French editions, even as late as the Rennes edition of 1853 and the Digne and Dijon editions of 1858.

Although the chant was in process of decadence from at least the thirteenth century on, some new chants were being added. The Vatican edition preserves some of these, particularly the widely known *Missa De Angelis* of which the *Kyrie* and *Gloria* are from the fifteenth and sixteenth centuries. The *Credo* (Vatican No. III) commonly used with this Mass dates from the seventeenth century. These chants clearly show the influence of the secular music of the period in which they were written. It is true that they are in the Gregorian modes and not in the modern modes, and that they employ many of the melodic figures known to Gregorian chant. Yet they barely qualify as chant. This is apparent by a comparison with the *Sanctus* used in that Mass which dates from the eleventh and twelfth cenutries and is characteristic of the chant. The lightness, flexibility in rhythm and nuance are missing from the *Missa De Angelis*. Perhaps this can best be summarized by saying the Mass is a perfect bridge of mensural music and the chant: it has one foot in each camp.

The resurrection of chant in the nineteenth century will be considered in Chapter IV.

[55] Müller, Hermann, "Solmisationssilben in der Medieäischen Choralausgabe," *Archiv für Musikurssenschaft I,* 127–134 (1918).

## THE WEDDING OF CHANT AND LITURGY

We are now in a position to examine the wedding of chant and liturgy. This is the principal concern of the chant – and of this chapter. Such a consideration necessarily involves an appraisal of chant as art.

The liturgical aim has been well expressed:[56]

> If the Catholic liturgy is in reality an act of Christ and of the whole Church, the liturgical chant can only fulfill its object entirely when it is connected as closely as possible with this act, when it interprets the various texts in accordance with the thoughts and sentiments that move Christ and the Church in their united action and embodies them in a tone-picture.

The attainment of this goal clearly requires that the melodies be subordinate to the liturgical purposes of the particular text. The melodies can never become ends in themselves or even distract in any way from the liturgy. But this does not require a lessening of artistic merit. The chant is concerned only with the expression of man's relation to God, and more particularly to Christ. That is a legitimate artistic goal. To introduce anything not a part of that relationship is not only unliturgical but inartistic. How the chant achieves that goal has been best described in simple terms by Pope Pius X in the *Motu Proprio* of November 22, 1903:

> This chant adapts itself to the liturgy better than any composition in the modern style. Its melodies are just the right length, neither too short nor too meager for solemn functions in a cathedral, neither too long nor impracticable in less favorable circumstances. Moreover, it gives the text without repetition or mutilation of the words, and omits none of them. Every syllable is enunciated by the whole choir at the same time. Though another system may be allowed or may often be necessary in polyphonic works, the

[56] Johner, Dominic, *A New School of Gregorian Chant* (New York: Pustet, 1925), p. 223.

simple style of plainsong deserves the preference in regard to the delivery of the words.

The musical techniques employed by the chant are seldom analyzed.[57] It would be surprising even to many who have some acquaintance with the chant to learn that the chant employs every device known to modern melody. Speaking somewhat arbitrarily we can classify the melodies into four groups: the psalmodic, the syllabic, the neumatic, and the melismatic.[58] A choice of style depends on many factors: first, there is the matter of the part of the liturgy involved. Chants for the Office are shorter than for the Mass. Then, the ability of the singer is considered. Chants for the clergy and the people are simpler and demand less musical training and skill (the psalmodic and syllabic). Those chants to be sung by the choir require training (neumatic and melismatic). The melismatic also serves for solo work by a skilled member of the choir (as in the melismatic *Alleluia* or *Deo Gratias*). Further discrimination in style is made in selecting melodies (*a*) between simpler melodies for ordinary ferial days and more replete melodies for Sundays, feasts of saints and solemn occasions, and (*b*) between the usual parts of the Office and the more solemn parts of the Office, Lauds and Vespers, which have fuller chants. Not only are particular melodies set to particular texts, but the melodies differ for the same text according as it is used in different parts of the liturgy. Sometimes the same "basic" melody may be used for the same

[57] The leading work is Paul Ferretti, *Estetica Gregoriana, Ossia Trattato delle Forme Musicali del Canto Gregoriano* (Rome: Pontificio Instituto di Musica Sacra, 1934), Vol. I, tr. into French by A. Agaesse.

[58] The definition of these terms can be recapitulated at this point. The psalmodic style involves an opening melodic figure, then one or two recitative tones (which may be broken by an occasional melodic figure: a semicadence) and a concluding melodic figure (the cadence). The syllabic style consists mostly of a different note to each syllable (such as in the *Pater Noster*). The neumatic style consists of a neum for each syllable (the neum being a compound note in Gregorian notation or a group of two to six notes in modern notation). The melismatic style involves extended passages over one syllable (such as the *Alleluia*).

text in different parts of the liturgy but at one part the melody is in neumatic style and at another part it is stripped to syllabic style. In such a case, the melody is seldom employed in different parts of the liturgy of the Mass or Office but is normally used in the same part. For example, the same melody is not usually employed as the basis for a *Graduale* and a *Communio* in a different Mass, but rather in several different *Communios.* There is a unity in the type of melodies employed in the *Introitus* as against those in the *Communio* for example. Thus the artistic "unities" cross each other in various ways. The melody in an *Introitus* may be in the *form* peculiar to the *Introitus* generally but may be related to a "basic" melody in the *Graduale* of the same Mass.

And yet we have covered only a part of the wedding of chant and liturgy. Gregorian melodies are fused to the text in a way that no other music is. Gregorian rhythm is "free," *i.e.,* it is oratorical rhythm. The text also is in oratorical rhythm. In this sense it would be correct to say that mensural music is correct only if it has a poetical text – because only then is there unity between the "regular" rhythm of the music and the "regular" rhythm of the text. Gregorian melodies follow the grammatical accents of the prose text.[59] The accented syllable has in general a higher note or notes than the neighboring syllables do – unless another unity cuts across. Besides using a higher note for emphasis, a prolonged note and a single note in the midst of elaborate melodies are also used for this purpose. The melody peaks correspond to the textual peaks. Not only is this true of syllables in the word but it is true of the word in relation to other words in the phrase or sentence. In this sense Gregorian chant is oratorical. The spoken liturgy itself is oratorical. The chanted liturgy is oratory upon oratory. The value of cheironomy (the

[59] Reference should be made at this point to the discussion earlier in this chapter of the dispute among today's scholars whether Gregorian rhythm is rigidly tied to grammatical accents.

use of the hand by the director to indicate visually the flow of the melody) for the chant is thus thoroughly understood.

The period as the unit in modern music is also found in the chant. Instead of the regular number of bars, however, the period in chant varies in length as the text does. The period is divided into phrases as in modern music. The phrases in a period may be two (forephrase and afterphrase) or three (forephrase, afterphrase, and afterphrase). The phrases are divided into members containing two or three incises. If there are two incises to the member, the pattern may be *aa* or *ab,* if three, the patterns primarily used are *abc, aab, abb,* or *aba.*

The metaphor of an arch has been used for the period in chant melody. Most Gregorian melodies rise to a peak at the middle of the period and descend to the final (in the plagal modes the "inverted" arch will be found). If the period is shortened, the melody may begin at the "top of the arch" and descend to the final. In some cases the arch is not used but the melody twines around a central note.

Cutting across this type of organization is another. There are formulae characteristics of (1) position (at intonation, in the middle section, and at the cadence); (2) style or tonality; and (3) of internal structure. Organization according to position we have already analyzed in discussing psalm tones, but it is common to all the chants. Organization by style or tonality is primarily demonstrated in the *parts* of the liturgy, e.g., the *Tractus* is written only in Modes II and VIII, the *Introitus* more commonly in Modes I and III, etc. Internal structure of the chant shows great care.[60] The two chief means of that structure are repetition and imitation. The repetition may be exactly of the melodic figure, or it may be transposed to begin on a different tone, or it may be repetition with an elaboration. Or instead of being melodic repetition, it may

[60] This is treated in detail with examples in Dominic Johner, *A New School of Gregorian Chant* (New York: Pustet, 1925), pp. 238–246.

be repetition of a rhythmic pattern with a different melody. The repetition may extend to larger sections.

Imitation is used in different ways: imitation in direct motion (e.g., a series of *porrectus,* continuously ascending), or in contrary motion (e.g., a *torculus* followed by a *porrectus,* thus alternately ascending and descending), or with an abbreviation or prolongation.

From the esthetic point of view, the climax is the great variation with which the different kinds of organization are employed, a variation *determined* by the text. There is a freedom from the monotonous structure to which modern music was long enslaved. It is at once a tribute to the chant that many are ignorant of the rules of organization in the chant. Its art is effortless in that sense.

Our viewpoint in looking at the smaller melodic figures has been microcosmic. Taking a macrocosmic view we find four different categories of *form* (as opposed to the psalmodic, syllabic, neumatic, and melismatic *styles* already discussed): (1) the strophic compositions, mainly the hymns and *Sequentiae,* involving stanza arrangement (the part of the chant closest to modern music and drawn from Greek sources); (2) psalmodic compositions, e.g., the psalm tones (drawn from the synagogue); (3) commatic or free compositions, most of the Mass and Office chants not included in groups (1) and (2) (the invention of the chant itself); and (4) the monologues and dialogues of the celebrant and congregation.

Gregorian chant also employs the "lesser" techniques known to modern music for contrast: the use of wide intervals for emphasis, for example. Some students even claim mnemonic instances can be found in the true chant (they are common in the corrupted chant). The use of liquescent neums for liquescent syllables might be cited. But there is little use of an ascending melody to accompany the word *ascendit,* for example, or of word painting such as some see, for example, in the imitation of cooing in the melody over a passage of the text referring to the dove. Much of the liturgy to which the chant is set comes verbatim from the Scriptures. Not only would it be adopting a "lower" standard to employ such devices in the chant but it would be divorcing the style of the music and of the text to admit word painting, for example, in the music when it does not occur in the text.

A homely metaphor may aid the understanding of one not a musician. Enough has already been said to establish that there is an analogy of the whole of the various chants to the structure and symmetry of architecture. Architecture does have one advantage over music, however. When a building falls, even the ignorant can understand that no matter how elaborate the structure and design were, they failed; music fails, too, when it is structurally faulty. The difficulty is that the failure is not so apparent as a collapsed building to one ignorant of the art.

## BIBLIOGRAPHY FOR CHAPTER II

### BOOKS

NOTE: The literature on Gregorian chant is very extensive. The best bibliography available in English (though by no means complete) is contained in Gustave Reese, *Music in the Middle Ages* (New York: Norton, 1940), pp. 431–445. The following is a selection of leading works arranged topically.

#### GENERAL

Birkle, P. Sintbertus, O.S.B., English trans. by A. Lemaistre: *A Complete and Practical Method of the Solesmes Plain Chant* (New York: Wagner, 1910).

Coussemaker, Charles E. H., *Scriptorum de Musica Medii Aevi Nova Series* (Paris: Durand, 1864–1876), 4 vols. New ed. (Paris: Durand, 1908). Facsimile ed. (Milan: Bolletino Bibliografico Musicale, 1931).

Dechevrens, Antoine, S.J., *Etudes de Science Musicale* (Paris: Chez liauteur, 1898), 3 vols.

Ferretti, Paul, O.S.B., *Principii Teorici e Pratici di Canto Gregoriano* (Rome: Desclee, 1933), 3 ed.

Gastoué, Amedee, *Cours Theorique et Pratique de Plain-chant Romain Gregorien* (Paris: Schola Cantorum, 1904).

—— *L'art Gregorien* (Paris: Alcan, 1911).

Gerbert, Martin, O.S.B., *De Cantu et Musica Sacra, a Prima Ecclesiae Aetate Usque ad Praesens Tempus* (St. Blasien, 1774), 2 vols.

—— *Scriptores Ecclesiastici de Musica* (St. Blasien, 1774), 3 vols. New ed. (Graz: Moser, 1904). Facsimile ed. (Milan: Bolletino Bibliografico Musicale, 1931).

Huegle, Gregory, O.S.B., *Catechism of Gregorian Chant* (New York: Fischer, 1928).

Jeannin, Jules C., O.S.B., *Melodies Liturgiques Syriennes et Chaldeenes* (Paris: Leroux, 1924–1928), 2 vols.

Johner, Dominic, O.S.B., *Neue Schule des Gregorianischen Choralgesanges* (Ratisbon: Pustet, 1906). English tr. from 5 ed. by H. S. Butterfield, *A New School of Gregorian Chant* (Ratisbon: Pustet, 1925).

Laroche, Teodoro, *Principe Tradizionali d'Esecuzione del Canto Gregoriano* (Rome: Desclee, 1935). French ed., *Principii Traditionelles d'Execution du Chant Gregorien* (Tournai: Desclee, 1935).

Mocquereau, Andre, O.S.B., *Le Nombre Musical Gregorien* (Tournai: Desclee, 1908–1927), 2 vols. English tr. by Aileen Tone of Part I, Vol. I (Tournai: Desclee, 1932).

*Monographies Gregoriennes* (Tournai: Desclee, 1910 – ), 13 vols. to 1938.

Pierik, Marie, *The Spirit of Gregorian Chant* (Boston: McLaughlin & Reilly, 1939).

—— *The Song of the Church* (New York: Longmans, 1947).

Pothier, Joseph, O.S.B., *Les Melodies Gregoriennes* (Tournai: Desclee, 1881).

Ravegnani, E., *Metodo Compilato di Canto Gregoriano* (Rome: Desclee, 1926), 5 ed.

Reese, Gustave, *Music in the Middle Ages* (New York: Norton, 1940).

Rousseau, Norbert, O.S.B., *L'Ecole Gregorienne de Solesmes* (Tournai: Desclee, 1910).

Sunol, Gregory, O.S.B., *Metodo Completo di Canto Gregoriano* (Rome: Desclee, 1905). English tr. by G. M. Durnford, *Textbook of Gregorian Chant* (Tournai: Desclee, 1930).

Ward, Justine B., *Gregorian Chant* (Washington, D. C.: Catholic Education Press, 1923).

Wagner, Peter, *Einführung in die Gregorianischen Melodien* (Leipzig: Breitkopf & Härtel, 1901–1921), 3 vols. English trans. by Agnes Orme and E. G. P. Wyatt of Vol. I, *Introduction to Gregorian Melodies* (London: Plainsong and Medieval Society, 1901).

*Ambrosian Chant*

Bas, Guilio, *Manule di Canto Ambrosiano* (Milan: Ambrosius, 1929).

Mocquereau, Andre, O.S.B., "Chant Ambrosien," in *Paléographie Musicale,* Vol. IX, cited below.

Pothier, Joseph, O.S.B., *Les Mélodies Grégoriennes* (Paris: Desclee, 1881).

*Chant Accompaniment*

Bragers, Achille P., *Short Treatise on Gregorian Accompaniment* (New York: Fischer, 1934).

Desroquettes, J. Herbert, O.S.B., *L'Accompagnement Rhythmique d'apres les Principes de Solesmes* (Tournai: Desclee, 1931).

Potier, Francis, *L'Art de l'accompagnement du Chant Gregorien* (Tournai: Desclee, 1946).

Potiron, Henri, *Cours D'Accompagnement du Chant Gregorien* (Paris: Desclee, 1927). English tr. by Ruth C. Gabain, *Treatise on the Accompaniment of Gregorian Chant* (Tournai: Desclee, 1933).

*Chant Modes*

Auda, Antoine: *Les Modes et les Tons de la Musique* (Bruxelles: M. Hayez, 1930).

Various authors in "General" section above.

*Chant Notation*

Benedictine of Stanbrook, *Gregorian Music: An Outline of Musical Paleography* (London: Burns & Oates, 1895).

Sunol, Gregory, O.S.B., *Introduction à la Paléographie Musicale Gregorienne* (Paris: Desclee, 1935).

Various articles in *Paléographie Musicale,* cited *infra.*

*Chant Rhythm*

*a*) Accentualist School

Pothier, Joseph, O.S.B., *Les Mélodies Grégoriennes* (Paris: Desclee, 1881).

*b*) Mensuralist School

Dechevrens, Antione, S.J., *Les Vraies Melodies Grégoriennes* (Paris: Beauchesne, 1902).

Jammers, Ewald, *Der Gregorianischen Rhythmus* (Strassburg: Heitz, 1937).

Jeannin, Jules C., O.S.B., *Etudes sur le Rhythme Grégorien* (Strassburg: Leroux, 1926).

*c*) Solesmes School

Mocquereau, Andre, O.S.B., *Le Nombre Musicale Grégorien ou Rhythmique Grégorienne,* cited above under "General."

Sunol, Gregory, O.S.B., *Introduction à la Paléographie Musicale,* cited above under "Chant Notation."

*Paléographie Musicale* cited *infra.*

## EDITIONS OF MUSIC

### *Ambrosian Chant*

*Antiphonale Missarum juxta ritum Sanctae Ecclesiae Mediolanensis* (Rome: Editio Typica Vaticana, 1935).

### *Gregorian Chant*

*Antiphonale. . . . pro Diurnis Horis* (Rome: Typis Polyglottis Vaticanis, 1912).

*Cantorinus Romanus* (Rome: Editio Typica Vaticana, 1911).

*Graduale Romanum* (Rome: Editio Typica Vaticana, 1924).

*Liber Usualis Missae et Officii pro Dominicis et Festis cum Cantu Gregoriano.* Published in three editions (Tournai: Desclee).

1) Gregorian notation with Latin rubrics, 1934
2) Gregorian notation with English rubrics, 1938
3) Modern notation with Latin rubrics, 1932

*Officium Defunctorum* (Rome: Editio Typica Vaticana, 1909).

*Officium Majoris Hebdomadae et Octavae Paschae* (Rome: Editio Typica Vaticana, 1923).

NOTE: The *Vesperale* (part of the *Antiphonale*) and the *Kyriale* (part of the *Graduale*) are published separately in numerous editions. In addition various of the older orders of the Church are authorized to use their own *Graduale* and *Antiphonale,* e.g., Dominican, Praemonstratensian, *etc.*

Particular mention should be made of the series, *Paleographie Musicale,* begun in 1889 by the Abbey of Solesmes and continued by Desclee of Tournai, of which sixteen volumes have appeared down to 1938. The series includes many papers on various technical aspects but more important, reproduces many of the original older codices and in a number of cases their modern translation.

# CHAPTER III

## *POLYPHONY FROM ITS BEGINNINGS TO ITS DENOUEMENT*

### THE DEVELOPMENT OF PART SINGING — ORGANUM

THE beginnings of polyphony in the Church date from Scotus Erigena (*c.* 815–*c.* 880), but the term *polyphony* has several meanings. In its broad meaning, polyphony (many voices simultaneously) is opposed to monody (unison or one-voiced music). In its narrower meaning it refers to that style of composition which employs the art of counterpoint.[1] For general purposes, counterpoint is distinguished from harmony, the other general scheme of polyphony, in that, in the latter, the several voices change notes simultaneously, whereas in counterpoint the changes of notes are not simultaneous but "staggered."[2]

Here and there in musical history before the ninth century, scholars have found traces of polyphony. Some references to it can even be found in early church music writings. Although few of the compositions of polyphony prior to 1200 have survived, some knowledge of theory and practice in this period is valuable for an understanding of the reasons for

[1] To avoid this confusion, the term "polyphony" will be used in its narrow meaning.

[2] This is only a rough distinction; it is sometimes expressed by referring to harmony as "vertical" music and counterpoint as "horizontal" music because in harmony the attention is directed to chords and in counterpoint to the contrasting lines of melody. The distinction is not accurate since it is possible to have simultaneous changing of notes in the different voices and yet produce a species of counterpoint, as for example at the very beginning of counterpoint in the *organum*.

chant decadence as well as of the matured contrapuntal school.[3]

The earliest attempts at polyphony are described by the philosopher Scotus Erigena in a treatise *De Divisione Naturae:* "The singing called *Organum* (also sometimes called diaphony) consists of voices that differ in quality and pitch, which sometimes are divided from each other by a large interval in a proportional relation and sometimes come together as dictated by certain fine artistic laws based on the differences in the ecclesiastical modes. The voices thus produce a natural and pleasing sound."[4] In a somewhat later work, *Musica Enchiriadis,*[5] formerly attributed to Hucbald, the *organum* is described as consisting of a leading voice (*cantus firmus*) and another voice *below* at an interval of a fourth.[6] The second voice is stated to be always parallel to the *cantus firmus* except that at the beginning and end of the composition the voices unite on the same tone. Later the interval employed was the fifth, due to the fact that the original *organum* was transposed an octave higher and thus placed above the *cantus firmus.*[7]

[3] Pratt, Waldo S., *The History of Music* (New York: G. Schirmer, 1907; rev. ed., 1930), is thoroughly unreliable in his section on ecclesiastical polyphony down to 1400 (pp. 77–85).

[4] Migne, *P.L.,* CXXII, 638.

[5] The *Musica Enchiriadis* is found in Martin Gerbert, *Scriptores Ecclesiastici de Musica Sacra Potissimum* (St. Blasien, 1774), Vol. I, pp. 152–172. The question of authorship is treated in Hans Muller, *Hucbald's Echte und Unechte Schriften über Musik* (Leipzig: Teubner, 1884).

[6] The *Scholia* of the *Musica Enchiriadis* are responsible for the frequent statement that the *Musica* describes *organum* at the fifth, some authors failing to distinguish between the *Musica* and its commentaries.

[7] A number of theories have been advanced to explain, psychologically, the origin of polyphony. Anselm Hughes, in *Anglo-French Sequelae, Edited from the Papers of the Late Dr. Henry Marriott Bannister* (Milwaukee: Morehouse, 1934) on page 99 advances the theory that since male or female voices fall into a high or low pitch, the interval of a fifth developed when the high voice was unable to sing a low melody or vice versa. Amedee Gastoué in *Encyclopedie de la Musique et Dictionnaire du Conservatoire, Partie I,* Vol. I, p. 572, argues that the voices took over polyphonic music from the organ (whence *organum*). Joseph Yasser in *A Theory of Evolving Tonality* (New York: American Library of Musicology, 1932), in Chapter VIII, thinks *organum*

Musicologists argue strenuously about whether free or strict *organum* came first. Erigena in the passage just quoted is describing free *organum,* in which the interval between the voices changes as the melody progresses. Strict *organum,* on the other hand, consists of the same interval throughout (except for the opening and closing notes). Whether *organum* at the fourth or fifth, free or strict, came first is unimportant; but the comment on the *function* of these beginnings is important. The author of the *Musica* says: the role of the early art was "a sort of layer of musical science intended for the embellishment of the ecclesiastical chants."[8] It has been suggested that this reference places *organum* in its relative role in church music but that it was much more widely used in secular music, and this may well have been so. The treatment of *organum* in the *Musica* is in many respects self-contradictory but one further fact worthy of note is reported. At one point the author says that to vitiate the undesirable tritone (the interval of an augmented fourth) which was sure to be involved in strict *organum,* the rule was laid down that in *organum* at the fourth, the *vox organalis* (the accompanying voice) should never pass below the fourth tone of the lower tetrachord. Whenever the range was so situated that the *vox organalis* would have to go lower than this, then the two voices would travel in unison until the rule could be met again. This is the first effort at rules in counterpoint.

Theoretical treatises such as the *Musica Enchiriadis* describe an *organum* of strict *limitations,* but manuscripts of

---

stems from the modal system. He argues that the ecclesiastical modes were originally made up of five whole tones and from this came the *organum* in the fifth. Armand Machabey, in *Histoire et Evolution Des Formules Musicales du Ier au XV$^e$ Siecle* (Paris: Payot, 1928), p. 52, bases the origin of *organum* on the fact that the four voices (soprano, alto, tenor, and bass) lie naturally about a fifth apart in their range. Karl Weinmann, in *History of Church Music* (New York: Pustet, 1925), p. 74, suggests the interval of the fourth developed from great respect for the Greeks (*via* Boethius) and their tetrachord.

[8] Gerbert, Martin, *Scriptores Ecclesiastici de Musica* (St. Blasien, 1774), Vol. I, p. 171.

the period (particularly chant manuscripts of tropes in which a second voice was freely added) show a much freer *organum.* Scholars seem agreed that the theorists were trying to establish frameworks for existing practices and as a result oversimplified the *organum.* This position is supported by Guido D'Arezzo's *Micrologus.* The unique Guido seems to have been able to perfect theoretical structures with skill. He recognizes *organum* at the fourth but banishes *organum* at the fifth. He gives preference to free *organum,* however. Where the author of the *Musica* set the fourth tone of each tetrachord as a lower limit for the *vox organalis,* Guido sets the third tone as that limit and does not give the reason that the augmented fourth is thereby avoided. None of the examples given by Guido shows more than three voices (with the *vox principalis,* the *vox organalis* below it, and the *vox organalis* doubled an octave higher). The interval of a minor second is prohibited, and no interval larger than a fourth is permitted between the *vox principalis* and the *vox organalis.* His examples show other important features: (1) crossing of parts — the *vox organalis* going above the *vox principalis* after beginning below, and vice versa; (2) one note of the *vox organalis* against more than one note of the *vox principalis* — the beginnings of modern organ point; (3) contrary motion particularly at the cadence — the *vox principalis* approaching the final from above and the *vox organalis* approaching from below. This was not the first instance of contrary motion since that had already appeared in the *Musica.* Guido was especially concerned about the cadence or *occursus,* as he called it, and laid down an extra rule prohibiting the employment of the interval of a minor third (the minor second always being forbidden).

What was once thought to be the earliest manuscript of *organum* extant, the Codex 572, Oxford Bodleian Library, was placed in the late tenth century.[9] This shows free *orga-*

[9] Printed in facsimile in Plainsong Society, *The Musical Notation of the*

*num*. There is an extended collection of *organum* dating from about Guido's time: the first half of the eleventh century. They are contained in the English Winchester Troper containing over 150 two-part *organums*[10] for various parts of the Mass. The most important feature of this collection is that the *vox organalis* appears *above* the *vox principalis*. This was to be important in later polyphony.

John Cotton (*c*. 1100) in his *Musica*[11] emphasizes the use of contrary motion at points other than the cadence, recognizes the use of two or three notes in the *vox organalis* against one note in the *vox principalis* (the reverse of Guido's "organ point"), and finds crossing of parts desirable and not merely permissible.

Thus down to the twelfth century we find the history of polyphony confined largely to the Church – as a new development traveling side by side with the trope. The melody used as *cantus firmus* was borrowed from the chant. Both these tendencies continued. But the situation with regard to polyphony demanded the development of some sort of system for measuring differences in values of notes. Practice again preceded theory, although without the books on theory it would be impossible to decipher the notation of the period from 1100 to 1400. The history of the development of the mensural system is intricate – but important.[12]

---

*Middle Ages* (London: Plainsong and Medieval Society, 1890). However, H. E. Wooldridge, *The Oxford History of Music* (London: Oxford, 2 ed., 1929), Vol. I, p. 91, places this manuscript as late as the twelfth century. Manuscripts of *organum* (outside the treatises of theorists) have not survived from an early date. In *Paleographie Musicale,* Vol. IV, p. 416, there is reproduced an antiphon in a tenth-century Einsiedeln manuscript which has two melodies that may have been meant for simultaneous singing. Outside of this, the *Micrologus* of Guido D'Arezzo includes the earliest substantial *organum* manuscripts.

10 Facsimile contained in Walter H. Frere, *The Winchester Troper* (London: Henry Bradford Society, 1884), Vol. VIII.

11 This work is in Martin Gerbert, *Scriptores Ecclesiastici de Musica* (St. Blasien, 1774), Vol. I, p. 263 ff.

12 This aspect is entirely ignored in Karl Weinmann, *History of Church Music* (New York: Pustet, 1906).

France was to take the principal part in the development of music until 1400. In the twelfth century the practice grew of putting a number of notes in the *vox organalis* against each note of the *vox principalis* which came to be called the tenor (*tenere,* to hold), as the voice which held its note. The center of this development, at least so far as can be judged from surviving manuscripts,[13] appears to have been the monastery of St. Martial in Limoges. Activity in Spain contributed the first genuinely three-part composition known — a three-part trope, *Congaudeant catholici,* on a *Benedicamus Domino.*[14]

## THE DEVELOPMENT OF NOTATION FOR MEASURED MUSIC

Much difficulty arises in this period due to ambiguous musical terms. *Discant,* for example, has been defined[15] as differing from *organum* in that the former employs contrary motion whereas the latter does not. The more commonly accepted difference, however, is that *organum* is nonmeasured polyphony whereas *discant* is measured polyphony.[16]

How did music develop a notation for time measurement? Not by the simple invention of different notes for different time values but through a long evolutionary process. The first step was the formation of rhythmic modes.[17] Rhythmic

13 There are four early twelfth-century manuscripts of this style surviving.

14 The authoritative work on St. Martial is Jacques Handschin, "Über den Ursprung der Motette," *Bericht über den Musikwissenschaftlichen Kongress in Basel* (Leipzig: Breitkopf & Härtel, 1924), pp. 189 ff.

15 There are earlier three-part works, but the third part is never independent but merely the *vox organalis* an octave removed. For a modern transcription of this work, see Friedrich Ludwig, *Die Geistliche Nichtliturgische, Weltliche Einstimmige und die Mehrstimmige Musik des Mittelalters bis zum Anfang des XV. Jahrhunderts* in the Adler *Festscript* (p. 182), cited at the end of this chapter.

16 Weinmann, Karl, *History of Church Music* (New York: Pustet, 1906), p. 79.

17 This use of the word "mode" is another equivocation that confounds music history. The ecclesiastical "modes" refer to tonality; the term "rhythmic modes" will be used to refer to the schema of rhythm employed in the twelfth and thirteenth centuries.

modes are schema of rhythm; they derive from the rhythm of classical poetry, which involves longs and shorts with the longs twice the length of the shorts. Music, however, employed three units: the extended long (*ultra mensuram*) was apparently equal to three shorts, the long (*longa recta*) was equal to two shorts, and the short (*breve*) was the unit. Thus the first rhythmic mode was based on a trochaic meter of a long followed by a short; the second rhythmic mode on the iambic meter of a short followed by a long; the third on the dactylic meter of an extended long, a short, and a long; the fourth on the anapestic meter of a short, a long, and an extended long; the fifth on the spondaic meter of all longs; and the sixth on the tribrachic meter of all shorts. Other rhythmic modes were developed by particular composers and theorists. There are three stages in the development. In the first stage there were no symbols for time values (this is the rhythmic mode stage just described); in the second stage there were no symbols to express time directly but the values are implied by the devices – the ligatures; in the third stage there are symbols for time values.

"Bars" were not employed to indicate "measures" until the sixteenth century and even then they were not used as in modern music. Modern editions of fifteenth- and sixteenth-century music employ bars but it must be remembered that this has nothing to do with stress. The first note after such "editorial" bars does not necessarily receive the accent. Rather, the accent must be gathered from special indications such as the textual meter. This is a key understanding to derive from the present short discussion.

The ligatures of the second stage are even more complicated than the rhythmic modes of the first stage. The ligatures came from the chant symbols for compound notes (see Plate I of Chapter II). The ligatures were different depending on whether the melody was ascending or descending, and ligatures could be (1) with propriety and with perfection, (2) without propriety, (3) without perfection, and (4) with opposite propriety. The four categories were distinguished from one another by tails added to the note or neum. The meaning of the different categories of ligatures varied from mode to mode. Thus a "three note ligature with propriety and perfection could imply long-breve-long in the first mode, breve-breve-long in the third and fourth modes, long-long-long in the fifth mode, or breve-breve-breve in the sixth."[18] The first task of the singer or director was to determine the mode, and this he did from the ligature groups! As if this were not enough, special systems were employed by various composers to indicate a "breaking" (i.e., change) of the mode. Add to this that rules as to rests were developed and the complexity of the system breaks down under its own weight. In the case of ligatures, as with rhythmic modes, much remained for oral tradition. It was possible to change modes in a single composition, and this usually came at natural points where one section ended and another began. The device of ligatures could be used in this way. Different rhythmic modes could be assigned, for example, to each voice of a two-part composition.

The scene was ripe for codification and simplification. Franco of Cologne (*c.* 1230–after 1280) is credited with this achievement and from him come the principles of modern rhythmic notation. His *Ars Cantus Mensurabilis*[19] became the standard work on rhythm. His basic notes were the semibreve (◆), the breve (■), the long (▀▌), and the double long (▀▀▌). The unit of time was the *brevis recta.* The *brevis altera* was two units, the perfect long was three units, the imperfect long two units, the minor semibreve was 1/3 unit, and the major semibreve was 2/3 unit. A parallel system obtained for

18 Reese, Gustave, *Music in the Middle Ages* (New York: Norton, 1940), p. 279.

19 Gerbert, Martin, O.S.B., *Scriptores Ecclesiastici de Musica* (St. Blasien, 1774), Vol. III, p. 1; Charles E. H. Coussemaker, *Scriptorum De Musica Medii Aevi Nova Series* (Paris: Durand, 1864–1876), Vol. I, p. 117.

rests. Whether a breve was *recta* or *altera,* whether a long was perfect or imperfect, and whether a semibreve was major or minor was determined by location with respect to the note which preceded or followed. Thus if a long followed a long, the first long was a perfect long whether the second was a note or a rest, or if a single breve came before or after a long, the long was imperfect. A change of mode could still, however, make changes in the time. Franco similarily reduced the ligatures to a uniform system.

The logic of these events bears recapitulation. The development of *organum* opened up great possibilities, particularly when it was realized that different rhythmic schemes could be employed in the different parts in part singing. This required a system of notation for time measurement. And throughout the development, practical music was always in advance of theory. Until Franco's time, the notation was imperfect, and music depended on oral tradition and personal interpretation.

## THE DEVELOPMENT OF DISCANT, CONDUCTUS, MOTETUS, AND CANTILENA

The *organum,* the *discant,* the *conductus,* the *motetus,* and the *cantilena* are not different "forms" in the sense in which we today understand "musical forms." Rather, they are different styles.

The twins: *organum* in unmeasured rhythm and *discant* in measured rhythm have already been traced to the point where intervals of the third and the sixth were introduced. After early prominence, the fourth had yielded to the unison, fifth, and octave as the basis for harmony. The third was admitted gradually through a role that modern music calls "the passing note" and was definitely recognized by the thirteenth century. Three-part writing came to be the commonest form of composition though two-part writing continued and four-part writing began to appear.

In the middle of the twelfth century the school of Notre Dame of Paris took the lead in musical composition, and it continued to hold the position of leadership throughout the thirteenth century. The two great figures of the school were Leonin, *optimus organista* (twelfth century), and Perotin, *optimus discantus* (*c.* 1160–*c.* 1240). By and large individual names were omitted from manuscripts during this period. But in an anonymous work[20] it is stated that Leonin, whose title indicates he was considered the greatest master of *organum,* composed the *Magnus Liber Organi de Graduali et Antiphonario pro Servitio Divino Multiplicando* which was a complete set of two-part compositions for the liturgy of the entire year. Leonin continued in the St. Martial tradition, his style being alternately note against note and then a sustained tone in one voice. When using the former technique, Leonin sometimes introduces short melismas which employ the rhythmic modes. Thus this part of the work is discant. The works of Leonin are designed to be used in conjunction with the chant, e.g., part of the *Graduale* would be supplied by a composition of Leonin and the balance would be chant. He seldom employs melodic intervals greater than a third and frequently uses sections running continuously through an octave or more in what approaches the *glissando* in modern music. Leonin employs the sequence[21] frequently.

Perotin, whose title indicates he was considered the greatest master of discant, achieved his renown by taking the *Liber* of Leonin and substituting new sections throughout the work. Perotin's compositions are less dissonant than those of Leonin, being built on chords. His range in the running passages is not as great as that of Leonin. Among his composi-

20 Coussemaker, Charles E. H., *Scriptorum de Musica Medii Aevi Nova Series* (Paris: Durand, 1864–1876), Vol. I, p. 342 f.

21 A sequence may be defined as a repetition of a motive or theme, beginning the second time on either the same tone or a different tone. Repetitions may be more than two and need not be exact.

tions can be found examples of the canon.[22] Also to be found are examples of the ground bass.[23] These illustrate the chief contribution of Perotin: making the several voices completely independent of each other rhythmically. This was an important addition to the equipment of polyphony.

The *conductus* seems to have originated as early as the eleventh century as a trope sung during the procession from one part of the church to another (whence the term possibly derives). By the end of the twelfth century the term had lost its original meaning. In the polyphonic *conductus,* developed at Notre Dame, the tenor voice[24] does not have sustained notes but all the voices move in approximately the same rhythm. The text is usually metrical, and the same text is sung by all the voices, thus distinguishing it from the early *motetus* which used a different text for each voice. In the *Discantus Positio Vulgaris,*[25] the *conductus* is defined as a polyphonic composition *"super unum metrum . . . consonans."* Thus the *conductus* is distinguished from the *organum* and *discant* which do not have uniform rhythm and from the *motetus* which has several texts. For polyphony, however, the most important characteristic of the *conductus* is that the tenor is no longer a Gregorian melody as in the *organum, discant,* and *motetus* but an original composition. Thus the *conductus* is the first polyphonic form in church

[22] The canon may be defined as the strictest type of imitative form in music. The subject or antecedent is stated by one voice and then an answer or consequent (being the exact repetition of the subject though not necessarily beginning on the same tone) follows in the next voice at any point after the beginning of the subject. More than one such subject may be used in the composition and any number of voices can be employed.

[23] The ground bass may be defined as the continuous repetition in the bass throughout a composition of a short melodic figure.

[24] It will be remembered that the "tenor voice" in medieval music does not mean the high male voice but rather the voice which has more sustained notes (from *tenere,* to hold).

[25] This is an anonymous work (*c.* 1230–1240) found in Charles E. H. Coussemaker, *Scriptorum de Musica Medii Aevi Nova Series* (Paris: Durand, 1864–1876), Vol. I, p. 96.

music in which the composer is completely free from the chant. While Leonin wrote no *conductus,* Perotin did. The form proved fertile ground for invention and many secular numbers were composed in it. The earliest example of double counterpoint[26] is found in a *conductus* of the St. Victor manuscript (*c.* 1245, now Paris National Library, Latin, 15139).

By the middle of the thirteenth century the *motetus* had replaced the *conductus,* and it became the leading form of that century. The chief characteristics of the *motetus* are, as already mentioned, a different text for each voice and a tenor drawn from existing melodies.[27] The mixing of texts had already appeared in the *organum* and *discant.* There is an easy explanation for polytextuality in the *motetus.* Rhythmic independence of the several voices would be immeasurably aided by assigning a different text to each voice. On liturgical grounds, of course, the objection is that the primary text is thus thoroughly obscured. The objection was probably advanced early, and this may explain why polytextuality made such slow progress in the Notre Dame school. About this time instruments were introduced to handle some of the voices—possibly as a solution to the liturgical objection to polytextuality. Another development of the *motetus* was the introduction of the vernacular into the accompanying voices while the tenor was in Latin. In the beginning the vernacular accompaniment consisted of a paraphrase of the Latin text of the tenor in the manner of a trope. In the *motetus,* the tenor always appeared at the bottom. The next voice above it was known as the *motetus,* the next higher as the first *triplum,* the next as the second *triplum,* etc. The *motetus* was widely used in the thirteenth century, the same *motetus* being found in different locations. The form was not confined to liturgical

26 Double counterpoint, a term frequently misused, is defined as the interchange upon repetition of the theme of a higher voice with the theme of a lower voice.

27 The *motetus* is thus completely different from the motet known to Palestrina.

uses but was employed in secular music as well, which by and large during this period of the Middle Ages tagged along behind the learning of the ecclesiastics.

As an embellishment of the *motetus,* the *hoquetus* appeared; it involved two or more voices (or groups of voices) staggered so that while the first sings a note, the second is silent and vice versa, with the notes being short. It is true that there are some compositions entirely in the *hoquetus* form, but the significance of the technique has been overrated. Such frivolity was calculated to draw the wrath of the liturgical musicians, such as the condemnation expressed in the Constitution of Pope John XXII in 1324–1325.

The *cantilena* was essentially a secular form that in some instances found its way into the Church. It involved a dance-song form such as the rondeau, virelai, or ballade and characteristically employed a refrain. Instruments likewise were brought in with the *cantilena.*[28] From all this it is easy to understand that from the end of the thirteenth century the return of true Gregorian chant was impossible. Likewise one can appreciate the famous decree of Pope John XXII, released in 1324 and 1325 at Avignon,[29] which forbade the adding of *motetus* and *triplum* parts to the chant and forbade all polyphony except such *organum* as was not overelaborate. How effective the reform was is another question.

Throughout the fourteenth century, France maintained its leadership in music although the other nations kept abreast of the new French developments, with Italy in particular coming to the fore. The two French leaders were Philippe de

[28] The history of instrumental music in the Church will be considered in Chapter V. In the thirteenth century we again find mention of dancing in the church of Notre Dame – something not found since the time of Augustine. See Handschin, Jacques, "Zur Geschichte von Notre Dame," *Acta Musicologica,* IV, 5, and 49 (1932).

[29] Reprinted in Latin and English in Wooldridge, H. E., *The Oxford History of Music,* 2 ed. (London: Oxford, 1929), Vol. I, pp. 294 ff., and *The White List of the Society of St. Gregory of America,* 4 ed. (New York: The Society of St. Gregory of America, 1947), p. 3.

Vitri (1291–1361), author of the famous *Ars Nova,* and Guillaume de Machaut (*c.* 1300–*c.* 1377). Although there are many references to him, few of Vitri's works are extant. These few, however, show a new and vigorous character – the isorhythmic structure.[30] What was intended as a reform volume, the *Roman de Fauvel,*[31] achieved wide usage. It shows a tendency – the dominant note of the fourteenth century – toward chordal or harmonic treatment and uniformity in rhythm. The effort is toward subtlety, e.g., the development of the *canon cancrizans* (crab canon), which is nothing but a treating of the theme backwards.

Continuous progress was made in the fourteenth century in rhythmic notation. The beginnings of the ideas underlying the use of the bar and the measure can be traced from this time, as well as some evidences of syncopation.[32] The outstanding composer of this century was undoubtedly Guillaume de Machaut.[33] Whether as a reaction to the decree of

30 Isorhythmic structure may be defined as a repetition of the rhythm of an entire section (though the melody of the repetition may change); it is related to the rhythmic mode in its repetitive aspect, but differs from it in that the pattern repeated is much more elaborate. The unifying effect of this device is clear. Such a *rhythmic* pattern was known as a *talea* (cutting). A similar repetition of the melodic scheme was known as *color.* As an illustration of the subtlety of the fourteenth century, we might cite a composition with the *talea* repeated but the melody different in the first repetition. Then in the third repetition there might be a new *talea* but the melody of the first *talea* might be repeated.

31 Edition by Pierre Aubry, *Le Roman de Fauvel* (Paris: Geuthner, 1907). The text of the work states the word "Fauvel" is derived from the first letters of *Flaterie, Avarice, Vilanie, Variete, Envie, Laschete.*

32 Syncopation can be defined as irregular rhythm, i.e., beginning a note at a point where it would not normally have an accent and carrying the note over to the point where it would normally be accented. One can imagine what theoretical complexities would result in a treatment of the subject in a period when *regular* rhythm was interminably complex in its notation. Syncopation is first actually defined in Phillipe de Vitri's *Ars Perfecta;* Charles E. H. Coussemaker, *Scriptorum de Musica Medii Aevi Nova Series* (Paris: Durand, 1864–1876), Vol. III, p. 34. There is some doubt whether De Vitri actually wrote this work.

33 Many of his works are extant, and an edition and transcription into modern music was finished by Friedrich Ludwig but has not yet been completely published (see bibliography at end of this chapter).

Pope John XXII or not, Machaut wrote principally secular music. He was a priest, but as Reese says "must have been a fairly active, jolly and worldly ecclesiastic,"[34] whose travels took him through every country in Europe. He knew and used practically every musical technique known up to his time – and he reached forward into the future. For church music, the item of greatest interest and importance is his *Messe Notre-Dame,* which is the first complete polyphonic composition for the *Ordinarium* of the Mass.[35] Written in *motetus* style with the use of a tenor, *motetus,* and *triplum,* its most significant aspect is the use of a motive to bind all the parts of the *Ordinarium* into an artistic unit – the first treatment of the Mass as an art form. It includes a section, *Ite Missa Est,* in addition to the standard parts of today. Machaut broadened the rhythm in the *Et incarnatus est* of the *Credo* – a practice carried over to the present day. Isorhythmic structure is found in his *Messe* as well as in 20 of his 23 *motetus* forms, in addition to the appearance of frequent imitations. Several of the sections of the Machaut *Messe* are based on Gregorian themes: the *Kyrie* on Mass IV, the *Sanctus* and *Agnus Dei* on Mass XVII.

## FAUX BOURDON, GYMEL, THE GERMAN HYMN AND MUSICA FICTA

The polyphonic contributions so far discussed came principally from French musicians. In general, Spain and Italy followed French ideas closely. Other countries, however, made individual contributions. There is no doubt that the three-part polyphony with intervals of the third and the sixth was an important part of early English polyphony at the end

[34] Reese, Gustave, *Music in the Middle Ages* (New York: Norton, 1940), p. 347.

[35] It is true that a so-called *Messe de Tournai* from the first half of the fourteenth century is a complete polyphonic *Ordinarium,* but it was not the composition of any one composer but rather a gathering of the several parts from various sources. See Charles E. H. Coussemaker, *Messe du XIII^e^ Siecle* (Paris: Durand, 1861).

of the fourteenth century. Wooldridge[36] gives an interesting account of its prominence. The decree of Pope John XXII in 1324 and 1325 had banned all polyphony except *organum*.[37] The decree was long observed but finally to avoid the decree, the French wrote music in simple, two-part *organum* at the fifth with a third part inserted in the middle at the interval of a third from each of these two parts. However, the upper two parts were sung as written but the third part was sung an octave higher than written. Thus the lowest voice (*bourdon*) was sung "falsely." Hence *faux bourdon*.[38] The composition ended in a concord of the voices. There had been considerable dispute among other authorities as to the origin of the 6–3 chord (*faux bourdon*). The authoritative treatise on the subject, by Bukofzer,[39] appears to settle things in this fashion: the English were the first (at the end of the thirteenth century) to develop the 6–3 chord but with the *cantus firmus* as the *lowest* voice. In the early fifteenth century the French developed the 6–3 chord with the *highest* voice as the *cantus firmus*. Thus the French development is deservedly termed *faux bourdon* (false bass).

The English predeliction for the interval of the third gave rise in the period from the thirteenth to the fifteenth cen-

36 *Oxford History of Music,* 2 ed. (London: Oxford, 1929), Vol. I, p. 298 ff.

37 Non-Catholic authors are inclined to find evidence of the "suppression" of musical development in this decree of Pope John XXII. The exact language is here set out and the reader can evaluate it for himself: "However, we do not intend to forbid the occasional use – principally on solemn feasts at Mass and at divine office – of certain consonant intervals superposed upon the simple ecclesiastical chant, provided these harmonies are in the spirit and character of the melodies themselves, as, for instance, the consonance of the octave, the fifth, the fourth, and others of this nature; but always on condition that the melodies themselves remain intact in the pure integrity of their form, and that no innovation take place against true musical discipline; for such consonances are pleasing to the ear and arouse devotion, and they prevent torpor among these who sing in honor of God."

38 Today the term *faux bourdon* or *falso bordone* has a different meaning in church music: the harmonized reciting tone with chord changes at the cadences (cf. Manfred Bukofzer, *Geschichte des Englischen Diskants und des Fauxbourdons nach den Theoretischen Quellen* (Strassburg: Heitz, 1936).

39 *Ibid.*

turies to two-part writing frequently employing this interval. To this style the term *gymel* (from *gemellus,* twin) was applied.

The development of music in the vernacular for church purposes occurred earlier and more frequently in Germany and England. This development, in precisely those countries, is not unnatural because of the dissimilarity of the English and German languages from Latin.

The *Kyrie eleison* has a peculiar history in Germany. It appears to have been a popular acclamation in processions and pilgrimages, and even on the battlefield.[40] It is from this practice that the early hymns were called *Leisen.* Weinmann[41] gives such an old German hymn:

| *German* | *Translation* |
|---|---|
| Unsar trohtin hat farsalt | The Lord has given over |
| Sancte Petre ginualt | Supreme power to St. Peter |
| Daz er mac ginerjan | That he may save from perdition |
| Ze imo dingenten man. | The man who puts his trust in him. |
| Kyrie eleison, Christe eleison. | Kyrie eleison, Christe eleison. |

From the twelfth century dates the famous hymn *Christ, der Du Geboren Bist* (sung at the battle of Tusculum in 1167). In 1848, Gerhoh, the Provost of Reichensberg, wrote: "The whole world sings the praises of the Saviour, even in the vernacular. This is particularly the case among the Germans whose language is best adapted for sonorous songs."[42] The

[40] At the removal of St. Boniface's relics from Mainz to Fulda in 819, on the entry of Dethmar into Prague, at the battle of Saucourt in 881, the *Kyrie* was used interspersed with ejaculations in the vernacular. This became so common that the Statutes of Strassburg laid down the injunction "That the people shall learn to sing *Kyrie eleison* properly and not in the clumsy fashion hitherto in vogue." See Karl Weinmann, *The History of Church Music* (New York: Pustet, 1906), p. 50.

[41] *Ibid.,* p. 52.

[42] Janssen, Johannes, *Geschichte des Deutschen Volkes,* 8 vols. (Freiburg: Herder, 1896–1904), Vol. I, p. 220. Translation mine.

movement toward the vernacular continued strong with the Germans — often involving abuses — until the fifteenth century when frequent condemnations were issued, e.g., by the Council of Basle in 1453, by the Synod of Schwerin in 1492, and by the Synod of Cologne in 1536. The greatest poet of the period was Walter von der Vogelweide (*c.* 1200).

The vernacular hymns or songs were mainly in monodic form and employed the ecclesiastical modes. In Germany it is rather difficult to draw a line between the secular and the religious — the secular songs of the period being more idealistic than those of the other countries. One particular development was carried further in Germany than elsewhere. Not only were the Latin texts beautifully translated into the vernacular[43] but the Latin and German lines were alternated as in the macaronic:

In dulci jubilo
Nu singet und sit froh
Unsres Herzens Wonne
Leit in praesepio
Und leuchtet als die Sonne
Matris in gremio
Alpha es et O

In the nineteenth century it was the fashion to credit the German hymn and its development to Martin Luther. Modern research has shown not only that the development long antedated Luther but that many of the hymns credited to Luther are not his and many of them have origins trace-

[43] The best treatises are: Hans J. Moser, *Geschichte der Deutschen Musik* (Stuttgart: Cotta, 1928–1930); Hoffmann von Fallersleben, *Geschichte des Deutschen Kirchenliedes bis auf Luthers Zeit* (Breslau: Grass, Barth, 1832); Philipp Mand Wackernagel, *Das Deutsche Kirchenlied von der Ältesten Zeit bis zu Anfang des XVII. Jahrhunderts* (Leipzig: Teubner, 1864–1877), 5 vols. The greatest at this art was the famous Hermann der Münch von Salzburg who belongs to the last half of the fourteenth century. His hymns include *Kum Sanfter Trost Heiliger Geist* (*Veni, Sancte Spiritus*), *Lob o Sion, Deinen Hailer* (*Lauda Sion Salvatorem*), and *Lobt All Sungen des Ernreichen* (*Pange Lingua Gloriosi*).

able to chant materials. This does not detract from the credit due Luther for emphasizing the value of music in the church, particularly by contrast with the leaders of other Protestant movements. The German Protestant church did develop a new style — the chorale — from the Catholic polyphonic motet.[44]

The important development of a system of semitones leading to the "keys" of modern music is known in the medieval books as *music ficta* or *musica falsa.* The theoretical beginnings date from Johannes de Garlandia[45] and the *Introductio Musicae* which appropriately defines *musica falsa* (the older of the two terms) as consisting in the substitution of a semitone for a whole tone (and conversely of a whole tone for a semitone) in the modal system. The situation created by the use of *B flat* and *B natural* in the chant to avoid the augmented fourth has already been mentioned. The new substitution was recognized as owing to necessity or art demands (*causa necessitatis sive causa pulchritudinis*). The necessity arose from the frequent occurrence of the augmented fourth in the new polyphonic art — at many places instead of only at the tone of *B* as in monodic modes, since the fourth could occur not only in the melodic line but in the relationship of one voice to another. This meant the more frequent use of flats. Sharps, on the other hand, came through an embellishment where, for example, the melody went from *G* to *F* and back to *G.* The sharpening of *F* in this case was a matter of "beauty." The same principle lowered *B* when it occurred in the melodic progression *A, B, A.* At the beginning of the fifteenth century we find Ugolino d'Orvieto and other theorists laying down polyphonic rules that fifths, octaves, and

[44] Music peculiar to the Protestant churches, of course, lies beyond the scope of the present volume.

[45] There is a considerable literature about this author, who lived in the thirteenth century: the authenticity of works attributed to him and the question of a fourteenth-century author by the same name. The treatise mentioned can be found in Charles E. H. Coussemaker, *Scriptorum de Musica Medii Aevi Nova Series* (Paris: Durand, 1864–1876), Vol. I, p. 166.

twelfths must be perfect, and if they would "normally" appear as diminished they ought to be augmented. Similarly if the interval of a sixth proceeded to an octave the interval should be major and not minor, thus laying the basis for the leading tone and its half step between the seventh and the octave. And if the third proceeded to a unison, the interval should be minor and not major. Prosdocimus de Beldomandis early in the fifteenth century had arrived at a chromatic scale in which all progressions are by half tones. This subject was made the more intricate because the rules were left to application by the performer — no separate notation indicated a sharp or a flat. Finally composers became disgusted with the increasing ignorance (!) of singers of their day and began to supply the chromatic signs.

## THE POLYPHONIC SCHOOLS

### THE NETHERLAND SCHOOL

In the period of the development of polyphony down to 1400 can be found the origins of all the devices later employed in the mature art. In the achievement of maturity there were four great schools of polyphony: the Netherland, the Roman, the Spanish, and the English.[46] The Netherland school grew from English sources. Reference has been made to the great popularity of *faux bourdon* and its debt to the English for the 6–3 chord. John Dunstable marked the link between the English and the Netherland school.[47] Certain

[46] Sometimes a Venetian polyphonic school is mentioned by historians. This is taken up in the next chapter together with the reasons for not recognizing that classification.

[47] Considerable emphasis is placed on John Dunstable (?–1453) particularly by English writers. Cf. Charles H. E. Wooldridge, *The Oxford History of Music* 2 ed. (London: Oxford, 1929), Vol. II. And not without reason, since he is truly the first great English musician. But viewed from our present purpose his principal significance is as a link in the development of the Netherland school. Though an Englishman by birth, Dunstable spent most of his life on the continent and was scarcely mentioned in contemporary England. His principal achievement is the free flow of many of his works — away from the pedantic and toward harmonic expression.

characteristics of the latter stand out for church music purposes. There is no question that the weaknesses of this school have been overemphasized. The greatest weakness, growing from the very strength of the school, is the basic emphasis on music and problem solving to the disregard of the text. This is part of another dominant feature, the reduction of the *cantus firmus* or melody line so that no one voice is more significant than another.

In the early years of the fourteenth century, composers were not content to draw on Gregorian chant for the *cantus firmus* but took secular melodies as the basis for motets and Masses, labeling the new composition with the secular title. Thus liturgical texts were entitled *Adieu, Mes Amours, Baisez Moi,* or *Fortuna Desperata.* On the folk-song tune of *L'Homme Arme,* all of the Netherlanders have written a Mass, and Josquin des Pres (*c.* 1450–1521), the greatest of the early Netherland school, did two Masses on the theme.

Ecclesiastical authorities promptly took exception to such names, and the composers then concealed the source of their *cantus firmus* or invented new themes and used such titles as *Missa sine Nomine, Missa Primi Toni, Missa ut, re, fa, sol, la* or *Missa ad Fugam,* and so on. This raises the question of the liturgical attitude toward the use in church music of motives from secular compositions. In the cases under consideration the borrowed motives were so interwoven that no one voice, by itself, sounded to the ear as a complete melody – hence the secular connotation was not present. Thus the composers seem to have been justified in their practice and the Church authorities were guilty of formalism. As the Netherland school used these secular motives, nothing but the name remained; the textual significance of the words was gone.

The other "weakness" of the school is more valid. Text meant nothing to the composer – in fact he frequently left it out altogether, particularly in the Masses (whose text was well known). The singer could fit the text in as his judgment dictated. The Requiem as written by the school was in a special style, and it was customary to write funeral motets on the death of some prominent figure. It mattered nothing that the composer used genealogical tables as his texts. In Greek music, in chant, and in folk song, text and melody were united. In the contrapuntal school of the Netherlanders only the composite sound of the several voices mattered.

The tendency was carried so far as to be roundly condemned by the Council of Trent (1545–1563). From the practice of tropes, the Netherlanders went further. Not only was the liturgical text freely interspersed with additional language but different voices were assigned different texts. These were known as *Farciturae*. For example, in the text of a *Missa Beatae Mariae Virginis,* part of the Gloria reads as follows: *Domine Deus, Agnus Dei, Filius Patris, primogenitus Mariae virginis matris, qui tollis peccata mundi, suscipe deprecationem nostram ad Mariae gloriam, quoniam tu solus sanctus Mariam sanctificans, tu solus Dominus, Mariam gubernans,* whereas the correct, liturgical text for this part is: *Domine Deus, Agnus Dei, Filius Patris. Qui tollis peccata mundi, miserere nobis. Qui tollis peccata mundi, suscipe deprecationem nostram. Qui sedes ad dexteram Patris, miserere nobis. Quoniam tu solus sanctus. Tu solus Dominus.* Ecclesiastical authorities were certainly justified in criticizing such practices. Yet the music itself was suitable for the church if the text were properly arranged.

Musically, the Netherlanders attained great skill. They employed the strict forms of counterpoint: canon and fugue and every device in imitation. No longer did repetition or simple imitation of the theme in different voices suffice. The rules for structure were embodied in the canon – that term being used in a different sense than today. The pattern was called the *Fuga* or *Conseguenza.*

First we shall examine the extremes to which the ingenuity of the Netherland school was carried. The note values of the tenor are doubled or tripled, or the tenor has changing time values in the measures, or the melody or the space distance between the entry of the different voices is shortened to a minimum thus creating the *Fuga ad minimam,* or even all voices begun at the same time but in different measures of the theme or the music sheet was reversed or read backward, or the thirds sung downward instead of upward. The capstone of all was the *Canon oenigmaticus* (the riddle canon) with the title indicating the way it was to be performed, or the canon was left for the performer to figure out. Such a title appears as *In gyrum imus nocte et consumimur igni* (We go in a circle at night and are consumed by fire) which reads the same if read backward — and likewise with the music.[48] Small wonder that Emperor Maximilian said "They read differently from what they write, sing differently from what they note down, speak differently from what is in their hearts."

The more serious work of the Netherlanders is of great value, however. It is customary to recognize three groups. The leaders of the first group were Gillis Binchois (*c.* 1400–1460) and Guillaume Dufay (1400–1474). Only fragments of Binchois' works are extant. In the case of Dufay, however, many Masses and motets are extant. He was the first of the Netherlanders to employ the canon seriously in a Mass composition. The *cantus firmus* still stands out, however, as the important melodic line. His best-known church music is *Missa Se la face ay pale*. His style until 1436, as in Binchois', is simple, with none of the elaborate structures of the later Netherlanders. From 1436, he began to experiment with his

[48] Weinmann, Karl, *The History of Church Music* (New York: Pustet, 1906), p. 90, collects others: "The skipping of rests was enjoined by *Clama ne cessas,* inversion of intervals by *Qui se exultat, humiliabitur,* the omission of all minims by *De minimis non curat praetor,* the change of the black notes into white by *Caecus non judicat de colore, etc.*"

ecclesiastical music although he has secular works in the *faux bourdon* and other more fluent styles.

The first group was essentially engaged in experimentation.[49] Structure was slowly developing, i.e., the rhetorical use of the canon and fugue as forms. This is shown by the tentative appearance of strettos[50] and cadence formulae and in the effort to make each voice as important melodically as the *cantus firmus.* Despite such structural weakness the school made great strides in fluency, making frequent use of thirds, sixths, and tenths in noncanonical forms.

The second school was dominated by Jean de Okeghem (*c.* 1430–1495) and includes among others, Jacques Barbireau (?–1491), Antoine Busnois (?–1492), and Jakob Obrecht (*c.* 1430–1505). Okeghem deals with more intricate problems than the earlier school. His most famous works, *Missa Cuiusvis Toni* and *Missa Prolationum,* are two of the few extant. In the *Missa Prolationum,* he has two concurrent canons, one for high voices and the other for low, and in the lower voice

49 The final steps in mensural theory came during the fifteenth century by the establishment of the Ratio and Proportion system. The system comprised five genera, three simple and two compound, which embraced all possible mensuration. Only the first two genera have survived into modern music: *genus multiplex* and *genus superparticulare:*

*Multiplex* ratio:

| | | | | |
|---|---|---|---|---|
| Dupla: | 2/1. | 4/2. | 6/3 | or 8/4 |
| Tripla: | 3/1. | 6/2. | 9/3 | or 12/4 |
| Quadrupla: | 4/1. | 8/2. | 12/3 | or 16/4 |

*Superparticulare* ratio:

| | | | | |
|---|---|---|---|---|
| Sesquialtera: | 3/2. | 6/4. | 9/6 | or 12/8 |
| Sesquitertia: | 4/3. | 8/6. | 12/9 | or 16/12 |
| Sesquiquarta: | 5/4. | 10/8. | 15/12 | or 20/16 |

The signature could, of course, be inverted, in which case the prefix *sub* was placed before the name, e.g., *subsesquialtera.*

50 The stretto may be defined as a telescoping or overlapping of the subject and the answer. Its rhetorical use is one of emphasis and climax. Instead of repetition or imitation, as so many "chunks" following each other, the stretto furnishes contrast. In classical (sixteenth century) form the stretto occurs in the development section of the fugue (after the statement of the theme and its answer) and in the coda or final section.

of each canon he augments the subject. Despite this difficult plan, the melodies do not suffer. Okeghem devised a new form – the *Catholica.* This was a polyphonic composition which could be sung in *any* mode at the discretion of the singers. The *Missa Cuiusvis Toni* – as its name indicates – is in this form and furnishes an example of the great efforts at ingenuity.[51] It is particularly worth noting that the accented syllable (and tone) bears no relation to the location of the bar. Okeghem continued the work of Dufay in developing the rhetorical use of the canon, getting away from the mechanical method of answer by one voice to the subject at a great distance after the subject.

A great number of Masses and motets by Obrecht are extant. Whereas previously the imitation had been confined to two voices usually, Obrecht and Busnois employ imitation in all the parts and the answer comes at other intervals than the customary octave. The accompaniment is dropped from the statement of the subject.

The last group, which centered around the great Josquin des Pres (1450–1521), included Pierre de La Rue (?–1518) and many others. The volume of Josquin's works remaining is very great, although only thirty-two Masses are extant. His works may be divided into two classes. The first is the canonic in which he continues the work of Okeghem but with more beautiful results. The tools fashioned by Okeghem are worked in a more effortless way – but no new additions are made to the structure of the canon.[52] More in his personal style are Josquin's two great motets, *Planxit autem David* and *Absalon fili mi.* In these he overcomes the greatest weakness of polyphony – the want of expression to which it tends. In

[51] Interesting experimentation can be had with this composition printed in the Okeghem collection cited in bibliography at the end of this chapter.

[52] All of the Netherlanders were blessed with humor. It is related that Josquin prodded the memory of a king who had made an unkept promise by composing to the 118th psalm (*Memor esto verbi tui servo tuo, in quo mihi spem dedisti*) a motet in which the tenor and bass carry on a jibbering counterpoint with the reiteration of *Memor esto verbi tui.*

them he anticipates the masters of the sixteenth century in their ability to make polyphony vibrant — to achieve once again the wedding of music and text that is the beauty of the chant. With him, polyphony begins maturity — after seven centuries of development.

Other contemporaries made similar progress. Pierre de La Rue left 36 Masses, Alexander Agricola (1445–1505) 31 works printed by Petrucci, Antoine de Fevin (1473–1516), and Loyset Compere (?–1518) who is sometimes called the "romantic" of the group because of his harmonic preferences. All exhibit skill in the canon which was used particularly in Masses. In motets they show a fine musicianship, being free from the desire to create problems for solving. The motets definitely contain sections written in harmonic style, i.e., with chordal arrangement and with changes in the syllables of the text uniform rather than staggered.

The generation following Josquin showed a realization that contrapuntal tricks were to be frowned upon and the effort is to obtain purity of sound and expression. The works of Nicholas Gombert (*c.* 1510–*c.* 1560), pupil of Josquin; Jacques Clemens (usually described as *non Papa* to distinguish him from Pope Clement VII [pontificate: 1523–1534], who was also a musician), and Adrian Willaert (*c.* 1490–1562) are extensive and made notable progress toward the goal of rhetoric in polyphony. Their names would stand higher if they were not overshadowed by the greater achievements of Lassus, Palestrina, and Victoria. In some of their works, it would be difficult to draw a line separating them from the great masters. The Netherlanders, through their wide travels and through the pupils attracted by their fame, had by now established descendants or branches in most of the countries of Europe and particularly in Italy. The names by this time have become so numerous as to require a monograph for any treatment even in sketch.

The great masters of the art are usually reckoned as Orlandus Lassus (*c.* 1525–1594) and Philippe de Monte (1521–1603) of the Netherland school, Giovanni da Palestrina (1526–1594) of the Roman school, Tomas da Victoria (*c.* 1540–1615) of the Spanish school, and William Byrd (1542–1623) of the English school. Classing Lassus as the last great Netherlander is somewhat arbitrary. Although born in Hainault, he spent most of his career in Germany at the court chapel in Munich.[53] Lassus was one of the most prolific composers of all time. He penned over 1250 works, about two thirds of which are sacred music, including 52 Masses, about 1100 motets, and about 100 magnificats, psalms, lamentations, etc. His greatest achievement is generally considered to be the *Seven Penitential Psalms* brought out in 1565. Lassus achieved rhetorical expression in polyphony. The text stands out as expressed in the music. He is considered to be characteristically lacking in melodic beauty but rather intentionally so because he was interested in the harmonic effect of the several voices taken together. His music expresses personal feeling for the text without becoming subjective. The technical devices developed by the Netherlanders are all there but not the spirit of setting problems just to show that they can be solved.

De Monte was the composer of two volumes of Masses and motets as well as some 600 madrigals.

## THE ROMAN SCHOOL

The *Schola Cantorum* of the Vatican had a continuity in Rome from the fifth century. The *Schola* remained in Rome

[53] Though we are late in mentioning it, the court chapel had been a most important phenomenon for all members of the Netherland school, in fact for all Europe from the beginning of the fifteenth century. Cathedrals were not capable of the economic burden involved and the monasteries still abided with the chant as best they could. At the court chapel were usually assembled several score of singers, and the master gathered select pupils. Honors and reward made the post even more attractive. It was an ideal setting for creative work. Cf. Higginson, J. V., "Orlando Lasso – the Musician and His Times," *The Catholic Choirmaster,* XXXIII, 7–10, 15 (1947).

during the period the popes were established at Avignon (1300–1377) and a new choir was organized at Avignon. Upon the return to Rome, in 1377, of Pope Gregory XI he brought the new choir with him and the addition stimulated music at Rome. During his pontificate (1471–1484), Pope Sixtus IV built the Sistine Chapel and the St. Peter's Chapel which was reorganized under Pope Julius II (pontificate: 1503–1513) whence the name Julian Chapel. From the pontificate of Pope Paul III (1513–1534) laymen were admitted to the choirs whereas previously only priests were admitted except for boy sopranos.

We cannot speak of a Roman school in the same sense as a Netherland school because Palestrina is, in reality, the first of the Roman school, and musically he derives from the Netherland school. Dufay had been at the Vatican from 1428 to 1437 and likewise Josquin des Pres from 1486 to 1494, thus establishing direct contact from the Netherland school. The first Italian of note was Costanzo Festa (?–1545) whose *Te Deum* is still used at the election of a pope. About this time another contact was built between the Vatican and Spain from which the Palestrina-Victoria relationship developed. This contact involved the Spaniard Cristobal Morales (1512–1553) who served in the Vatican from 1535 to 1540 when he returned to Spain. Coming from the Netherlands, Jacob Arcadelt (*c.* 1514–*c.* 1560) remained at the Vatican from 1540 to 1549 and then went to Paris. The most important predecessor of Palestrina, however, was Giovanni Animuccia (?–*c.* 1570) who was choirmaster at St. Peter's from 1555 to 1571 or between the two terms of Palestrina. He is credited with the founding of a new art form — the Oratorio, though his *Laudi Spirituali* (1563–1570) written for St. Philip Neri's Oratory were simple hymnlike pieces. Of Palestrina's predecessors, none wrote as great music but each was distinguished by one quality — a style devoid of secular influence.

From age 14 to 18, Giovanni Pierluigi da Palestrina (*c.* 1524–1594) was in Rome to study music with the Netherlander, Gaudio Mell. At 18 he became chapelmaster at the cathedral in his native town, Palestrina. In 1550, when he was 25, he was called to be choirmaster of the Julian choir. In January, 1555, he was appointed director of the Sistine Choir by Pope Julius III (pontificate 1550–1555), but in May of the same year he yielded this position, when the rule against married men was enforced by the new Pope Paul IV (pontificate 1555–1559). He stayed as choirmaster in Rome's other churches until recalled to St. Peter's by the new pope in 1571. He remained at that post until his death in 1594. He received the title of Composer of the Papal Choir – an honor accorded to only one other in history, his successor, Felice Anerio (?–1614). His compositions include 93 Masses, 139 motets and like forms, and over 100 madrigals. His two most famous works are the *Missa Papae Marcelli* and the *Improperia.* The latter has been sung every Good Friday at the Vatican since 1560.

Palestrina is generally conceded to be the greatest church music composer of all time. It is true that Lassus, Victoria, and Byrd are ranked with him, each being known as great in one aspect but weak in another (e.g., Lassus is great in harmonic effects but weaker in melody; Victoria's music is mystic, original, and warm, but he does not employ the great structures of Palestrina and Byrd). Palestrina is equal in greatness to the peculiarity of each of the other three but he does not have the slight drawback peculiar to each.

Palestrina had before him all the developments of polyphony. His own task was primarily a matter of judgment – to weld together all the various elements. He knew how to evolve a fine melody, the value of expression and harmonic effect, the ways of adapting elaborate contrapuntal structures to his purposes. The great canonic and proportional devices of the Netherlanders and the smooth flowing melodies of his

Italian and Spanish predecessors met in Palestrina. More especially he developed conjunct movement, i.e., step-wise or short-interval movement of the voices. Variety in his music comes with frequent change of note values and by occasional disjunct (wide) intervals. In the wide jump, Palestrina always immediately changes the direction of the melody back toward the original note. Further, he treats the melody of each voice in such a way as to emphasize the mode in its plagal and authentic forms. Here is a close relationship to plain chant. He employs cadences with as great effectiveness as any cadence in modern music. The unity of the mode is preserved by using the endings peculiar to each of the psalm tones of the chant; but this still left variety, for he had twelve modes and three or four endings characteristic to each mode. So perfectly are the separate melodies developed that it is difficult to realize that each is also merely a part of the plan with its neighboring melodies.

It has been a favorite theme for some historians to argue that Palestrina was pointed to his goal by the reverberations of the Council of Trent which threatened to outlaw all music except chant from the church. From the accident of coincidence, it was argued that the *Missa Papae Marcelli* was written to demonstrate to the Council the liturgical possibilities of the polyphonic style. There is no direct evidence to support this thesis. It is clear, moreover, that Palestrina had embarked on his path long before the thunder began to rumble.

The excellence of Palestrina's compositions from a liturgical point of view is recognized in the *Motu Proprio* of Pius X, of 1903, and by others before him. In the *Motu Proprio* his works are placed on a par with the chant in that respect. The liturgical text is correctly expressed with none of the repetitiousness or incidental character attached to it by the early Netherlanders. The wedding of music and liturgy in Palestrina is quite as perfect as in the chant.

Plate XI. Palestrina Manuscript.

This manuscript is considered by the leading authority on Palestrina to be in Palestrina's own handwriting. Casimiri, Raffaele C., *Il "Codice 59" dell'Archivio Musicale Lateranense, autografo di Giov. Pierluigi da Palestrina* (Roma: Tipografia poliglotta vaticana, 1919).

As is usual with a great man, his progeny was great. Contemporaneous with him were Giovanni Maria Nanino (1545–1607) and Giovanni Bernardino Nanino (1560–1624). The former was not as productive as Palestrina and his works tend toward efficiency in technique and the beginnings of decadence in the liturgical spirit. The younger Nanino pushes further along this path. Felice Anerio (?–1614), the only other holder of the title of Composer of the Papal Choir, has not left many works, but their merit may be gauged by the fact that historians have sometimes confused his compositions, in particular the *Ingegneri Responsories,* with those of Palestrina. Giovanni Francesco Anerio (*c.* 1567–*c.* 1670) stayed within the bounds of good liturgical music in polyphonic style but in his work we find the influence of the rising secular tide. Lodovico Grossi da Viadana (1564–1627) wrote a number of compositions in polyphonic and ecclesiastical style, but he has also left a number which show the new influences. He is the inventor and chief proponent of the *basso continuo*[54] for organ – the origin of the figured bass so common in the day of J. S. Bach. Giovanni Croce (?–1609) also has left many works in all forms of the Roman tradition. Francesco Suriano (1549–1620), a pupil of Palestrina and G. M. Nanino, was choirmaster at St. Peter's from 1603. His liturgical compositions rank with those of Felice Anerio and G. M. Nanino as fine continuations of the style of Palestrina though Suriano, too, betrays a tendency toward the dramatic. Luca Marenzio (1550–1599) is known principally for his secular work in madrigal form, but he has a number of motets in the Roman style. The last two great composers of the Roman school were Gregorio Allegri (1584–1652) and Francesco Foggia (?–1688). Allegri is particularly famous for the *Miserere* in four and five parts sung every Good Friday by

[54] The *basso continuo* consists of writing out the bass melody and placing above it numbers indicating the intervals at which the other voices are to appear.

the papal choir. It is this work to which a penal decree applied for removal of a copy from the Vatican, and which Mozart heard at the age of 14 and later transcribed from memory. In a thoroughly acceptable style Foggia blended many of the new ideas in music (to be considered in the next chapter) with the traditions of the Roman school. With his death in 1688, the Roman school ceased even though occasional works of the next generation achieved merit. Only one hundred years after the death of Palestrina the great polyphony that was over 700 years in building had disappeared. Many works, it is true, continued to be written *a la Palestrina* both before and after Foggia's death, some by Casciolini, Pasquini, Bai, Pitoni, Biordi, Agostini, Benevoli, Mazzocchi, Antonelli, Bernabei, Abbatini, and Valentini, but while they speak the language of Palestrina, the expression and ideal are gone in favor of mass effects – one composition appearing in as many as 48 parts! The cycle in composition returned to the early Netherlanders and the creation of problems to be solved was again the dominant note.

## THE SPANISH SCHOOL

Mention was made in the discussion of the Roman school of the interchange of the Spanish with the Vatican and the Netherland school. In 1890 there was uncovered a collection of four to five hundred secular compositions by more than sixty Spanish composers[55] of the period 1490–1520 which demonstrate great ability in harmony and a typical Spanish melancholy. This collection shows the influence of the Netherland school. Andres Torrentes (?–1544) and Cristobal Morales (?–1553)[56] both had been in Rome for some time and returned to Toledo. They were thoroughly familiar with

55 Barbieri, Francisco A., *Cancionero Musical de los Siglos XV y XVI* (Madrid: Huerfanos, 1890).

56 Some of their works appear in Eslava, Miguel H., *Lira Sacro Hispana,* 10 vols. (Madrid: Salazar, 1869), Vol. I, and Pedrell, Francesco, *Hispaniae Schola Musica Sacra,* 8 vols. (Barcelona: Pujol, 1894–1898).

contrapuntal methods and their works still survive in Spain as typical of the Spanish polyphony with more expression and meaning attached to the text than is the case with the Netherlanders. Both are well within liturgical standards. Escobedo was another contact of Spain with Italy. Of the next generation, Francisco Guerrero (1527–1599) first at Seville and then Morales' successor at Toledo, and Francisco Salinas (?–1590), for a while at Naples and then at Salamanca, both stand out. Most of the works of Guerrero are church music and Salinas brought out a treatise, in 1577, on the subject of musical rhythm in relation to poetic rhythm. This clearly shows the Spanish concern with expression of the text. The other great concern of the Spanish was with fluency in music. Contrapuntal devices were employed only when they were readily digested. Accordingly, the Spanish musical structure was the simplest of the polyphonic schools.

The great master of the Spanish school, however, was Tomas Luis da Victoria (1540–1613). At an early age he went to Rome and returned to Spain at the age of 49; he was a close friend of Palestrina and his music is the closest of any composer to that of the master of the Roman school. As was true with the leader of each school, the quantity of his works was large. His most famous works are the *Officium Defunctorum* in six voices and his *Improperia.* He carries on the Spanish tradition of greater warmth in expression (but never approaching the dramatic style) and a somewhat simpler structure than that of Palestrina. Otherwise all the remarks about Palestrina would apply to Victoria: purely ecclesiastical in style, a master of melody and harmony. It is difficult to place Palestrina ahead of Victoria. In a sense, Palestrina travels the middle road, Lassus the road on one side which is more interested in the music itself and its devices, and Victoria the road on the other side which views the devices of music as something to be employed sparingly lest they get in the way of the exact expression of the text.

The process of decadence after Victoria follows the Italian pattern though it is accelerated by the Spanish tendency to lyricism. Very few of the post-Victoria works are published but some from composers who were of the generation immediately after Victoria still survive and are in the true style.[57] Portugal shared the Spanish development and produced some composers of merit at this time also.

### THE ENGLISH SCHOOL

The English school was the least of the four great schools — and for a very good reason. The Reformation snuffed the English school as its fire began to burn — but not entirely.

While John Dunstable (?–1453) the Englishman-on-the-continent was the link funneling the accrued knowledge of polyphony to the early Netherlanders, England itself was quite unprepared for the new developments. Thus Tinctoris (*c.* 1475) speaks[58] of the English students now coming to learn from the Netherlanders who had originally learned from the English. Until the second decade of the sixteenth century, however, the English rejected the new devices of the Netherlanders: canon and harmonic progression of chords. Instead they followed strict counterpoint with note against note style and occasional passing notes. Generally accepted as the leader of this era was Robert Fayrfax (?–1529). Masses and motets were composed in this rigid and inexpressive style. Eventually the Netherland ideas prevailed, however,[59] and the English began to imitate the continental movement. The leaders in this development were: Christopher Tye (*c.*

[57] E.g., the works of Sebastino de Heredia of Saragossa (?–1618) and Carlos Patino of Madrid (?–1683). Cf. Chase, Gilbert, *Music of Spain* (New York: Norton, 1941), on this subject, and on the church music of Portugal, *ibid.,* p. 273. Cf. Sister Lucy Marie, "Tomás Luis de Victoria, Priest-Composer," *The Catholic Choirmaster,* XXXII, 149–152, 182–184 (1946).

[58] Coussemaker, Charles E. H., *Scriptorum de Musica Medii Aevi Nova Series* (Paris: Durand, 1864–1876), Vol. IV, p. 77.

[59] Wooldridge, Charles H. E., *The Oxford History of Music,* 1 ed. (London: Oxford, 1901), p. 322, places this date at about 1516.

1490–1572) and his pupil, Robert Thomas Tallis (*c.* 1510–1585) and his pupil, William Byrd (1543–1623), the great master of English polyphony.

Tye was the first Englishman to employ canon and fugue extensively. He left many Masses and motets in manuscript. His best-known work is a six-voiced Mass, *Euge bone,*[60] which is fully abreast of the Netherland developments. To an extent, he shows more creativeness. The subjects for his canons and fugues are material more carefully designed melodically than that typical of the Netherlanders. He also attempts variety by introducing some passages in strict counterpoint. He is also more careful, particularly in later works, than the Netherlanders in how he respects the liturgical text. Robert Whyte is the *alter ego* of Tye whose pupil he was.

The achievements of Tallis were greater, however. He left a Mass, *Sine Nomine,* and a number of motets and similar compositions. The extent to which he followed the Netherlanders is shown in a motet, *Spem in Alium non Habui,* for eight five-voiced choirs. He more fully digested the devices than did Tye and in his maturity forgets about them and strives for beauty and expression. The Reformation disturbed both Tye and Tallis. Though the latter continued at his post through the changes in religion under Henry VIII, Edward, Mary, and Elizabeth, he left Waltham Abbey when it was dissolved. There was considerable pressure exerted by both Catholics and Protestants for a return to strict counterpoint, and, in the case of the Protestants, an English text was required. After Mary, music in any form was strongly opposed by one segment of English Protestantism. To what extent Tye and Tallis supplied compositions in the emasculated form demanded is uncertain but they did not abandon their development of the new methods. Some of these "forced" works show that both met the formalism by

60 Tye, Christopher, *Missa Euge Bone,* ed. G. E. R., Arkwright (Oxford: Parker, 1893).

writing note for note but actually employed "limited" canons — not unlike the Netherlanders in their evasion of formalism by naming Masses *"Sine Nomine,"* etc. Tallis, at least, soon abandoned this position and returned to writing for the Catholic liturgy and published the works as *Cantiones Sacrae* under a printing monopoly he held jointly with Byrd. Tye became a Protestant clergyman, about 1466, and apparently abandoned music. Many of the Protestant composers saw their escape from the new restrictions in instrumental music — particularly for the organ.

William Byrd remained a Catholic[61] and composed for the Catholic liturgy though he was a member of the Royal Chapel from 1569. He left three Masses and many motets and like forms in two volumes entitled *Cantiones Sacrae* and two entitled *Gradualia,* as well as considerable instrumental music. Byrd's music does not fall into traditional polyphonic categories. He makes frequent use of chromatics and does not remain consistently in the ecclesiastical modes. His style has strong harmonic effects, and he uses the devices of canon, fugue, and imitation freely, but in his own way and not as the traditional rules would require. His music is rugged and vigorous, yet entirely liturgical. His life was hardly conducive to serenity.

In concluding this chapter, we are aware of the many names omitted — but as stated in the Preface the present volume is not primarily a history of music.

## BIBLIOGRAPHY FOR CHAPTER III

### BOOKS

Adler, Guido, *Handbuch der Musikgeschichte,* 2 ed. (Berlin: H. Heller, 1930), Vol. I.

[61] Byrd is known to have suffered considerably for his religion but seems to have been saved from worse by his fame as a musician. His capabilities as a performer on the organ and virginal and his many compositions for these instruments were probably his ticket to life.

Aigrain, Rene, *Religious Music,* tr. from French by Charles Mulcahy (London: Sands, 1931).

Ambros, August, and Leichtentritt, Hugo, *Geschichte der Musik* (Leipzig: F. E. C. Leuckart, 1909), Vol. IV.

Apel, Willi, *The Notation of Polyphonic Music, 900–1600,* 2 ed. (Cambridge: Medieval Society of America, 1942).

Bannister, Henry M., *Monumenti Vaticani di Paleografia Musicale Latina* (Leipzig: Harrassowitz, 1913).

Besseler, Heinrich, *Die Musik des Mittelalters und der Renaissance* (Potsdam: Akademische Verlagsgesellschaft Athenaion, 1931–1935).

Bukofzer, Manfred, *Music in the Baroque Era* (New York: Norton, 1947).

Coussemaker, Charles E. H. Work cited at end of Chapter II.

D'Indy, Vincent, *Cours de Composition Musicale,* 5 ed. (Paris: Durand et fils, 1912), Vol. I.

Gastoué, Amedee, *Les Primitifs de la Musique Francaise* (Paris: Laurens, 1922).

Gerbert, Martin, O.S.B. Works cited at end of Chapter II.

Gerold, Theodore, *La Musique au Moyen Age* (Paris: Champion, 1932).

——— *Histoire de la Musique des Origines a la Fin du XIV*e (Paris: Renouard, 1936).

Jeppesen, Knud, *Kontrapunkt* (Leipzig: Breitkopf & Härtel, 1935); English tr. by Glen Haydon, *Counterpoint* (New York: Prentice-Hall, 1939).

——— *Palestrina and the Dissonance* (Oxford: Oxford University Press).

Leichtentritt, Hugo, *Geschichte der Motette* (Leipzig: Breitkopf & Härtel, 1908).

Merritt, Arthur T., *Sixteenth Century Polyphony,* 2 ed. (Cambridge: Harvard University Press, 1944).

Morris, R. O., *Contrapuntal Technique in the Sixteenth Century* (London: Oxford, 1922).

Reese, Gustave. Work cited at end of Chapter II, pp. 249–424.

Riemann, Hugo, *Geschichte der Musiktheorie vom IX.-XIX. Jahrhundert,* 2 ed. (Leipzig: Breitkopf & Härtel, 1921).

*Studien zur Musik-Geschichte: Festschrift für Guido Adler zum 75. Geburtstag* (Vienna, Universal Edition, 1930).

Wolf, Johannes, *Geschichte der Mensural Notation von 1250–1460,* 3 vols. (Leipzig: Breitkopf & Härtel, 1904).

Wooldridge, Charles H. E. Work cited at end of Chapter II, Vol. II.

EDITIONS OF MUSIC

Byrd, William, *Collected Vocal Works,* ed. Fellowes (London: Stainer and Bell, 1937–1939), 9 vols.

——— *Tudor Church Music* (London: Oxford University Press, 1922–1929), 10 vols.

*Denkmäler Deutscher Tonkunst* (Leipzig: Breitkopf & Härtel, 1892–1937).

*Denkmäler der Tonkunst in Bayern* (Leipzig: Breitkopf & Härtel, 1894–1937).

*Denkmäler der Tonkunst in Osterreich* (Vienna: Artaria, 1894–1937).

Des Pres, Josquin, *Werken,* ed. Smijers (Leipzig: Breitkopf & Härtel, 1925–1937), 17 vols.

*Hispaniae Schola Musica Sacra,* ed. Pedrell (Barcelona: Pujol, 1894–1898), 8 vols.

Lassus, Orlandus, *Sämmtliche Werke* (Leipzig: Breitkopf & Härtel, 1894–1926), 21 vols. thus far.

*Les Maitres Musiciens de la Renaissance Francaise,* ed. Expert (Paris: Senart, 1894–1908), 23 vols.

Machaut, Guillaume, *Musikalische Werke,* ed. Ludwig in *Publikationen Älterer Musik* (Leipzig: Breitkopf & Härtel, 1926–1929), 3 vols.

Monte, Philippe de, *Werke* (Düsseldorf: Schwann, 1930–1935), 26 vols.

Monteverdi, Claudio, *Tutte le Opere,* ed. Malipiero (Asolo, 1926–1932), 14 vols.

Obrecht, Jakob, *Werken,* ed. Wolf (Leipzig: Breitkopf & Härtel, 1912–1921).

Okeghem, Johannes, *Sämmtliche Werke* in *Publikationen Älterer Musik* (Leipzig: Breitkopf & Härtel, 1927– ).

Palestrina, Giovanni Pierluigi da, *Opera Omnia,* ed. Haberl (Leipzig: Breitkopf & Härtel, 1862–1903), 33 vols.

Petrucci, Ottaviano de, *Harmonice Musices Odhecaton,* Venice, 1501, Canti B, 1502, Canti C, 1504. Modern ed. by Helen Hewitt and Isabel Pope (Cambridge: Medieval Academy of America, 1942).

Victoria, Tomás Luis de, *Opera Omnia,* ed. Pedrell (Leipzig: Breitkopf & Härtel, 1902–1913), 8 vols.

# CHAPTER IV

## *MODERN CHURCH MUSIC*

IN THIS chapter there are not the continuous developments in church music to be found in each of the other chapters — except from the point at the beginning of the nineteenth century which marks the resurrection of liturgical music. This chapter, with that exception, is the dismal story of the disintegration of the liturgical ideal due to a number of influences of which two stand out: (1) the Reformation in religion, and (2) the new technical developments in music.

### THE VENETIAN SCHOOL

It may have surprised some readers that no mention was made of the Venetian school in the preceding chapter since histories of music often group it with the four polyphonic schools. But it is no exaggeration to say that contemporaneous existence was the one element common to the Venetian school and the others. The Venetian school marks the beginning of modern music.

The founder of the Venetian school was the Netherlander, Adrian Willaert (*c.* 1490–1562), who was mentioned earlier as a member of the Netherland polyphonic school. Willaert, a pupil of Josquin, left Paris for Rome, in 1516, and, in 1527, won the appointment as choirmaster at the important St. Mark's in Venice which was to be the center of new ideas for almost two centuries. There is some truth in the statement generally made in histories of music that the new ideas were developed because of the fact that St. Mark's had two opposing choir lofts, each with its own organ. At any rate, the initial Venetian efforts were in mass effects. Two choirs were used separately and then in unison. Willaert still remained clear in his music and was careful with the handling of texts as is shown in his two-choir *Magnificat Sexti Toni* and his three-choir works. His most famous compositions besides the *Magnificat* are the psalms *Confitebor Tibi, Lauda Jerusalem,* and *Laudate Pueri* besides many Masses, motets and like church music, as well as secular works (which at one time caused him to be termed the Father of the Madrigal). Although he wrote for four, five, and six voices and developed the new mass effects, Willaert not only rose above the wallowing in contrapuntal devices characteristic of the Netherlanders at this time but made definite advances in treating the text more concisely and giving it more expression through a greater emphasis on harmony, e.g., more definite cadences.

After Willaert, however, changes become rapid. He was succeeded at St. Mark's by his pupil, Cyprian De Rore (1516–1565), also a Netherlander. De Rore wrote some church music but most of his work was in secular forms. From his time on the secular influence in church music grows. De Rore was enamoured of chromatics. As an innovator, he never achieved mastery of the technique – being in this respect like the early Netherland school in its treatment of contrapuntal devices, mainly concerned with problem solving. Yet his secular compositions were very popular. His successor, Gioseffo Zarlino (1517–1590), has left few works, mostly motets and madrigals, which show a growing mastery of chromatics. His fame rests mainly on his theoretical treatise, *Istituzioni Harmoniche,* which established him as the leading theorist of the sixteenth century. In his work he presents the rules of counterpoint so successfully that for more than a century they remained standard. But more important, he shows the distinction between major and minor chords and their relations to each other. He is thus the founder of the science of Harmony.[1] Hence, even before the death of Palestrina, an entirely new idiom of music was well along in its development. The idiom progressed mainly in secular composition and particularly in the madrigal form. Zarlino's successor was Baldassare Donato (?–1609) who continued mainly in secular composition. Donato was succeeded by Giovanni Croce (1539–1609), a pupil of Zarlino. Croce has left many works in all the forms. Like Willaert he preferred counterpoint and used chromatics and the new idea of chords sparingly and with purpose. His style is simple and expressive, and his compositions endure in popularity today, particularly in Germany.

Throughout the period we have discussed, important contributions were made by the Venetian school to instrumental literature, but this will be considered separately in Chapter V. Two of the leading organ composers of the school were the two Gabrieli: Andrea (1510–1586) and his nephew, Giovanni (1557–1612), but they also brought out vocal works in all the forms. Andrea considered the six-voiced *Penitential Psalms* his greatest work but the three-choir *Deus Misereatur Nostri* surpasses it in effectiveness. To the ordinary choir he added another choir in higher range and one in lower, welding the three in a fine result. While Willaert used two choirs, each of four mixed voices, Giovanni grouped his choirs into male and female and added an orchestra which did not duplicate the choirs but was another independent

[1] Harmony is distinguished from counterpoint (or polyphony in the narrow sense) in that the several voices are considered from the point of view of chords — i.e., different triads in which the upper voices (in the original position of the chord) are an interval of a third above each other. The chords may be "inverted," i.e., the lowest tone of the triad may appear above the other tones. For example, the tonic triad of the key of *C major,* in its original position, would be *C* in the lowest voice, *E* in the middle voice, and *G* in the top voice. In its inverted form, *E* (first inversion) or *G* (second inversion) may appear in the lowest voice and the other tones in the higher voices. Thus in harmony, the composer thinks of the several voices "vertically," but in counterpoint he thinks "horizontally," i.e., in terms of the flow of melody in one voice against the flow of melody in the other voices.

unit. Not content with this, his expression is subjective and dramatic with the freest use of chromatics to be found up to his time. His most famous work is the *Symphoniae Sacrae* of two volumes involving from six to sixteen voices. He clearly oversteps the liturgical limits at almost every point — but that he achieved great fame in the process is beyond dispute.

With the Gabrieli, true church music ceased in the Venetian school though St. Mark's continued for another century to develop important musicians. Most of their efforts, however, were directed to the opera, the orchestra, and the oratorio. They are worth discussing in passing because their works often pass as good church music "in the Venetian style." The most famous of the seventeenth century at St. Mark's undoubtedly was Claudio Monteverdi (1567–1643), who is accounted the father of the opera, though there had been previous efforts at this form. Monteverdi wrote twelve such "operas" and much other secular music. Perhaps out of deference to his post at St. Mark's, he wrote much church music, including Masses, vespers, and motets. But the style and spirit of his work is entirely secular. Then follow the three "C's": Giovanni Carissimi (1604–1674), composer of more than 15 oratorios and many cantatas; Francesco Cavalli (*c.* 1600–1676), composer of 42 operas; and Marc Antonio Cesti (*c.* 1620–1669), composer of 12 operas. Carissimi and Cavalli have left music for sacred texts, but it is entirely in the idiom of the stage. The same is true of Antonio Caldera (*c.* 1670–1736), composer of 69 operas, although his church music is closer to acceptable limits. Antonio Lotti (1667–1740) was likewise an opera composer, but he devoted considerable time to the composition of church music, and his style is acceptable. Earlier, Giovanni Legrenzi (1626–1690) had composed a considerable number of works for the Church.

## OTHER NORTHERN ITALIAN CITIES

Drawing from the Venetian school, a musical center developed at Naples, headed by Alessandro Scarlatti (1659–1726), who is justly famous in the history of opera, having 115 works in that form. He is reputed to have written over 200 Masses but only a few of them survive — replete with arias and all the paraphernalia of the stage. Yet one of his students, Giovanni Battista Pergolesi (1710–1736), is the composer of the *Stabat Mater* which enjoys more fame, perhaps, than it deserves.

At Cremona, Marco Antonio Ingegneri (1545–1592) left much church music in the style of the Roman school. So like Palestrina are his works that his *Responsoria Hebdomadae Sanctae* was for a long time credited to Palestrina. At Modena, Orazio Vecchi (1550–1603) rests his reputation mainly on secular works. He composed a number of pieces for sacred texts, but they are not expressive of the liturgy and are in operatic style. His namesake, Orfeo Vecchi (1540–1604), who wrote church music exclusively, produced more practical works with artistic expression.

## POLISH CHURCH MUSIC IN THE SIXTEENTH CENTURY

Polish church music of this period has not been entirely uncovered. There are reasons for believing that much more lies buried in libraries.[2] The German, Heinrich Finck (1527–1579), probably a pupil of Dufay, founded the Polish school which bears all the marks of Netherland influence. From 1492 to 1506, Finck was choirmaster at the royal chapel in Cracow. The earliest native composers were Sebastian Felstin (*c.* 1490–*c.* 1543) with a book of hymns in 1522 and Christopher Borek (?–1557) with a Mass and hymns. The best of the school, however, were Martinus Lwowczyk (1540–1589) with three Masses extant and Waclav Szamotulczyk

[2] The best edition of early Polish music is Joseph Surzynski, *Monumenta Musicae Sacrae in Polonia* (Posen, 1885), 4 vols.

(*c.* 1525–1572) with a number of motets, some of which have been resurrected today. Polish compositions are in the Netherland contrapuntal style but show the sense of strong rhythm found in all early German music as well. Polish church music composition continued until the eighteenth century and in the seventeenth century showed strong Venetian influence with arias and elaborate accompaniments.

### GERMANY

Because of Luther and the Reformation, no polyphonic school developed in Germany, but this was also partly due to the German predeliction for hymns already discussed in Chapter III. Heinrich Isaac (*c.* 1450–1517) is the leader of the German musicians. His secular songs have merited for him the title of the "German Orpheus." In addition, he composed much church music. His Masses are largely in contrapuntal style with Gregorian chant melodies for the *cantus firmus.* His best-known church works, uncovered in the resurrection of church music in the nineteenth century, are *Choralis Constantinus,* being the offices for Sundays and holydays, and the *Oratio Jeremiae Prophetae.* Some of his songs, with different texts, were adapted as both Protestant chorales and Catholic hymns. Other names of the period are Thomas Stottzer (?–1526), Paul Hofhaimer (1459–1537), Leonhard Paminger (1495–1567), and Ludwig Senfl (1492–1555).

The greatest composer of the last part of the century was Hans Leo Hassler (1564–1612), who followed the Venetian school with many instrumental works and songs. To this period belong Adam Gumpeltzhaimer (1559–1625), Christian Erbach (1573–1635), Gregor Aichinger (1564–1628) with his *Sacrae Cantiones* and *Tricinia* for four to ten voices, and Jacob Gallus (1550–1591) with his *Opus Musicum.* The hymns of all these composers show originality and the simple but profound expression characteristic of German music. Their admissibility as correct church music gave rise to many contradictory decrees by the hierarchy – not surprising in view of the turmoil in religion in Germany during the period and the Wars of Liberation. Thus Archbishop Karl Joseph of Mainz ordered that only German hymns be sung during High Mass whereas scarcely a century earlier councils and synods had condemned the singing of hymns in German at High Mass, insisting that such hymns were proper only outside the liturgy, e.g., in processions and pilgrimages. The process of Germanizing everything (known as Josephinism) went far beyond any bounds. Thus in the eighteenth century, such songs became popular for use at High Mass as the *Jager und Echo* (Hunter and Echo) by Lindenborn, a duet portraying a hunting scene which has its ecclesiastical connection in the echo's guidance of the hunter to the Christmas crib.

What is to be said of the role of the vernacular hymn in church music? In view of the complete Latin texts of the Mass and the Office, there is not much occasion for the vernacular hymn except during the Low Mass, at the beginning or end of Mass, or in the services other than the Mass and the Office. The liturgical principles governing music for the vernacular hymn are the same as those governing music for the Latin text except that, in addition, the text itself must be appropriate. The most common exceptions are taken to certain hymn music because of (1) its sentimentality – and in this it violates the standards of art quite as much as those of the liturgy, (2) its worldliness – such as transferring waltz or dance tunes to vernacular texts,[3] or (3) its distractiveness – such as elaborate solos centering the attention of the congregation on the choir loft rather than on the altar. The standards governing music of the vernacular hymn are quite the same as those governing any other music in the modern[4]

[3] This is not to say that all music written with the dance time signature (e.g., the 3/4 signature) is *ipso facto* unliturgical.

[4] The term "modern music" is always used in the present volume to mean music in the modern (i.e., major and minor) modes.

style for the church, whether it be for the *Ordinarium,* for solo, organ, or whatever its type or form. This is demonstrated in our next section. There is nothing in modern music *per se* in conflict with the principles of liturgical music.

## THE EIGHTEENTH AND NINETEENTH CENTURIES — THE MUSIC OF BACH, MOZART, HAYDN, BEETHOVEN, AND THE CLASSICAL MASTERS

Richard Wagner, as an artist, recognizes what must be the judgment of the modern masters as church music composers:[5]

> The first step in the decay of true sacred music was the introduction into it of orchestral instruments. Through them and by their freer and more independent use religious utterance was forced to assume a sensuous character, greatly to its own detriment and to that of singing as well. The virtuosity of the instrumentalists at length called forth in the singers a similar virtuosity, and ere long the secular operatic taste penetrated into the Church. Certain passages of the sacred text were marked out as standard texts for operatic airs, and singers trained in the manner of the Italian opera were brought into Church to deliver them. . . . To the human voice, the immediate vehicle of the sacred word belongs the first place in churches, and not to instrumental additions or the trivial scraping found in most church pieces today. Church music can regain its former purity only by a return to the purely vocal style. If an accompaniment is considered absolutely necessary, the genius of Christianity has provided the instrument worthy of such function, the organ.

Not that any argument from authority is necessary, but the comments of Wagner are certainly impartial.

There are two positions that must be kept separate. The first is that the "religious" compositions of Mozart and the masters do not meet the requirements of the liturgy. The

[5] Wagner, Richard, *Gesammelte Schriften und Dichtungen* (Leipzig: Fritzsch, 1871), II, pp. 336–337. This is not a translation but a synopsis of a passage several times as long.

second is that their "sacred" compositions are defective, as a matter of art, because they do not express the texts. This argument is that, essentially, such compositions fall under the same censure as the early Netherlanders with their problem solving and disregard of texts. The argument, of course, concedes that the different composers violate true art in different degrees, e.g., J. S. Bach less so than any other. The entire second position is beyond the scope of this book.[6]

Characteristically, those who advance Mozart and the other masters as acceptable liturgically do not contend that all their "sacred" music is liturgical but rather select only certain works as acceptable.[7] Wolfgang Amadeus Mozart (1756–1791) left 15 Masses, 4 *Kyries,* 4 Litanies, 9 Offertories, a *Te Deum,* and miscellaneous pieces. Those usually advanced as liturgical are the Requiem and the *Mass in F* and the *Mass in D* (Köchel numbers 192 and 194). In the early days of the church music revival in the nineteenth century these works were admitted. But exception is taken to them on several grounds. First, the length of the compositions is inadmissible. Frequent repetitions and extended musical treatment place the *Ordinarium* out of proportion to the other liturgical texts of the Mass. Efforts have been made to meet this difficulty by the publication of abridged editions. Such practice, however, destroys the artistic merit of the work since the "piecing together" produces an unnatural and illogical composition.

6 Attention can be directed to the confusion of these two positions by Wagner in the quotation just given. He is, at least impliedly, assuming the second position as well as the first.

7 At the outset, mention should be made of the categoric decision of the Society of St. Gregory of America (and similar societies in almost all the countries) to exclude from the church all the compositions of Mozart, Haydn, Schubert, Weber, and many others of lesser caliber. The basis of the decision, of course, is not that most of the compositions by these masters are unliturgical and therefore all of them ought to be excluded, but rather results from a judgment of each individual composition. This is clearly shown by the fact that some of the compositions of other composers are approved and others disapproved, e.g., only the Masses St. Cecilia, Sacred Heart, and De Paques of Charles Gounod are disapproved.

The second ground of objection is the florid style, the use of brilliant solos, elaborate cadences, etc., which are calculated to distract the devotion of the congregation. This necessarily implies that the spirit of the text is not conveyed by the music. Elegant and brilliant contrapuntal passages are not consistent with the liturgical words. If the words are to be understood as conveying a "natural" religion or lofty sentiments, then the music would, perhaps, be appropriate. But the music is not expressive of a divinely revealed text.

Joseph Haydn (1732–1809), the creator of the modern symphony, left 13 Masses, 13 Offertories, 2 *Te Deum's,* a *Stabat Mater,* and miscellaneous sacred compositions. His works, though in a grander vein, are even less liturgical than those of Mozart. A statement attributed to him: "that the thought of God made his heart leap with joy, and his music into the bargain," may offer some explanation of his spirit.[8] His pupil, Ludwig von Beethoven (1770–1827) composed a *Missa Solemnis* and a *Mass in C.* Of them, his biographer states[9] that they have "in common with the Church only what we have called the origin of all religions, namely, deep and fervent devotion to the Godhead, the nostalgia of the soul for its Eternal Home. . . . It is so independent of the words affixed, that the composer himself wished to assign another [German] text to the music. He certainly only retained the words at all because without words it could not be sung. His work is primarily instrumental music."

Of the group, Michael Haydn (1737–1806), the brother of Joseph, approaches closest to liturgical acceptability. Both his brother and Mozart freely admitted the superiority of his sacred music. He has many Masses, Graduals, Offertories, and other forms, of which the *Tenebrae* and two *Missa Quadragesimalis* are best known.

8 Weinmann, Karl, *History of Church Music* (New York: Pustet, 1906), p. 192.
9 *Ibid.*

John Sebastian Bach (1685–1750) employed the Catholic liturgy only in five Masses, the most famous being the *Mass in B Minor,* and four "short" Masses containing only the *Kyrie, Gloria,* and *Sanctus.* He presents a better expression of the text than the masters just discussed. The inspiration is more thoroughly that of revealed religion, but the structure is far too elaborate for the liturgy, with organ interludes, arias, and duets in the Italian form and lengthy choruses. It could not be said of Bach, however, that he would just as soon have other words than those actually employed. Bach's contemporary, Frederick Handel (1685–1759), left 5 *Te Deum's* and 12 psalms which are similarly unsuited for liturgical use.

## RESURRECTION OF CHURCH MUSIC

Continuously from shortly after the death of Palestrina, there were efforts at restoring liturgical music but none were successful in any degree until that of the nineteenth century — just as there had been repeated unsuccessful efforts from the thirteenth century on to revive the chant in its pure form. With the turmoil of the Reformation everywhere in evidence, the failure at revival is not surprising.

The first figure in the church music revival that succeeded was Kasper Ett (1788–1847), organist from 1816 at the Court Church of St. Michael's in Munich under Ludwig I, King of Bavaria. He revived works from the seventeenth century beginning with Allegri's *Miserere.* He had progressed so far by 1821, that the papal legate to Bavaria, the Duke of Lero Cassano, who was a musician, is credited with the comment that the singing in Munich was better than in Rome. The few compositions left by Ett are all in liturgical style. The center of the revival soon shifted to Ratisbon (Regensburg) under Dr. Karl Proske (1794–1861), a medical graduate of Halle who became a priest in 1826. With the co-operation of Bishop Sailer of Ratisbon and King Ludwig the movement was given official impetus by the Royal Decree of 1830. Proske spent most of his life in research and gathered the famous Proske Library of publications and manuscripts of the polyphonic schools known as *Antiquitates Musicae Ratisbonenses.* Gradually these works were reintroduced at the Ratisbon cathedral. Other leaders there were John Mettenleiter (1812–1858), the composer; Dominic Mettenleiter (1822–1868), the research scholar; Joseph Schrems (1815–1872); and Joseph Hanisch (1812–1892). In 1853, they began the publication of selected polyphonic works in a collection, *Musica Divina.*

The movement continued under Franz Witt (1834–1888), a true reformer, with the issuance of a pamphlet on the state of church music, in 1868, at Bamberg and with the periodical *Musica Sacra* originated by Proske at Ratisbon. The reform was defined as applying to the use of Gregorian chant, the revival of congregational singing, the reintroduction of the polyphonic music, and the reform of modern church music. The efforts were recognized in a brief of sanction, *Multum ad Commovendos Animos* by Pope Pius IX on December 16, 1870.

Almost contemporaneous with the German movement came the French restoration of the chant outlined by the Benedictine, Prosper Gueranger (1805–1875), in 1835, and continued by his successors at the Abbey of Solesmes, as already described in the beginning of Chapter II. His efforts had been preceded by those of the Jesuit Louis Lambillotte (1797–1855) who made diligent researches.[10] Contemporaneously in Belgium we find the researches of Francois J. Fetis (1784–1871).

The German and French groups came into unfortunate conflict on the subject of the chant. In 1883, appeared the *Liber Gradualis* of the Benedictine Joseph Pothier (1835–

[10] Unfortunately his tentative *Graduale* was published posthumously. The chant it contains is still in abbreviated and altered form and not the true original. Similarly with the Rheims-Cambrai *Graduale* published, in 1851, at Paris.

1923), successor to Gueranger.[11] Previously (in 1848) the *Mechlin Graduale* had appeared as a substantial reprint of the *Medicaean Graduale* of 1614.[12] An edition of the *Graduale* was undertaken at Ratisbon by Pustet in 1868 under a thirty-year exclusive license from the Vatican. It was declared the official edition by Pope Pius IX, in 1873, and again by Pope Leo XIII, in 1878. The *Vesperale* of the series was based on the *Antiphonale* of Venice, in 1585, and of Antwerp, in 1611. These editions of the corrupt chant became known particularly because of their mensural notation as the Ratisbon notation. Though it was apparent before the expiration of the thirty years that this edition was unsound, the exclusive printing privilege granted Pustet, in 1868, was observed by the Vatican.

Finally Pope Pius X divested the Ratisbon edition of its official character and established an international commission to edit the official edition. The result was the *Graduale* published in 1907.[13] For a while confusion existed particularly on the subject of whether the rhythm was "free" or "mensural" at the option of the individual. This prompted the Prefect of the Congregation of Rites to address a letter on February 18, 1910, to the President of the *Cecilienverein* in Germany instructing him that "free" rhythm is necessarily implied in the official edition of 1907.

The restoration of church music culminated in the establishment of the Pontifical Institute of Sacred Music at the Vatican in 1910. The Institute has been successively under the direction of the Jesuit, Angelo de Santi, 1910 to 1922, and the Benedictines Paul Ferretti, 1922 to 1938, and Gregory Sunol, 1938 to 1946, and Msgr. Igino Anglés since 1947. The most important "school" previously had been that

11 Almost always overlooked is Paul Jausions (1834–1870), the first researcher of the Solesmes school, whose untimely death, however, occurred only after he had made great strides in a little more than a decade of work.

12 Discussed in Chapter II.

13 Followed by the other books as mentioned in the beginning of Chapter II.

established by Witt, in 1870, at Ratisbon and continued under Dr. F. X. Haberl (1840–1910). Other schools – offshoots of the Ratisbon school – were established at St. Francis, Wisconsin, in 1873; at Laibach, Jugoslavia, in 1877; at Malines, Belgium, in 1879; at Posen, Poland, in 1889; and at Utrecht, Holland. The leading texts were Dr. Haberl's *Magister Choralis* and the *Chorale Schule* of Ambrose Kienle.

The nub of the entire restoration, however, was the *Motu Proprio* of Pope Pius X on Sacred Music issued on St. Cecilia's Day, November 22, 1903. The *Motu Proprio* describes itself as a "juridical code of sacred music."[14] The instruction is so succinct as to defy a synopsis. Accordingly, it is given as an appendix to the present volume. From the historical viewpoint, the *Motu Proprio* is supported in every sentence by the evidence of history.[15] All of the difficulty and confusion, to say nothing of the conflict, which has developed about the *Motu Proprio* stems from the inadequate historical background of those reading and attempting to interpret it.

Following the lead of Belgium, Germany, and France, restoration movements were underway in almost all countries before the close of the nineteenth century, usually by

[14] The immediate drafting of the *Motu Proprio* is frequently said to have been in the hands of the Jesuit, Angelo de Santi (1849–1922).

[15] The historical facts supporting the *Motu Proprio* include, of course, besides the writings of the ecclesiastics, the official documents of the Vatican on the subject. Mention has been made of the Constitution of Pope John XXII in 1316 (in Chapters II and III) and of the Rules of Sacred Music of the Council of Trent in 1545–1563 (in Chapters II and III). In addition, the leading documents include the Constitution of Pope Alexander VII in 1657; the Decree on Sacred Music by the Sacra Vista Apostolica in 1665; the Encyclical Letter of Pope Benedict XIV in 1749; the Decree of Cardinal Placido Zurla, Vicar of Pope Leo XII in 1824; and the Regulations for Sacred Music of Pope Leo XIII in 1884. Since the *Motu Proprio,* the Constitution of Pope Pius XI was issued in 1928. All of these are available in English translation in *The White List of the Society of St. Gregory of America,* 4 ed. (New York: The Society of St. Gregory of America, 1947).

The authoritative work on ecclesiastical legislation about music is Fiorenzo Romita, *Jus Musicae Liturgicae* (Tourini: M. E. Marietti, 1936), pp. 319.

means of a Society of St. Gregory or St. Cecilia Society accompanied by a periodical,[16] as set out in Table I, p. 144. With these societies came an effort to establish catalogues, or, as they are more commonly called, "White Lists" of approved music. These efforts introduced a new element of danger best described in the words of Dr. Karl Weinmann, the successor of Dr. Haberl as head of the Ratisbon school:[17]

> Only if it [the approving authority] were to set up the idea that in the choice of sacred compositions its Catalogue should be regarded as sole criterion, so that works not found in the Catalog should not deserve the appellation of "sacred" or, on the other hand, that pieces included therein absolutely fulfill the demands of art, the reproaches of its opponents would become justified and, moreover, its pretentions would not be borne out by fact. For excellent and worthy sacred music exists outside the Catalogue, while much finds a place within it that can claim no artistic merit but merely liturgical correctness.

## NINETEENTH-CENTURY REFORM COMPOSERS

Kasper Ett wrote only a few compositions but Franz Witt (1834–1888) in addition to his other efforts composed more than fifty works, the most famous being the *Exultet,* St. Lucis, St. Xavier, and St. Raphael Masses, the Lamentations, and the Stations of the Cross. Because reprints of the polyphonic masters were not immediately available and choirs were not at that time capable of such works, there was a dearth of practicable compositions. The result was a deluge of simple compositions with little intrinsic merit and barely qualifying for the liturgy. Those who have since fallen by the wayside wrote in the heavy, pedantic style of Germany at this time,

16 Because a list of the leading periodicals in church music is not available in English (except for a partial list in *The White List of the Society of St. Gregory of America*), the leading church music periodicals are presented in Appendix III. The exact status of these periodicals since World War II is difficult to ascertain.

17 Weinmann, Karl, *History of Church Music* (New York: Pustet, 1906), p. 175 f.

without original melody and with mechanical and routine succession of chords. Witt's efforts rise above these, as is indicated by their survival. His style goes further and is indi-

## TABLE I

LIST OF PRINCIPAL SOCIETIES PROMOTING CHURCH MUSIC RESTORATION AND THEIR PERIODICALS

| *Country* | *Name of Group* | *Date founded* | *Periodical* |
|---|---|---|---|
| Germany, Austria, and Switzerland | Cecilienverein | 1868 | Musica Sacra and Die Kirchenmusik |
| United States | Society of St. Gregory of America (Preceded by Caecilian Society of 1873) | 1914 | The Catholic Choirmaster |
| Czechoslovakia | St. Cyril Society | 1873 | Cyril |
| Holland | Dutch Society of St. Gregory | 1875 | St. Gregorius Blad |
| Jugoslavia | Caecilian Society | 1877 | Sveta Cecilija |
| England and Ireland | Society of St. Gregory of Great Britain and Ireland | 1876 again in 1929 | Liturgy |
| Belgium | Society of St. Gregory of Belgium | 1879 | Musica Sacra |
| Italy | Society of St. Cecilia of Italy | 1880 | Bolletino Ceciliano |
| France | Schola Cantorum | 1894 | Tribune de St. Gervais |
| Hungary | Hungarian Cecilian Society | 1897 | Magyar Körnes |
| Poland | Association of Organists and Choir Directors | 1898 | Muzyka Koscielna |
| Spain | Spanish Cecilian Society | 1912 | None |

vidual, always the badge of a master.[18] He took the materials of the polyphonic school and became the first liturgical composer in modern times.

Other composers whose work appears destined to become a part of the liturgical repertoire are shown in Table II.

## TABLE II

### Leading Church Music Composers of the Late Nineteenth and Early Twentieth Centuries

*(Excluding those born since 1900 and those composing exclusively for organ. For the latter see Chapter V.)*

*United States*

Richard K. Biggs (1886–living)
Ludwig Bonvin, S.J. (1849–1939)
Lambert A. Dobbelsteen, O.Praem. (1878–1947)
Martin Dummler (1868–living)
John Farnsworth (1879–living ?)
Hubert Gruender, S.J. (1870–1940)
J. Vincent Higginson: pen name — Cyr de Brant (1896–living)
Philip G. Kreckel (1886–living)
Joseph McGrath (1889–living)
Nicola A. Montani (1880–1948)
Michael L. Nemmers (1855–1929)
Carlo Rossini (1890–living)
J. Alfred Schehl (1882–living)
John B. Singenberger (1848–1924)
Henry Tappert (1855–1929)
Paul C. Tonner (1892–living)
Mathias J. Vanden Elsen, O.Praem. (1870-living)
Pietro A. Yon (1886–1943)

*Italy*

Ernesto Boezi (1856–1918)
Enrico Bossi (1861–1925)

18 Franz Liszt is reported to have complimented Witt in the presence of Cardinal Hohenlohe "Let people curse and steal as they will, only write us twenty measures such as you have already given us." Karl Weinmann, *History of Church Music* (New York: Pustet, 1906), p. 173 f.

Luigi Bottazzo (1845–1924)
Filippo Capocci (1840–1910)
Raffaele Casimiri (1880–1943)
Pietro Magri (1873–1937)
Lorenzo Perosi (1872–living)
Oreste Ravanello (1836–1938)
Licino Refice (1885–living)
Giuseppe Terrabugio (1842–1933)
Jacopo Tomandini (1820–1883)

*Holland and Belgium*

Hendrik Andriessen (1892–living)
Matthias Beltjens (1820–1909)
Joseph Borremans (1775–1858)
G. L. Bots (1859–1941)
Joseph Callaerts (1838–1903)
Hubert Cuypers (1873–living)
Alfons Diepenbrock (1862–1921)
Evert Haak (1897–living)
Michael A. Lans (1845–1908)
Philip Loots (1865–1916)
Anton Ponten (1870–living)
Anton J. van Schaik (1862–1927)
Alfons Vranken (1879–living)
Jaap Vranken (1897–living)
Joseph Vranken (1870–living)
John Winnubst (1885–1934)

*Poland*

Waclaw Giebrowski (1879–living)
Joseph Stefani (1880–living)
Joseph Surzynski (1851–1919)
Mieczyslav Surczynski (1866–living ?)
Franz B. Walczynski (1852–1923)

*England*

Richard Terry (1865–1938)
A. Edmonds Tozer (1857–1910)
Ambrose Turner (18—-1905)

*France*

Jacques L. Battmann (1818–1886)
Charles Bordes (1863–1909)
Henri Dallier (1849–1934)
Pierre Dietsch (1808–1865)

Gabriel Faure (1845–1924)
Ferdinand de la Tombelle (1854–1928)
Confined otherwise to Gregorian chant except for organ composers listed in Chapter V

*Germany, Austria, and Switzerland*

Joseph Auer (1856–1911)
Joseph H. Beltgens (1820–1909)
Jacob Blied (1844–1884)
Eduard Brunner (1843–1903)
Albert H. Dietrich (1829–1908)
Joseph H. Dietrich (1874–living)
Ludwig Ebner (1858–1903)
Franz X. Engelhart (1861–1924)
Max Filke (1855–1911)
Heinrich Goetze (1836–1906)
Vincenz Goller (1873–living)
Carl Greith (1828–1887)
Peter Griesbacher (1864–1933)
John E. Habert (1833–1896)
Michael Haller (1840–1915)
Joseph Hanish (1811–1892)
Karl Jaspers (1835–1882)
Frederick Koenen (1829–1887)
Otto Kornmuller (1824–1907)
Aloys Kothe (1828–1868)
Bernhard Kothe (1821–1897)
Carl A. Leitner (1837–1904)
Alban Lipp (1866–1903)
Franz X. Mathias (1871–living)
Bernard Mettenleiter (1882–1901)
John Mettenleiter (1812–1858)
Ignatius Mitterer (1850–1924)
Joseph Mohr (1834–1892)
John B. Molitor (1834–1900)
Franz Nekes (1844–1914)
Heinrich Oberhoffer (1824–1885)
Peter Piel (1835–1904)
Eduard Pilland (1887–living)
John Plag (1863–1921)
Gerhard J. Quadflieg (1854–1915)
George Rathgeber (1869–living)

Joseph Renner, Jr. (1868–1934)
Joseph Renner, Sr. (1832–1895)
Carl Santner (1819–1885)
Ferdinand Schaller (1835–1884)
Joseph Schildknecht (1861–1899)
Gustave E. Stehle (1839–1915)
Bruno Stein (1873–1915)
Joseph Stein (1845–1915)
Karl Theil (1862–1940)
Peter H. Thielen (1839–1908)
Johann Vieth (1872–1935)
William Weitzel (1884–living)
August Wiltberger (1850–1928)
Heinrich Wiltberger (1841–1916)

*Spain*

Miguel Eslava (1807–1878)
Felipe R. Piquera (1881–living)

## BIBLIOGRAPHY FOR CHAPTER IV

Adler, Guido. Work cited at end of Chapter III.

Baumker, William, *Das Katholische Deutsche Kirchenlied in Seinen Stufweisen,* 4 vols. (Freiburg: Herder, 1883–1911).

Bukofzer, Manfred. Work cited at end of Chapter III, Bibliography.

Fellerer, Karl G., *Der Palestrinastil und Seine Bedeutung in der Vokalen Kirchenmusik des Achtzehnten Jahrhunderts* (Augsburg: B. Felser, 1929).

Haberl, Franz X., *Magister Choralis, A Theoretical and Practical Manual of Gregorian Chant* (New York: Pustet, 1877), English tr. by Nicholas Donnelly from the German.

Kienle, Ambrose, O.S.B., *Choralschule, Ein Handbuch zur Erlernung des Choralgesanges* (Freiburg: Herder, 1890).

Riemann, Hugo. Work cited at end of Chapter III, Bibliography.

Walter, Anton, *Franz Witt, Ein Lebensbild* (Regensburg: Pustet, 1906).

Weinmann, Karl. Work cited at end of Chapter I, Bibliography, pp. 168–207.

Witt, Franz, *Das Kgl. Bayer. Kultusministerium, die Bayer. Abgeordnetenkammer und der Cecilienverein* (Regensburg: Pustet, 1886).

# CHAPTER V

## *ORGAN MUSIC FOR THE CHURCH*

THE organ is the traditional instrument in the church. While the *Motu Proprio* admits[1] other instruments on special occasions, there has never been any considerable use of them even in the most decadent periods of church music.

The organ has a long history and has always been a favorite subject for the visual arts, painting, and sculpture. The organ was known to the Egyptian, Roman, and Greek worlds long before the time of Christ.[2] At that time organs were hydraulic, the effect of the modern bellows being achieved by a water device to put air under pressure. The pneumatic organ was known, however, in Byzantium before the ninth century, and by this time there were two types of organ, the portative and the positive, distinguished on the basis of whether they were playable while carried or only when stationary. This points to the theory, as regards the portative organ, that it descends from the bagpipe.

The early Christian fathers make mention of other instruments, stringed and wood wind, introduced into the church on occasion. Even when instruments were common in Byzantium, they were never used to accompany the chant. It is fre-

1 "In some special cases, with due limits and with proper safeguards, other instruments may be allowed, but never without the special permission of the Ordinary. . . . The employment of the piano is forbidden in church, as is also that of noisy or frivolous instruments such as drums, cymbals, bells and the like. . . . It is strictly forbidden to have bands play in church, and only in special cases with the consent of the Ordinary, will it be permissible to admit wind instruments, limited in number, judiciously used, and proportioned to the size of the place. . . ."

2 A standard reference on the early history of the organ is Farmer, Henry G., *The Organ of the Ancients From Eastern Sources (Hebrew, Syriac and Arabic)* (New York: Dutton, 1931).

quently stated that Pope Vitalian (pontificate: 657–672) introduced the organ to improve congregational singing and that Charlemagne received an organ from the Arabs. But there is no evidence to support either statement. However, there is a ninth-century German treatise on organ construction,[3] and it is known that St. Dunstan (952–988) installed several organs in England. The monk Wulfstan (?–963) describes an organ at Winchester for two organists with 400 pipes supplied by 26 bellows requiring pumping by 70 men.[4] Reference to organs from this time on is frequent.

By the thirteenth century, organs themselves were common. Until this time, organs were "played" by removing a wooden slide which admitted air into the pipe and by reinserting the slide to stop the tone. In the thirteenth century, however, the organ received its greatest impetus — the discovery of the keyboard. Vocal music began to be arranged for the organ. The development of *musica ficta* (the use of semitones instead of the regular whole tones of the scale and whole tones in place of the regular semitones) was closely related to organ and other instrumental music. At the end of the thirteenth century, pedals were added. Until this time, no evidence can be found of the organ being used to accompany voices. The closest to that is the use of the organ for short interludes between singing. Even as late as the polyphonic masters of the sixteenth century, whose works contain such directions as "Intended for human voices and for instruments of every kind," the organ was merely intended to duplicate or to act in place of a missing voice.

### EARLY ORGAN COMPOSERS

Several hundred pieces for organ by Francesco Landino (1325–1397) survive in European libraries, and there is extant

[3] Gerbert, Martin, *Scriptores Ecclesiastici de Musica* (St. Blasien, 1774), Vol. I, p. 107.

[4] On the organ at this period, see Bittermann, Helen K., "The Organ in the Early Middle Ages," *Speculum*, Vol. IV, p. 390 (1929).

a fourteenth-century English collection of pure organ pieces and of *intervolatures* or adaptations of vocal pieces for the organ.[5] St. Mark's in Venice had organists from the fourteenth century. In the fifteenth century the line of organists beginning with Zuane (1406–1419) was Bernardino (1419–1445), Bernardo di Stefanino Murer (1445–1459), and Bartolomeo Vielmis (1459–1490). From 1490, St. Mark's had two organs. The choirmaster did not function as organist. Though Willaert was at Venice, from 1527 to 1562, and wrote organ music, the true beginnings of organ music composition date from the terms of the two Gabrieli, Andrea (1556–1586) and Giovanni (1585–1612). Andrea composed many organ pieces called *Intonazioni d'Organo*. The style is experimental with works in contrapuntal form, interspersed with passages of scales and the use of chromatics. With differences in registers uncommon and no *crescendo* and *decrescendo,* the instrument was limited. Giovanni left a number of pieces called *canzoni* which are in fugue fashion, not strict in development but with frequent shifting of themes. Various names are applied to the organ compositions, e.g., fantasies, contrapunti, intonations, ricercari, toccati, passacaglias, etc., and differences are apparent in the music itself. Previously Konrad Paumann (1410–1473) at Nuremberg and Munich wrote studies for organ called *Fundamentum Organisandi* but they do not illustrate the possibilities of the organ.

In southern Germany developed the second great organ school, its style being essentially an experimentation in embellishing contrapuntal works, or "coloring" as it was then known. The growth of secular music with songs and dance tunes had an important influence in expanding the organ style. A sort of fusion of these melodies with polyphony led to the use of chords and harmonic treatment.

Two leading students of the Gabrieli went to Germany,

[5] Ritter, A. G., *Zur Geschichte des Orgelspiels im XIV–XVIII. Jahrhundert* (Leipzig: Hesse, 1884).

Jan Sweelinck (1562–1621) of Amsterdam and Heinrich Schutz (1585–1672) of Dresden. It is somewhat a matter of choice whether Sweelinck or Claudio Merulo (1533–1604) of Parma is named the developer of a style of organ music which corresponds to the technique of the instrument. The Gabrieli had made efforts in this direction. By now not only did all the court chapels have organs and competent organists but each of the large churches harbored men engaged in new composition. The experimentation also evolved an organistic treatment of forms that were originally vocal, such as the fugue and the chorale.

Besides the Netherlander and the German, there is a leading Italian composer for the organ in this period, Girolamo Frescobaldi (1583–1644), the organist of St. Peter's at Rome from 1608 to 1614. Frescobaldi was remarkable for his technical ability as an organist, and his compositions show great variety. Those for the church are largely founded on the ecclesiastical modes, but he wrote many dances and preludes calculated to bring out the different effects of which an organ at that time was capable. He introduced the "tonal" fugue.[6] Many of his compositions survive today in anthologies for the organ.[7]

## THE GOLDEN AGE OF ORGAN COMPOSITION

From the viewpoint of *church* music the greatest achievement in the seventeenth century undoubtedly was the growth in organ music which culminated in the Bach family of the eighteenth century. Two students of Frescobaldi achieved distinction in what is called the south German school. Johann

[6] The "tonal" fugue is distinguished from the "real" fugue in that the answer to the subject is altered slightly to remain in the same key whereas in the real fugue the answer is an exact imitation of the subject, which except for an unison fugue, necessarily involves another key.

[7] If the statement is correctly understood, it can be said that Frescobaldi brought to a maximum development the organ possibilities inherent in the chant and the modes, but further development of organ music depended on the German progress with the organ chorale and fugue.

Froberger (1605–1667) of Vienna and Johann K. Kerll (1627–1693) of Munich wrote elaborate works in a true organ fashion. They abandoned the modes and yet did not confine themselves to dance forms but struck out in original chordal work. The other two leaders of this school were Georg Muffat (*c.* 1645–1704) and Johann Pachelbel (1653–1706). It is characteristic of all four that they drew from all countries for their materials. Muffat was trained in Paris under Lully, who was principally concerned with the opera and the orchestra. Pachelbel particularly developed the prelude for chorales and hymns, and he was a model for many of the early works of J. S. Bach. Johann J. Fux composed many works, and his *Gradus ad Parnassum* (not to be confused with that of Clementi for piano) had a strong influence on composers and organists for the next hundred years. His works do not rise to the height of Bach, but they are sacred in spirit and polyphonic in style. Johann E. Eberlin (1702–1762) of Salzburg left many organ works in the Bach idiom some of which survive today in anthologies.

The north German school was bound to Italy principally through Sweelinck who had many brilliant pupils: Jakob Praetorius (1586–1651), Heinrich Scheidemann (1596–1663), and Jan Reinken (1623–1722), all of Hamburg; the three great "S's," Johann H. Schein (1586–1630) of Leipzig, Samuel Scheidt (1587–1654) of Halle, and Heinrich Schutz, the student of the Gabrieli; and at Hanover Melchior Schildt (1593–1667) who was considered the best pupil of Sweelinck. Only Scheidt and Schutz wrote any considerable number of works. Scheidt began the work of adapting the vocal chorale to the organ. The master of the north German school, however, was Dietrich Buxtehude (1637–1707), a Dane who spent his career at Lübeck. He has left about 70 organ works, most of them in enlarged chorale style, but including 13 fugues and 3 toccatas. With him organ composition becomes mature with extensive independent use of the pedals, varied registration, and dynamic effects. His use of themes and their elaborate development brings harmony and counterpoint together in expression that is solid and characteristic of the organ. His influence was great, particularly upon Bach, and his works are used today.

The central German school (Thuringia and Saxony) was subject to the influence of both the north and the south. Through it runs the Bach family, famous as musicians for three centuries (1550–1850). Some 60 members of the family achieved musical reputations. Besides Johann Sebastian Bach, those ranked as composers include the brothers, Johann Christian Bach (1642–1703) and Johann Michael Bach (1648–1694), both in the sincere tradition of the family and devoted to church music, and the son of Johann Sebastian, Carl Philipp Emanuel Bach (1714–1788). Their organ compositions follow the chorale and fugue forms and show not only learning but originality in ideas. Important organ works are also credited to Johann H. Buttstett (1666–1727).

The other nations of Europe were not idle in organ composition but were overshadowed by Germany. Significant compositions survive by the Frenchmen Guillaume G. Nivers (1617–1701), Nicholas A. Le Begue (?–1702), and Andre Raison (?–1714), the Portuguese Manuoel Coelho (sixteenth century to the seventeenth century), and the Englishman William Byrd (1546–1623).

The greatest master of organ music composition was Johann Sebastian Bach (1685–1750). At Weimar (1708–1717) his compositions were mainly for organ; at Cothen (1717–1723) mainly instrumental, chamber, and piano music; and at Leipzig (1723–1750) mainly sacred (not liturgical) vocal music. He was great as a performer and mastered the Italian and French as well as the considerable German literature of organ music. Though he achieved great heights in the other fields of music, the cornerstone of his music was the organ. The toccata and fugue and the expanded chorale were brought to perfection as organ music. He blended harmony and counterpoint, marshaled the forms in contrast with one another, built cumulative effects and great climaxes — but all to serve religious sentiment. There is counterpoint throughout his works, but, for example, in the statement of a subject for a fugue, there is immediately present a harmonic idea. There is telescoping of parts in the stretto and elaborate development of material, but all bound by unity. Every rhythmic and melodic device known to music is there. While it is possible to describe the particular merits of lesser composers in words, the compositions of Bach (as of Lassus and Palestrina) cannot be reduced to words. Analyses of particular qualities can be made, but no synthesis of words will be effective in describing the result.

This immediately poses the question why the organ works of Bach are admissible to the church and not his vocal works. In the previous chapter, it was conceded that the vocal compositions of Bach are sacred in spirit and in that respect satisfactory but that their length (definitely impeding the progress of the liturgy and transferring attention to themselves) as well as their failure to follow the sentiments of the particular liturgical text disqualify them liturgically. The use of the organ music of Bach does not suffer from these two disqualifications and hence is appropriate, particularly for processionals and recessionals. This immediately establishes the liturgical test for all organ music.

George Frederick Händel (1685–1759) left fantasias, suites, fugues, and concertos for the organ. His style is not characteristically sacred although some of his works qualify as church music. With his interest in operas (of which he wrote over 40) and oratorios (of which he wrote about 20), his organ music is essentially dramatic, and, though his artistry is great, his work will not stand the close inspection that Bach's music can.

Johann G. Walther (1684–1748), a close friend and relative

of Bach, has left many organ works in the Bach style and ranks as a great composer for the organ although he is not widely known. Similarly the work of Gottfried H. Stolzel (?–1749) was highly regarded by Bach though it is principally vocal composition.

Highly regarded in his own day was George P. Telemann (1681–1767) whose prolific works have since been considered superficial. It is often said that he was a primary influence in the eclipse of liturgical organ music in the last half of the eighteenth century. If an immediate cause must be found, that is true; but the real cause for the decline of organ music lay in the great development of secular music, particularly the opera and the orchestra about this time and the greater remuneration for musical talent in the secular field. Of the later group, some wrote in a satisfactory liturgical style and with some artistic merit. No longer is there the great intellectual vigor and sublimity of Bach, but the music is still truly organistic, always melodious, and with a tendency to harmonic treatment. Organ compositions constitute only a small part of the works of members of this group, and most of them wrote vocal music for the liturgy which cannot qualify for the church. Johann G. Albrechtsberger (1736–1809), the teacher of Beethoven, belongs to this group. His works are frequently found in today's anthologies. Another was Abbe G. J. Vogler (1749–1814), the teacher of Weber and Meyerbeer, who roamed Europe. More famous than either of these is Johann C. H. Rinck (1770–1846) whose reputation rests primarily on his organ music, particularly his *Orgelschule,* a standard pedagogical work. Fugues are not found among his works. Rather the style is harmonic and full, bringing out the capability of the organ for great changes in color. Though mention is seldom made of Mendelssohn's (1809–1847) organ works, he composed six organ sonatas (that form being adapted to the organ from the piano) and several preludes and fugues. Most of these are acceptable as liturgical music, following the style of his oratorios which rise to the highest religious spirit displayed by that form in the nineteenth century.[8]

Nothing is here said of the art of organ building which developed greatly in the nineteenth century. That subject is too complex for a synopsis.

## THE LITURGICAL REFORMATION IN ORGAN MUSIC

More important, however, is the stimulus to liturgical organ music created by the resurrection of church music begun by Kasper Ett (1788–1847) in the vocal forms. Ett himself started the organ movement also, though the results were not as drastic because the liturgical requirements for organ music did not involve problems of the text and liturgy itself found in vocal music. The style of liturgical music in the nineteenth century was far removed from that of Bach, for the organ was now capable of new effects. The style is more clearly harmonic with the strictures of counterpoint gone and with the fugue replaced by the imitation[9] and its greater freedom. The sonata form of the harmonic school replaced the fugue of the polyphonic school. Instead of the subject, its answer and development, the sonata consisted of three or four sections with contrasting rhythms and related keys. The role of the answer in the fugue was taken by a contrasting theme.

The development of the organ sonata is principally due to Joseph G. Rheinberger (1837–1901) who composed some 20 organ sonatas as well as many other works. Writing in the smaller forms were Johann G. Herzog (1822–1909) with his

[8] This, of course, does not infer that the use of music from *Midsummer Night's Dream* as a wedding march is in any sense liturgical – Mendelssohn himself would have granted that.

[9] The imitative style involves a much shorter subject, or if the subject is longer, then the repetitions involve only snatches of the subject. The whole composition has greater flexibility – and accordingly requires a higher degree of structure than the fugue which, in a sense, supplies a good deal of its own structure.

*Preludienbuch* and *Handbuch für Organisten.* Paralleling Rheinberger in many ways was Gustav Merkel (1827–1885) who has a large number of works. Merkel harks back somewhat to the style of Bach and carries the latter's spirit over to the harmonic style. Anton Bruckner (1824–1896) developed a style that is perhaps best termed "mystical." Even his symphonic music carries a message of religious fervor. Writing on a level requiring less skill of the performer were Moritz Brosig (1815–1887), August G. Ritter (1811–1885), and Peter Piel (1835–1903), many of whose works are found in anthologies for the less skilled organist.

Germany and Austria, however, do not stand so much alone in organ music of the nineteenth century as was the case in the seventeenth and eighteenth centuries. A great French school developed whose liturgically great names include César Franck (1882–1890), Charles Widor (1845–1937), Theodore Dubois (1837–1924), Gabriel Faure (1845–1924), Henry Pierne (1863–1937), and the greatest, perhaps, Alexander Guilmant (1837–1911). Belgium produced the great Nicholas J. Lemmens (1823–1881), and Italy produced Enrico Bossi (1861–1925) and Gaetano Capocci (1811–1898). Lemmens established the College at Malines, in 1879, under the auspices of the Belgian hierarchy for the reconstruction of Catholic music. About 60 of his organ works are widely used, and his *Ecole d'Orgue* is a standard manual. In the United States, the principal organ composers have been Philip Kreckel (1886–living) and Carlo Rossini (1890–living).

The French school shows the influence of a new era in secular music, the romantic age. The fantasia and pastorale became favorite forms. The introduction of chromatics and very free modulation from key to key opened opportunities to slip to mediocrity or sentimentalism. However, the new ideas were absorbed by the French organists just named without compromising the truly religious spirit. All of them were too thoroughly trained in the works of Bach to lose sight of the central purpose of organ music in the church.

The present treatment of organ music for the church has dealt little with the use of the organ during Mass, being rather concerned with organ music before and after Mass. During the Mass, aside from the accompaniment of singing, the role of the organ is limited to very short interludes with the principal occasion for any extended playing being during the distribution of Holy Communion. That period may well be employed for hymns and motets, but if organ music is used, many of the works appropriate for processional or recessional are not within the requirements of the liturgy at this point. Accordingly a number of works, usually titled "Communion" or the like, have been written for the occasion.

There is a corollary principle applicable to the use of the organ to accompany vocal music of the liturgy. When the organ is so used, it cannot interrupt the liturgy, e.g., by interludes within the *Credo*. However, this does not deny the organ an independent status musically, nor reduce it to the duplication of the vocal music.

## BIBLIOGRAPHY FOR CHAPTER V

DeBrisay, Aubrey C., *The Organ and Its Music* (New York: Dutton, 1935).

Farmer, Henry G., *The Organ of the Ancients from Eastern Sources (Hebrew, Syriac and Arabic)* (London: Reeves, 1931).

Frotscher, Gotthold, *Geschichte des Orgelspiels und der Orgelkomposition,* 2 vols. (Leipzig: Hesse, 1934–1935).

Lahu, Henry C., *The Organ and Its Masters,* rev. ed. (Boston: L. C. Page & Co., 1927).

Ritter, August G., *Zur Geschichte des Orgelspiels im XIV. bis XVIII. Jahrhundert* (Leipzig: Hesse, 1884).

Rokseth, Yvonne, *La Musique d'Orgue au XV$^{e}$ Siecle et au Debut du XVI$^{e}$* (Paris: Droz, 1930).

Schering, Arnold, *Alte Meister aus der Frühzeit des Organspiels* (Leipzig: Hesse, 1884).

# CHAPTER VI

## *THE HISTORY OF AMERICAN CATHOLIC CHURCH MUSIC*

IT IS difficult to reconstruct Catholic church music in America. One path can be marked out with some certainty although there is the limitation that very little work has been done in this virgin territory. That path traces the publication of church music.[1] Aside from the fact that what is published is not always a fair indication (and certainly not a proportioned indication) of what is actually sung, there is the added difficulty that throughout the history of American Catholic church music, a high proportion of the music sung has been imported from Europe. The present chapter accordingly is devoted more to what has been published but does not omit the other aspects.

### MEXICO

It is commonly stated that the Protestant *Bay Psalm Book* of 1640[2] was the first book containing music to be printed

1 For this reason a more complete bibliography has been appended to the present chapter.

2 E.g., in Foote, Henry W., *Three Centuries of American Hymnody* (Cambridge: Harvard University Press, 1940); Frank J. Metcalf, *American Writers and Compilers of Sacred Music* (New York: The Abingdon Press, 1925); and Frank J. Metcalf, *American Psalmody, Or, Titles of Books Containing Tunes Printed in America from 1721 to 1820* (New York: Heartman, 1917). The trustworthiness of the last named may be gauged by the fact that of the 11 items, antedating 1820, shown in the list in Table IV, p. 181, Metcalf is familiar with only 4. These and other "standard" histories of American church music uniformly pass over the music of the Catholic Church with only incidental mention.

No music appeared in the *Bay Psalm Book* until its ninth edition in 1698.

in America. However, before the founding of Jamestown, in 1607, at least ten[3] books containing music had been published in Mexico — and all that music was music of the Catholic Church. The first American printing press was set up by the Spanish, in 1539, in Mexico City by one Juan Pablos who held an exclusive license for several decades to print in the New World.

The first book to be printed in America was the *Breve Y Nias Compendiosa Doctrina Christiana en Lengua Mexicana Y Castellana* of Juan de Zumarraga, first bishop in the New World. It was a catechism and printed, in 1539, at Mexico City. The first publication containing music was an *Ordinarium* published, in 1556, at Mexico City, undoubtedly by Juan Pablos although no publisher is indicated. It consisted of forty pages with black notes on red lines and was a manual of chant. There followed nine more music books closing with the *Liber in quo quattuor passiones Christi Domini continentur* in 1604. But from then until after 1700, no more music was printed in Mexico. The most likely explanation for the hiatus is that music was imported from Europe during this time. Some of the ten Mexican books referred to and listed in Table III are excellent examples of printing, being in several colors and with beautifully engraved initial letters. By and large, they contain chant after the notation common in sixteenth-century Spain. However, the *Liber* just referred to consists of original composition by Juan Navarro, the choirmaster of the Cathedral in Mexico City, for the passion of Christ. It was evidently intended for Holy Week.

As to the performance of church music in the first two centuries of colonization in Mexico all that can be said is that the Indians had a music of their own but the missionary fathers early determined to replace this with the chant. The objection taken to the use of the native music for church services was that it was interwoven with the superstitious

[3] See Table III, p. 180.

practices of the Indians and therefore dangerous to use if the superstitions were to be eradicated.

It goes without saying that the chief contact between Mexican civilization and that of the United States came through the extension of the missions of northern Mexico and lower California to what are now the states of Arizona, New Mexico, and Texas.

### PUERTO RICO

Recently[3a] attention has been directed to a history of sacred music in Puerto Rico written in 1915, *Musica y Musicos Portorriqueños* by Fernando Vallejo. Although the first settlement on Puerto Rico dates from 1509 and the first ecclesiastical establishment from 1513, all records of the cathedral at San Juan, the capital, were lost in the Dutch invasion of 1625. Later records of the seventeenth century show that music played a part in the early history of the island. Existing records trace the names of the organists from 1660. Little is known beyond the fact that instruction in chant was given.

In the nineteenth century, through the influence of the military and the theater, an orchestra was introduced at the Cathedral. The orchestra consisted of complete strings, woodwinds, and even brass. Two organists of the period, Domingo Belgado (organist from 1848 to 1858) and his pupil, Felipe Gutierrez, did original compositions for the Cathedral. Some compositions were also set at a later date by Gregorio Ledesma. These compositions reflected the theatrical episode in Europe during the nineteenth century. The music performed included works by Mercadante, Mine, Miller, Calahorra, and others of that era in Europe.

With the transfer of Puerto Rico from Spain to the United States in 1898, Church and state were separated resulting in

[3a] Guisa, Marcelino, "La America Latina: Funiculus Triplex Historia de la Musica Sagradã en Puerto Rico," *Schola Cantorum* (Mexico), Vol. VIII, pp. 2–4, 18 and 19, 34 and 35 (1946).

confusion for a considerable period. With the issuance of the *Motu Proprio* in 1903, Puerto Rico began a return to liturgical music.

## CALIFORNIA

In 1813, at Mission San Jose, California, Padre Narciso Duran compiled a *Choir Book* to which he wrote an introductory *Prologo* describing his efforts at music with the Indians. The *Choir Book* contains a *Misa de Cataluna* (V mode); a *Misa Viscaine* (VI mode); a *Credo Parisiense* (VI mode); a *Misa de Soledad,* two part; a *Misa de San Antonio,* two part; a *Misa a 4 Voces IV Tono;* a *Requiem Mass,* four part; and a number of hymns, such as *Padre Nuestro, Ave Maria, Dies Te Salve Maria,* and *Santo, Santo, Santo,* for a total of 179 pages. There is reason to believe that a good share of the music was composed by the compiler, Padre Narciso Duran.[4] The notation of the chant is in the "old Spanish" style, a first cousin to the Ratisbon notation. There are other manuscripts extant of the music used in California missions[5] from the time that they were first extended into the present territory of the United States by the establishment of Mission San Diego de Alcala in 1769. Much of this music is similar to that used in Mexico and in the earlier missions to the east. The missions in California established by Fra Junipero Serra in the last third of the eighteenth century reached their zenith shortly after the turn of the century. In their efforts to instill a knowledge of music in the Indians, the Franciscan friars developed a technique of their own. After the Indians had been taught to read a line of music and to sing in unison, singing in several parts and the playing of instruments in small bands were begun. The music

[4] See Da Silva, Owen, *Mission Music of California* (Los Angeles: W. F. Lewis, 1941), p. 14 f.

[5] For the most part these have been gathered by Father Owen da Silva at the Santa Barbara Mission although a few manuscripts are to be found in the Stanford University Library and the Bancroft Library of the University of California.

was written for the several voices on one staff, and to enable the Indians to follow readily the separate voices, the friars wrote the music for each voice or instrument in a different color so that each voice or instrument had only to follow the "red" notes or the "blue" notes or another color, as the case might be. For the most part the melodies are of chant origin with parts put to them in harmony.

### TEXAS, NEW MEXICO, AND ARIZONA

Missions were established in the territory of what are today the states of Texas, New Mexico, and Arizona well in advance of the missions in California. Although the territory had been visited from Mexico as early as 1530, no permanent settlement was made until 1598, when Mission San Juan de los Caballeros was established about 40 miles north of Santa Fe. By 1630, there were 25 missions in New Mexico and, in 1659, the Mission of Our Lady of Guadalupe was established at El Paso by Fra Garcia de San Francisco. Music was brought to all the missions by the friars, much in the manner already described for the missions of California. Fra Antonio Margil is particularly associated with the melody *Alabado* that was the most popular tune and common to all the missions of the Southwest, from Louisiana to, and including, California.[6] The authorship of the *Alabado* is in doubt but it was translated from the Spanish into Mexican and the Indian dialects, including Aztec, and the surviving manuscripts indicate that four-part singing to chant melodies was practiced as in California. Particular efforts were made in the Christmas and Lenten seasons to enact plays — *Los Pastores, Las Posadas,* and *Dimas, El Buen Ladron.* Some of the materials for these plays, including the music, still survive.

6 The text of the *Alabado* reads *Alabado sea el Santisimo Sacramento del Altar! Bendita sea la Limpia y Purisima Concepcion de Nuestra Senora Maria Santisima sin Mancha de pecado original.*

## FLORIDA

Although European contact with Florida dates from 1513, and the famous settlement at St. Augustine dates from 1565, there is no record of any music printed in Florida before the nineteenth century. Nor is there extant anything of music brought from Europe.[7]

## LOUISIANA

Similarly, although Louisiana can trace its history from a visit to that vicinity in 1519, and a settlement in 1699, no permanent location was made until 1718. Nothing as yet has been unearthed from which we can get an idea of the early musical history of that colony. In the nineteenth century the church music used in New Orleans was only an adaptation of operatic music to church purposes by the scissors and paste method.

## CANADA

Another early civilization to develop on the North American continent was that of French Canada. Quebec was founded in 1608. But strange to say, the first book to be printed in Canada came in 1767,[8] by Brown, a printer who came from Philadelphia. That was a catechism again; this time for the Montaguais Indians in their language under the title *Nehiro-Irinini, etc.* Nothing approaching music was printed until the appearance of the *Officium in honorem Domini Nostri J. C. summi sacerdotis et omnium sanctorum sacerdotium ac levitarum* in 1777. Again, no doubt, the gap was filled by importing music from France.

## THE EASTERN SEABOARD OF THE UNITED STATES

The expectation for the first Catholic church music to be printed in the United States might logically point to Balti-

[7] See, for example, Geiger, Maynard, *The Franciscan Conquest of Florida (1573–1618)* (Washington, D. C.: Catholic University Press, 1937).

[8] Stratton, F. M., and Tremaine, Grace, *A Bibliography of Canadiana* (Toronto: The Public Library, 1934).

more. That logic is defeated only by some curious developments. In 1787, John Aitken of Philadelphia printed the first Catholic church music in the United States. It was a substantial quarto volume of 136 pages entitled *A Compilation of the Litanies and Vesper Hymns and Anthems As They Are Sung in the Catholic Church.* The work has many curious features. First, John Aitken was not a Catholic, but he was an enterprising tradesman. That he uncovered a market is shown by the fact that two subsequent editions of the work were printed in 1791 and 1814. The fact that Aitken was not a Catholic is clearly indicated by internal evidence. First of all, there are a number of outright Protestant hymns included, and the *O Salutaris* and *Adeste Fideles* are omitted. But this is not conclusive since even today many "Catholic" music collections include Protestant hymns. More conclusive, however, is the haphazard arrangement of the music. There are two Masses: *Holy Mass of the Blessed Trinity* and *The Mass for the Dead* in addition to 49 other numbers. The parts of the Mass (*Kyrie, Gloria, Credo, Sanctus, Benedictus,* and *Agnus Dei*) are interspersed with hymns in an illogical fashion. No Catholic editor would have printed the music for the Mass in that way. Further, a number of important phrases of the *Gloria* and *Credo* are deleted. But most conclusive of all is the fact that in the 1791 and 1814 editions, the parts of the Mass are printed as a unit – evidently the criticism of the customers called that to the editor's attention. The title page of the first edition shows that the music is "Adapted to the Voice or Organ." But strangely enough the music has only two voices: the melody and a bass. That peculiarity was removed in the later editions by adding a third voice. In view of what has already been said, it would be expected that the musical quality of the work (by *any* standard) would be poor. It is so.

The second edition of 180 pages contains several additional hymns and also a Mass in the modern (i.e., nonchant) style, but the Protestant hymns are carried over and the deletions in the *Gloria* and *Credo* go uncorrected. In the third edition, brought out in 1814, by Charles Taws, the number of pages is reduced to 88 and the number of items to 45.

The first Catholic church music by a Catholic editor was that of Bishop John Cheverus,[9] *Anthems, Hymns, &c Usually Sung at the Catholick Church in Boston,* a collection of 72 pages printed at Boston in 1800. A second and enlarged edition of 112 pages was brought out in Baltimore, in 1807, under a slightly different title. Cheverus also edited the *Roman Catholic Manual, or Collection of Prayers, Anthems, Hymns, &c.* of 287 pages at Boston in 1803. A second and abbreviated edition of this work with 184 pages was brought out at Boston in 1807 and a third edition at Boston in 1823.

The reason for the early appearance of Catholic church music at Boston, which, by comparison with such centers as Philadelphia and Baltimore, had few Catholics at this time, has a ready explanation. The bulk of the Protestant service – and the Protestant religions were vigorous in the New England states – was hymn singing. It was only a natural reaction for the Catholic population of the New England states centered at Boston to use music in the church to a greater degree than elsewhere in the colonies. Moreover, in the eighteenth century in America, most of the immigrants came from England where the suppression of Catholicism had been so severe that the use of music in English Catholic churches had practically ceased.

While little is known of John Aitken as a musician (his principal occupation being, to all appearances, that of printer), another Philadelphian furnishes a curious history. In 1793, Joseph Carr and two of his sons, Thomas and Benjamin, came from England to the United States and promptly

[9] John Lefevre de Cheverus was consecrated first bishop of Boston in November, 1810. He was transferred to Montauban in 1823, and then to Bordeaux where he died as cardinal archbishop, July 19, 1836.

established three music publishing houses: Joseph and Thomas Carr began in Baltimore in 1794, and Benjamin set up two houses, one in Philadelphia in 1793, and the other in New York City also in 1793.[10] The latter he sold in 1797. The family was and remained Episcopalians. Benjamin had a variegated career as composer, organist, publisher, teacher, and promoter. Sometime after his arrival he became organist at St. Joseph's Catholic Church in Philadelphia and continued there until 1801. In that year he took up the position of organist for St. Augustine's Catholic Church, in which post he continued until his death in 1831. He published operas, popular songs, and church music for both Catholics and Episcopalians. In 1805, he brought out his *Masses, Vespers, Hymns, Psalms, Anthems and Motetts . . . for . . . the Catholic Church* of 128 pages and dedicated it ("with permission") to Bishop John Carroll, the first bishop in the United States. The work contains a Mass and a *Te Deum* composed by Carr together with a number of Protestant hymns. They represent, musically, the best work to appear in the first half of the nineteenth century in American Catholic church music. Carr taught two of the leaders in later Philadelphia church music: Benjamin Cross and William A. Newland, the latter a composer whose works were performed in Philadelphia churches but not published.[11] In the *Records of the*

10 The Carr family holds a unique place in American history. Thomas Carr (1780–1849) is credited with the arrangement of the *Star Spangled Banner* for Francis Scott Key, bringing out the first edition in 1814. Benjamin Carr (1769–1831) brought out the first edition of *Yankee Doodle* in 1795 (though it was sung earlier) and also of *Hail Columbia* in 1798 (the tune had originally been composed as the president's march for Washington's inauguration).

11 See Reuss, Francis X., "Sketch of Prof. William Augustine Newland," *Records of American Catholic Historical Society,* XIII, 285–324 (1902) which contains a list of Newland's compositions. It is interesting that as late as 1902, in Philadelphia there still was no appreciation of liturgical music (if we can assume Reuss as familiar with the opinions of his time). Cf. the descriptions of Newland's music at pp. 305 and 306. Newland taught Gregorian chant at St. Charles Seminary from 1852 to 1864. Whether this should be understood as being limited to the chants required of the priest is not clear. The absence of any mention of the use of Gregorian chant in the full discus-

*American Catholic Historical Society* we have a fairly complete account of church music actually used in Philadelphia churches throughout the nineteenth century. The compositions used most frequently are those of Mozart, Haydn, Lederer, Carr, Mazzinhi, and De Monte. Toward the end of the century the more frequently used compositions also include those of: Farmer, Leonard, Rosewig, and Turner. None of the music was, of course, liturgical in any sense.

Of the music printed in the United States already described, none was of sufficient merit to survive the century. The collections were gotten together partly from Protestant hymnals with occasionally an original composition. The process seems to have been the expropriation of the melody from such hymnals and sometimes, perhaps by memory, from European sources. The melody was then harmonized after a fashion by anyone with a bare competence in notation. Not infrequently the harmony was furnished by a non-Catholic who had no knowledge of the liturgy of the Church. The inspiration was a desire to turn an honest penny by selling to a hungry market.

Another picture of the plight of church music is given to us by Benedict J. Fenwick, bishop of Boston from 1825 to 1846. In his unpublished *Memoirs to Serve for the Future Ecclesiastical History of the Diocese of Boston,* written from 1833 to 1836,[12] he estimates that in two thirds of the Catholic churches of America there was no singing at all. He states that the congregations "know as much about music of any kind as they do about Greek." Accordingly he sponsored an edition of church music in 1833, but it was destroyed by fire at the printing plant. Then, in 1840, he was largely responsible for the publication of *The Morning and Evening Service of the Catholic Church, Comprising a Choice Collection of*

sion of music used in the Philadelphia churches (see various articles listed in the bibliography) would seem to indicate so.

[12] *History of the Archdiocese of Boston,* 3 vols. (New York: Sheed & Ward, 1944), Vol. II, pp. 376–377.

*Gregorian and Other Masses; Litanies, Psalms, Sacred Hymns, Anthems, Versicles and Motets. . . . Compiled and Respectfully Dedicated to Rt. Rev. Dr. Fenwick by R. Garbett, Professor of Music.* This volume is a vast improvement over anything published up to this time except the work of Carr.

By now the question has certainly arisen in the reader's mind whether this was the music actually performed in the Catholic churches of the United States down to 1850. It would not be surprising if it was for several reasons. First, the music imported from Europe would not have been of much better caliber, at least from the liturgical standpoint, since we find the Vatican complaining of the use of drums and whistles in church music ensembles in Europe at this time. Further, except in the larger urban centers, pioneer conditions existed, and they do not admit of such development of the arts. In addition, the Catholic population in the United States at this time constituted the poorer segment financially. In the larger cities the degenerated European church music of the late eighteenth and early nineteenth centuries was used. Europe was under theatrical and operatic influences in its church music and the Gregorian chant was to all intents lost. The music of Scarlatti, Rossini, Mozart, Haydn, Gounod, and others was carried over to America. Another factor was that secular music had its beginnings in the United States at this time. Small orchestras for dances, chamber music, and lesser symphonic music and choral societies for the oratorios, particularly those of Handel, Haydn, and Mendelssohn were in active existence. Much of that music, being familiar to organist, players, and singers alike, was transferred to the church. By the scissors and paste method it could be adapted to reasonable lengths. Even today several of the Masses of Mozart adapted by this means are sung in many churches in the United States. Instruments, particularly strings and wood winds, were introduced into the church, and on occasion, even the "full" orchestra was used for Mass and other services.

## THE MIDDLE WEST

The germ of reform in church music began to develop in Europe by the middle of the nineteenth century. Naturally enough that movement was reflected in the United States which at this time was experiencing a great influx of immigrants. But here it was aided by another circumstance. Prior to the growth of the sisterhoods in the United States to sufficient numbers to take over teaching duties in parochial schools, it was customary in many parishes to have a layman serve as organist and choirmaster and "to double in brass" by teaching in the parochial school. This required the establishment of a Catholic normal school for the training of such laymen. In a few of the larger cities, the roles of organist and choirmaster were filled by musicians trained in Europe who were employed otherwise in the teaching of secular music, often in the early conservatories. As the sisterhoods grew to sufficient numbers they took over even the role of organist and choirmaster in many parishes. This, together with the development of Catholic colleges and universities, caused the Catholic normal school to be displaced shortly after the end of World War I.

The Catholic normal school was a phenomenon of the Middle West. The South has never had Catholics in numbers. In the West they did not develop in numbers until after 1885. New England, with the exception of Boston, had few Catholics. Such centers as New York, Philadelphia, Washington, and Baltimore were supplied with European-trained musicians.

Just as the movement for reform in church music received its greatest impetus in Europe from Germany, so the American reform was initiated by German immigrants largely in the Middle West.[13] The first American Caecilian Society[14] was

13 As used in this chapter, the term "Middle West" includes the western edges of New York and Pennsylvania, all of Ohio, Indiana, Michigan, Illinois,

established in Holy Trinity Church in Cincinnati on St. Caecilia's Day, November 22, 1838, by the Rev. J. Martin Henni. The society published a magazine, *Liedertafel.* Nothing remains to shed light on the situation beyond these bare facts.[15] Another Caecilian Society was formed in Cincinnati in 1856, by Frederic L. Ritter, which continued until about 1861. Cincinnati was at this time the largest German settlement in the United States and the European firm of Pustet established an American office there in 1867, after first opening in New York in 1865. This provided an American outlet for the liturgically satisfactory publications of Witt, Stehle, Schaller, Oberhoffer, Molitor, Haller, Diebold, Greith, Hassler, Kaim, and others.[16] At Dayton, Ohio, in 1864, the firm of J. Fischer & Bro. was begun. The first decades of publication by this house were devoted almost entirely to Catholic church music, and the business became, from 1873, particularly, known as publisher for John B. Singenberger.

---

Kentucky, Wisconsin, Missouri, Iowa, Minnesota, North and South Dakota, Nebraska, and Kansas.

14 There was a Caecilian Society established at Charlestown, South Carolina, in 1767, but it was of secular character. Similar Caecilian societies were established at Newport, Rhode Island, in 1793, and at New York City in 1791.

15 Sources for the information: Pattermann, H. A., *Deutsch Amerikanischen Biographikon und Dichter* (Cincinnati: Pustet, 1911), p. 318, and *Wahrheitsfreund,* Cincinnati, January 31, 1839 (the first Cincinnati Catholic newspaper).

16 The firm of Benziger Brothers brought out the "Hellebusch" (B. H. F. Hellebusch, *Katholisches Gesang- und Gebetbuch,* New York: Benziger Brothers, 1858). This remarkable German hymnal was used in thousands of churches. By 1874, it was in its sixty-ninth edition. No effort will be made to list or discuss the voluminous publications of church music in the United States since 1870. The subject is dealt with in the two periodicals, *The Caecilia* (from 1874) and *The Catholic Choirmaster* (from 1915). The number of Catholic hymnals published in the United States numbers well over one hundred and the number of separate publications (e.g., Masses, hymns, organ works, etc.) runs somewhere between five and ten thousand. The story of the battle between "unliturgical" and "liturgical" music on an individual composition level is recorded in the two periodicals. At times the acrimony has been extreme. The classical example is the dispute over the permissibility of the *St. Basil Hymnal* — which despite all has sold over one million copies.

Such was the background for the appearance of the greatest nineteenth-century center of Catholic church music in the United States — the Catholic Normal School of the Holy Family at St. Francis, Wisconsin. The same Father Henni who established the Caecilia Society at Cincinnati in 1838, became Milwaukee's first bishop, March 19, 1844.[17] He immediately began work to establish a seminary and induced the Rev. Dr. Joseph Salzmann to come from Germany to found The Salesianum, St. Francis Seminary, in 1856. As already pointed out, there was an urgent need for organists and teachers. Together, Henni and Salzmann planned such a teacher-training school as an adjunct to the seminary. With a gift of 3000 gulden from King Ludwig of Bavaria in 1865, and supported particularly by the German parishes throughout the Middle West, the cornerstone of the building was laid June 12, 1870, and the school opened in September, 1871. Dr. Salzmann was well acquainted with the German Caecilian Society and sought adequate professors from Franz Witt at Regensburg. Witt responded by sending John B. Singenberger and Max Spiegler who arrived at St. Francis, April 11, 1873. Salzmann called a meeting of the faculty[18] and student body on May 7, 1873, at which the American Caecilian Society was founded.[19] The influence that developed from

[17] Elevated as first archbishop of Milwaukee on February 11, 1875, and died September 7, 1881.

[18] The faculty at this time included: Messrs. Buelsbach, Esswein, Duehmig, Singenberger, Spiegler, and Rev. R. Scholter. Spiegler returned to Germany after being with the school for three years.

[19] The Catholic Normal School of the Holy Family continued in existence until 1922. The school experienced difficulties in maintaining enrollment after 1885, and a business school was added to bolster the attendance. The business school was named Pio Nono College and ceased also in 1922. The Normal School was primarily a music school although it professed to prepare for general teaching. Accurate records are not available (no catalogues even are available before 1883) but reasonable estimates place the number of graduates of the Catholic Normal School at about 500 during its 51 year history. The greatest single factor in its passing was the rise of Catholic colleges and universities particularly after the turn of the century. The strong German affiliation also set limits to the school.

this fountainhead was great. Within the first four years, the Caecilian Society had 3000 members, and the school had 101 students from 11 states in 1885–1886.[20] By 1900, the Society numbered over 5000.

The Catholic Normal School offered courses in piano, organ, violin, harmony, counterpoint, chant, church music, and related subjects. In addition, courses in the classical and modern languages and literatures, and the various sciences were taught as well as religion and liturgy. Concerts and programs regularly showed the music of the leaders in the German Caecilian movement: Kasper Ett (1788–1847) of Munich, Karl Proske (1784–1861) of Regensburg, and Franz Witt (1834–1888) of Bamberg and the leading texts of the nineteenth century were used: Dr. F. X. Haberl's *Magister Choralis* and Beuron Abbot Ambrose Kienle's *Choral Schule.* Also appearing on the programs are the older masters such as Palestrina, Victoria, and Lassus. The chant is found on almost every program – the Ratisbon edition based on the old Medicean edition of the seventeenth century. This was promptly replaced at the school, in 1903, upon the adoption of the Vatican edition – indeed, the theories of the new edition had been anticipated for 15 years at the school through the contact of Kienle. Reference has already been made to the establishment of the firm of J. Fischer & Bro. at Dayton, Ohio, in 1864. Singenberger[21]

20 A Caecilian Society was organized, in 1872, at Vincennes, Indiana, by a Benedictine from St. Meinrad Abbey. It was not successful except locally.

21 John B. Singenberger was the principal figure in each of the movements: the Catholic Normal School, the Caecilian Society, and *The Caecilia.* He was born May 25, 1848, at Kirchberg, Switzerland, studied at the Jesuit Stella Matutina in Faldkirch, and for a time at the University of Innsbruck and then attended the church music school at Regensburg. He studied under Franz Witt, Rev. Dr. F. X. Haberl, Joseph Hanish, Rev. Augustine Link, S.J., Winnebald Briem, Rev. Michael Haller, and Carl Greith. Besides the articles published in *The Caecilia* he wrote *Guide to Catholic Church Music* (St. Francis, Wis., 1905), which is essentially an English translation of the German Caecilian catalogue, and his compositions include 17 Masses, several hundred hymns and motets, collections of organ music, etc. In 1882, Pope Leo XIII conferred upon him the title of Knight of St. Gregory. In 1905, Pope Pius X

worked with that firm and established *The Caecilia,* the organ of the Caecilian Society, in 1874. The magazine appeared monthly with articles in both German[22] and English, many of them by leading European authorities. It carried also a supplement of music, which permitted the development of musical composition within the Society. In 1875, J. Fischer & Bro. moved to New York and shortly afterward *The Caecilia* was published under Singenberger at St. Francis, Wisconsin.[23]

The Caecilian Society was active in holding conventions (or as they were known in the German, *Caecilienfeste*) at which hundreds of singers joined in programs that had been rehearsed by the individual choirs scattered over hundreds of miles. The first such choral festival was held on St. Caecilia's Day, November 22, 1873, at St. Francis, Wisconsin. The second choral program was given in St. John's Cathedral, Milwaukee, on June 17, 1874. The next general meeting was at Dayton, Ohio, in 1875. On this program appeared the Palestrina masterpiece *Missa Papae Marcelli:* sufficient evidence in itself of the caliber of the Caecilian Society. Conventions followed at Baltimore in 1876, at Rochester in 1877, at Detroit in 1878, at Milwaukee in 1879, at St. Louis in 1881,

---

conferred the Papal Cross *"pro ecclesia et pontifice"* and, in 1908, the title of Knight of St. Sylvester. In 1924, Pope Pius XI conferred the title of Knight Commander of the Order of St. Gregory. His death occurred May 29, 1924, and he is buried on the grounds of St. Francis Seminary. See bibliography for list of biographies of him.

22 In the earlier days, the articles were almost entirely in German — a feature that handicapped the development of the movement. The German disappeared from the magazine about the time of World War I.

23 Besides *The Caecilia,* Singenberger published his own and the works of many others. Upon his death in 1924, the publishing was continued by his son, Otto Singenberger, until 1930 when the catalogue was taken over by McLaughlin & Reilly Co. of Boston. This company was established, in 1906, by Dr. James A. Reilly and publishes school music as well as church music. Singenberger made an effort to carry the Caecilian movement to English-speaking Americans by launching two English language periodicals: *The Echo* and *Review of Church Music,* but both of these endeavors collapsed after short periods because of insufficient support.

at Philadelphia in 1882, at Cleveland in 1883, at Chicago in 1885, at Detroit in 1895, at St. Francis in 1898 (the twenty-fifth anniversary), at Belleville, Ill., in 1900, at Chicago in 1902, and the last at St. Louis in 1903.[24] As an outgrowth of the Caecilian Society, John B. Singenberger, in 1905, edited his *Guide to Catholic Church Music,* which consisted of a list of 270 pages of acceptable church music. A supplement was issued in 1911.

Bishop Henni requested papal approbation of the society in 1875, and the request was granted in 1876. The bishops of the various dioceses, in turn, issued their endorsements and gave impetus to the reform.

The Catholic Normal School produced the bulk of church musicians[25] in the United States during the last quarter of the nineteenth century and the early twentieth century. A graduate of the first class, Michael L. Nemmers, went on to become the first native-born composer of Catholic church music[26] and established, in 1895, the M. L. Nemmers Publishing Co., the oldest firm in the United States publishing Catholic church music exclusively.

24 As a corollary of the conventions, summer schools were conducted by the Catholic Normal School facutly: at Rochester in 1873; at Quincy, Illinois, in 1886; at Findlay, Ohio, in 1887; at Fort Wayne, Indiana, in 1889; at Defiance, Ohio, in 1890; and at Covington, Kentucky, in 1896.

25 The graduates of the school were thoroughly schooled in liturgical music and became the choirmasters and organists in the largest churches throughout the Middle West and even in the Southwest and Far West. Some rose to exceptional standing as concert artists, such as Dr. Casper Koch, the Pittsburg organist.

26 Since Michael L. Nemmers is the grandfather of the present writer, there may be objections to an evaluation of his place in history as a composer. Certain facts can be stated. His published compositions include 15 Masses; 78 hymns, Antiphons, Offertories, and other choral works; 63 organ numbers and numerous arrangements, as well as several secular pieces. The compositions have been approved by the various church music commissions and have shown remarkable vitality since fifty years after publication their sale and use are still increasing, e.g., *The Guardian Angel Mass* is now in its thirty-fourth edition. Setting the self-imposed, rigid limitations of easy performance and practicality to his liturgical compositions does not seem to have affected the musical quality of his work. See Nemmers, Erwin Esser, "Michael L. Nemmers," *The Catholic Choirmaster,* XXVIII, 112, 139 (1942).

## THE TWENTIETH CENTURY

The Second Council at Baltimore, in 1866, had stated:[27] "We consider it very desirable that the elements of Gregorian chant be taught and exercised in the parochial schools." But no effort to exercise the authority of the Church over church music was made in the United States until Archbishop William H. Elder of Cincinnati issued a catalogue of approved and disapproved church music on February 18, 1888. This was a natural outgrowth of the efforts of the Caecilian Society and marked a new type of movement: diocesan controls and commissions of church music. Bishop Henry J. Richter of the Grand Rapids diocese organized a synod and issued a catalogue of approved music on September 18, 1903.

The issuance of the *Motu Proprio* by Pope Pius X on St. Caecilia's Day, November 22, 1903, marked a new era in church music in the United States as throughout the Catholic world. The decree was mandatory and gave immediate impetus to diocesan controls. The Caecilian Society became to a large extent superfluous – its function now devolving upon diocesan authorities. But for various reasons there was still a need for a national organization. It would, for one thing, assure some degree of uniformity. In addition, many dioceses were not equipped to handle the problems. The function might have been handled by the Caecilian Society, but a separate organization was formed, in 1914, in the East: the Society of St. Gregory of America. The new society was the outgrowth of a meeting at Baltimore in June, 1913, of leading church musicians of the Eastern seaboard.[28] The original constitution of the society stated: "The main object and guiding principle of the Society is to foster fraternal assistance

27 Baltimore, II, p. 338.

28 The principal organizers were Rev. Leo P. Manzetti of Baltimore; Rev. Dr. John M. Petter of Rochester; Nicola A. Montani of Philadelphia; Rev. James McKeever of Pittsburg; Rev. Simon M. Yenn of Ft. Wayne, Ind.; Rev. James A. Boylan of Philadelphia; Dr. Harold B. Gibbs of New York City; and Mr. Hession of Boston. Rev. Dr. Petter continued for many years as president of the society.

and encouragement among the members thereof, in their endeavor to promote the cause of Sacred Music Reform according to the provisions of the *Motu Proprio* of the late Holy Father, Pius X." Two of the immediate purposes of the society were the publication of a periodical and of an acceptable hymnal. The first issue of *The Catholic Choirmaster,* the official bulletin of the Society of St. Gregory of America, appeared in February, 1915, under the editorship of Nicola A. Montani,[29] and it has continued as a quarterly with music supplement. The *St. Gregory Hymnal* appeared in 1921, with 430 pages and a revised and enlarged edition of 621 pages was brought out in 1940. The Society sought of Pope Benedict an approbation similar to the approval of the Caecilian Societies under the Constitution *Multum ad Movendos Animos.* By rescript No. 6194 of May 1, 1915, approval was granted, and Gaetano Cardinal Bisleti appointed first protector. Under the patronage of James Cardinal Gibbons the second convention was held in June, 1915, at Baltimore. The third convention was held in June, 1917 at Cincinnati. At this convention, the Society began to publish a list of approved and recommended church music – the so-called "White List." The list appeared serially in *The Catholic Choirmaster,* and, with the issues of 1922, a list of disapproved music was published – the so-called "Black List." These two lists were published in pamphlet form, in 1928, 1932, 1939, and 1947, by the Society and have been accepted by many dioceses. In 1920, the convention was held in New York City and attended by representatives from Canada, France, Australia, and South America, among them being French Benedictine scholars, Dom Mocquereau and Dom Gatard. In 1922, the convention was held at Rochester; in 1924, at Toronto; in 1927, at Cincinnati; in 1930, at Pitts-

[29] The labors of Nicola A. Montani were recognized by Pope Pius XI in 1928, by the conferring of the title of Knight Commander of the Order of St. Sylvester with the privilege of the Count's Cross.

burg; in 1934, at Washington; and in 1936, at Newark. The American Society gave an example which was followed in England by the establishment, in 1929, of the Society of St. Gregory of Great Britain and Ireland after previous efforts had failed. The English Society initiated its periodical, *Music and Liturgy,* now *Liturgy* in 1930. The strong activity of the American Society in the Eastern states resulted in the establishment of "subsidiary" guilds: The Rochester Organist and Choirmaster's Guild (from 1920), The Catholic Choir Guild and St. Caecilia Guild in Newark (from 1933), the St. Louis Catholic Organist's Guild (from 1933), the Paterson Guild (from 1938), the Chicago Organists and Choir Guild (from 1940), and the San Francisco Catholic Organists and Choir Guild (from 1941).

Side by side with the Society of St. Gregory many of the dioceses created their own commissions and regulations and published lists of approved and disapproved music. By and large the activities of the diocesan groups have been no more than sporadic.

Another important development in the field of American Catholic church music has been the establishment in the twentieth century of college and university courses in church music. The most significant of these has been the Pius X School of Liturgical Music of the College of the Sacred Heart in New York City. On November 6, 1924, Patrick Cardinal Hayes dedicated the new building of the school which had been in existence from the autumn of 1916. The Pius X School has been particularly interested in spreading the theory of Gregorian chant advanced by the Benedictines of Solesmes and in the renaissance of polyphonic music. The leading figures of the school have been Mrs. Justine B. Ward and Mother Georgia Stevens, R.S.C.J. Under Mrs. Ward[30]

30 Mrs. Ward has received the honorary degree of Doctor of Music from the Pontifical Institute of Sacred Music at Rome, and Pope Pius XI conferred the Cross *pro ecclesia et pontifice* and the Order of Malta.

was developed a system of teaching Gregorian chant to children of the elementary school level now known as the Ward Method and used throughout the United States. The system follows the theories of the Benedictines at Solesmes. Other colleges and universities have followed the lead of the Pius X School, particularly the Catholic University of America which is responsible for the Catholic Education Press, the publisher of the materials for the Ward Method.[31]

## TABLE III

### Catholic Church Music Published in Mexico 1556 to 1700

1. *Ordinarium sacri ordinis heremitaru sancti Augustini episcopi & regularis observatie, nunc denuo correctu, sicez no secundum more antiquu, ceremonie siant, sed secudu choros altos. Mexici, anno dni 1556 idibus Julij.*
   40 pp. Copy in New York Public Library.
2. *Manule sacramentorum secundum usum ecclesie Mexicane noviter impressum, cum quibusdam additionibus utilissimis: que omnia in sequete pagella reperies. 1560 Juan Pablos.*
   173 pp. Copy in British Museum.
3. *Missale Romanum Ordinarium. September 1561 Antonio de Espinosa.*
   330 pp. Copy in New York Public Library.
4. *Manuele Sacramentorum. 1568 Pedro Ocharte.*
   183 pp. Copy in New York Public Library.
5. *Graduale Dominicale. 1576 Antonio Spinosa.*
   208 pp. Copy in National Library of Mexico.
6. *Graduale Dominicale. 1576 Pedro Ocharte.*
   208 pp. Copy in Newberry Library, Chicago.

[31] The leading role of schools of church music seems now to have passed to the Alverno College of Music, Milwaukee, and the Gregorian Institute of America, Toledo, Ohio (the only schools in the United States conferring degrees in liturgical music). Other schools that should be mentioned are: the Catholic Summer School (Cliff Haven, N. Y.); De Paul University School of Music (Chicago, Ill.); Duquesne University School of Sacred Music (Pittsburgh, Pa.); St. John's University (Collegeville, Minn.); Marywood College (Scranton, Pa.); Teachers College of the Athenaeum (Cincinnati, Ohio); and Webster College (Webster Groves, Mo.).

This is practically the same as No. 5 but has a different publisher and some of the type is different.

7. *Graduale Dominicale.* Title page missing.
208 pp. Copy in National Library of Mexico.
This is similar to Nos. 5 and 6 but there are differences in type from both previous editions.
8. *Psalterium Amphonarium* (sic) *Sanctorale, eum Psalmis et Hymnis, positis in suis locis propriis uniuscujusque diei festi totius anni, nunc primo cum licentia excussum. Mexico: excudebat Petrus Ocharte 1584.*
300 pp. Copy in National Library of Mexico.
9. *Antiphonarium.* Mexico, 1589.
62 pp. Copy in National Library of Mexico.
10. *Liber in quo cuattuor passiones Christi Domini continentur. 1604 Diego Lopez Davalos.*
105 pp. Copy in Library of University of Texas (music by Juan Navarro, choirmaster, Cathedral of Mexico City).

No more music was printed in Mexico until after 1700.

NOTE: This table agrees as to number of items with Lota M. Spell, "The First Music Books Printed in America," *The Musical Quarterly,* XV, 50–54 (1929). The same items are given by Jose T. Medina, *La Imprenta en Mexico* (Santiago de Chile, 1905–1911), I and II except that Medina does not know of Nos. 5, 6, and 7. Joaquin Garcia Icazbalceta, *Bibliografia Mexicana del Siglo XVI* (Mexico: Libreria de Andrade Y Morale, 1886) is familiar with only Nos. 3, 8, and 9. Vicente de P. Andrade, *Ensayo bibliografio mexicano del signo XVII* (Mexico: Imprenta del Museo Nacional, 1899) shows nothing in music in the seventeenth century.

## TABLE IV

### CATHOLIC CHURCH MUSIC PUBLISHED IN THE UNITED STATES 1787–1860

1. Aitken, John:
*A Compilation of the Litanies and Vesper Hymns and Anthems as They Are Sung in the Catholic Church Adapted to the Voice or Organ* by John Aitken, Philadelphia, 1787, 136 pp.
Parsons, No. 62

2. ——
*A Compilation of the Litanies, Vesper Hymns and Anthems as They Are Sung in the Catholic Church.* Philadelphia: printed and sold by John Aitken, 1791, 180 pp.
Parsons, No. 92

3. Cheverus, John (Bishop):
*Anthems, Hymns, &c. Usually Sung at the Catholick Church in Boston.* Boston: printed by Manning & Loring, 1800. 72 pp.

4. ——
*Roman Catholic Manual, or Collection of Prayers, Anthems, Hymns, &c.* Boston: printed by Manning & Loring, No. 2, Cornhill, Dec. 1803, 287 pp.
Parsons, No. 249

5. Carr, Benjamin:
*Masses, Vespers, Hymns, Psalms, Anthems and Motetts composed, selected and arranged for the use of the Catholic Churches in the United States of America and respectfully dedicated by permission of the Right Reverend John Carroll, D.D., Bishop of Baltimore.* Baltimore: J. Carr, 1805, 128 pp.
Parsons does not list this item.

6. Cheverus, John (Bishop):
*Hymns, for the Use of the Catholic Church in the United States of America a New Edition, with additions and Improvements.* Baltimore: printed by John West Butler, 1807, 112 pp.
Parsons, No. 299

7. ——
*Roman Catholic Manual, or a collection of prayers, anthems, hymns, &c. With the approbation of the Rt. Rev. Bishop.* Boston: printed by J. T. Buckingham, Winter Street, 1811, 184 pp.
Parsons, No. 410

8. Anonymous:
*Receuil de Cantiques a l'usage de la Congregation etablie parmi les eleves du College de Ste. Marie Sous le Nom de societe de la Ste. Familie.* A Baltimore, de l'imprimerie G. Dobbin & Murphy, 4 Harrison Street, 1811, 154 pp.
Parsons, No. 409

9. Aitken, John:
*A Collection of Litanies, Vespers, Chants, Hymns, and Anthems. As Used in the Catholic Churches of the United States. A new Edition, Carefully revised and corrected from the former editions.* Philadelphia: published and sold by Charles Taws, at his music store No. 61, South Third Street, 1814, 87 pp.
Parsons, No. 465

10. David, J. B. (Rev.):
*Collection of Sacred Hymns for the Use of the Catholic Churches in Kentucky.* Bardstown: 1815.
Parsons does not list this item; Finotti does but had not seen a copy.

11. Carr, Benjamin:
*Collection of Sacred Music, Chants, Anthems, Hymns.* Philadelphia: B. Carr, 1816, 62 pp.
Parsons does not list this item.

12. Cheverus, John (Bishop):
*Roman Catholic Manual, or Collection of prayers, anthems, hymns, etc.* Boston: Ezra Lincoln, 1823, 287 pp.
Parsons, No. 800

13. Walter, Jacob:
*Ancient and Modern Music selected for the use of the Catholic Church consisting of litanies, masses, vespers, anthems, hymns, and choruses for the seasons, festivals & other occasions. Arranged for the pianoforte or organ.* Jacob Walter, Baltimore: published and sold by John Cole, Baltimore. (Date about 1825.) 124 pp.
Parsons does not list this item; a copy is in Nazareth College, Nazareth, Kentucky, inscribed "Presented to Sister Harriett by Mother Francis." Sister Harriett died in 1826.

14. Haliday, J. F.:
*A Collection of Psalms, Hymns, Anthems, &c. (With the Evening Office.) For the Use of the Catholic Church Throughout the United States Permissu Superiorum.* Washington: printed by J. F. Haliday, 1830, 289 pp.
Parsons, No. 1024

15. ——
Same as item 14, second edition, 1832.
Parsons, No. 1024

16. Garbett, R.:
*The Morning and Evening Service of the Catholic Church, Comprising a Choice Collection of Gregorian and Other Masses; Litanies, Psalms, Sacred Hymns, Anthems, Versicles and Motetts . . . Compiled and Respectfully Dedicated to Rt. Rev. Dr. Fenwick by R. Garbett, Professor of Music.* New York, 1840.

17. Horner, James (Rev.):
*Manual of Catholic Melodies.* Baltimore: John Murphy, 1846.

18. David, J. B. (Rev.):
*Collection of Sacred Hymns for the use of the children of the Catholic Church; compiled chiefly from a little work published by Father David in 1815, to which are added selections from other approved sources intended principally for the use of schools and academies &c.* Louisville: Webb & Levering, 1853.
Second edition, 1867.

19. Kirk, P. A.:
*The Catholic Harp, containing the morning and evening service.* New York, 1853.

20. Cunningham:
*Hymn Book.* Philadelphia, 1854.

21. Elliott, James (Rev.):
*The Catholic Melodist, a collection of masses, vespers, anthems and sacred hymns chiefly from the manuscripts of the late Right Rev. John B. David, coadjutor bishop of Bardstown, designed principally for the use of country congregations, small choirs and schools. Compiled and arranged by Rev. James Elliott with the approbation of the Right Rev. Bishop of Louisville.* Webb & Levering, 1855.

22. Werner, Anthony:
*The Memorare, a collection of Catholic Music containing six masses, a short requiem mass, vespers and a variety of miscellaneous by Anthony Werner.* Boston: O. Ditson, 1857.

23. Hellebusch, B. H. F.:
*Katholisches Gesang- und Gebetbuch eine Auswahl der vorzüglichsten Choräle und Kirchenlieder, für zwei Stim-*

*men gesetzt, mit den gewöhnlichen Andachtsübungen, von B. H. F. Hellebusch.* New York, Cincinnati, Chicago: Benziger Brothers, 1858.

NOTE: The reference to Parsons is Parsons, Wilfrid, *Early Catholic Americana* (New York: Macmillan, 1939) which purports to cover only down to 1830 and lists only works *by* Catholics. Hence he does not list items 5 and 11 above since Carr was not a Catholic.

## BIBLIOGRAPHY FOR CHAPTER VI

### BOOKS

*A Brief Exposition of the Caecilia Society* (Milwaukee, 1879).

Andrade, Vicente de P., *Ensayo bibliografio mexicano del siglo XVII* (Mexico: Imprenta del Museo Nacional, 1893).

Finotti, Joseph M., *Bibliographia Catholica Americana* (New York: The Catholic Publication House, 1872).

Foote, Henry W., *Three Centuries of American Hymnody* (Cambridge: Harvard University Press, 1940).

Garcia, Josquin Icazbalceta, *Bibliografio mexicano del siglo XVI* (Mexico: Libraria de Andrade Y Morale, 1886).

Gould, Nathaniel D., *Church Music in America* (Boston: A. N. Johnson, 1853).

Joan of Arc, Sister M., C.D.P., *Catholic Music and Musicians in Texas* (San Antonio: College of Our Lady of the Lake, 1936).

Metcalf, Frank J., *American Psalmody (1721–1820)* (New York: C. F. Heartman, 1917).

—— *American Writers and Compilers of Sacred Music* (New York: The Abingdon Press, 1925).

Parker, A. A., *Church Music and Musical Life in Pennsylvania in the Eighteenth Century,* 3 vols. (Philadelphia: Pennsylvania Society of Colonial Dames, 1926–1928).

Parsons, Wilfrid, S.J., *Early Catholic Americana* (New York: Macmillan, 1939).

Ritter, F. L., *Music America* (New York: Scribner, 1890).

Silva, Owen da, *Mission Music of California* (Los Angeles: W. F. Lewis, 1941).

Singenberger, John B., *Guide to Catholic Church Music* (St. Francis, Wis., 1905). Supplement, 1911.

*Souvenir und Addressbuch des Lehrers Seminar* (Dubuque, Iowa, 1898).

Stratton, F. M., and Tremaine, Grace, *A Bibliography of Canadiana* (Toronto: The Public Library, 1934).

## PERIODICALS

NOTE: There is much material in the two American periodicals of Catholic church music, *The Caecilia* (from 1874) and *The Catholic Choirmaster* (from 1915), which is not cited here, but care must be used in employing these two periodicals since there are inaccuracies. There also is the extinct periodical *Church Music* (from 1905 to 1909, Philadelphia).

*Annual Catalogs,* 1882–1922 (Catholic Normal School of the Holy Family, St. Francis, Wis.).

Campbell, Jane, "Notes on a Few Old Catholic Hymnbooks," *Records of American Catholic Historical Society,* XXXI, 129–143 (1920).

Cross, Michael H., "Catholic Choirs and Choir Music in Philadelphia," *Records of American Catholic Historical Society,* XXVIII, 208–223 (1915).

——— "Catholic Choirs and Choir Music in Philadelphia," *Records of American Catholic Historical Society,* II, 115–126 (1889).

Guisa, Marcelina, "La América Latina: Funiculus Triplex," *Schola Cantorum* (Mexico), VIII, 2–4, 18, 19, 34, 35 (1946).

Henry, Hugh T., "A Philadelphia Choir Book of 1787," *Records of American Catholic Historical Society,* XXVIII, 208–227 (1915); reprinted in *The Catholic Choirmaster,* XXV, 107–116 (1939).

——— "Philadelphia Choir Books of 1791 and 1814," *Records of American Catholic Historical Society,* XXVIII, 311–327 (1915).

Higginson, J. Vincent, "The American Caecilia Society," *The Catholic Choirmaster,* XXVIII, 107–109 (1942).

——— "History of the Society of St. Gregory," *The Catholic Choirmaster,* XXVI, 57–59 and 160–163 (1940).

——— "Professor John B. Singenberger," *The Catholic Choirmaster,* XXVII, 101–104 (1941).

Joan of Arc, Sister M., C.D.P., "Mission Music of the Southwest," *The Catholic Choirmaster,* XXVI, 102–104 (1940).

King, Percy, "Some Early Catholic Hymnals," *The Caecilia,* LXVI, 61–64 (1939).

McGill, Anna B., "Old Mission Music," *The Musical Quarterly,* XXIV, 186–193 (1938).

Metcalf, Frank J., "History of Sacred Music in the District of Columbia," *Records of the Catholic Historical Society,* XXVIII, 175–202 (1925).

Montani, Nicola A., "Early Church Music in America," *The Catholic Choirmaster,* XIV, 7–11 (1928).

Nemmers, Erwin E., "American Church Music Pathfinder—Rev. L. A. Dobbelsteen, O.Praem., Biography and Critique," *The Catholic Choirmaster,* XXXI, 81, 82, 91 (1945).

——— "Michael L. Nemmers," *The Catholic Choirmaster,* XXVIII, 112, 139 (1942).

——— "History of American Catholic Church Music," *The Catholic Choirmaster,* XXXII, 6–9, 43, 44, 46, 54–56, 88, 133–135, 138 (1946).

——— "Rev. M. J. Vanden Elsen, O.Praem." *The Catholic Choirmaster,* XXXIII, 129, 130 (1947).

Redway, Virginia L., "The Carrs, American Music Publishers," *The Musical Quarterly,* XVIII, 150–177 (1932).

Reuss, Francis X., "Sketch of the Life of Professor William Augustine Newland, Last of the Old-Time Philadelphia Organists," *Records of American Catholic Historical Society,* XIII, 285–324 (1902).

Schuster, George, "John Singenberger and the Caecilia Society" (unpublished A.M. thesis, St. Francis Major Seminary, St. Francis, Wis.).

Schuster, Valery P., "The Catholic Normal School of the Holy Family and Pio Nono College" (unpublished A.M. thesis, St. Francis Major Seminary, St. Francis, Wis.).

Shaver, Lillie T., "Spanish Mission Music," *Papers and Proceedings of the Music Teachers National Association,* XL (1919).

Vallejo, Fernando, *Musica y Musicos Portorriquenos* (S. Juan, Puerto Rico: Cantero Fenandiz y Cia, 1915).

Weller, Philip, "Early Church Music in the United States," *The Caecilia,* LXVI, 297–304 (1939) reprinted from *Liturgical Arts* (1938).

# APPENDIX I

## *GLOSSARY OF CERTAIN TERMS PECULIAR TO CHURCH MUSIC AND DEFINED IN THE TEXT*

(REPEATED HERE FOR CONVENIENCE)

*Antiphon* – originally a form involving the singing by two or more choirs of a recurring verse alternately with successively varying verses. Cf. *Responsory*.

*Antiphonale* – in early church music used to describe the book containing all the chants; in modern times used to describe the book containing the Office, as distinguished from the *Graduale* containing the Mass.

*Authentic and plagal modes* – descriptive of the ecclesiastical modes. The authentic mode began as melodies concentrated within a span of five notes. The plagal modes extended the range. Each plagal mode has a related authentic mode with the same final tone but the two have different dominant notes. One plagal mode is distinguished from another by having its half tones differently located and by having different dominant and final tones.

*Basso continuo* – a system in which the upper voices are indicated simply by figures above the bass voice which is written out in full.

*Canon and fugue* – the principal art form of the polyphonic school; strict imitation in several voices of a subject (antecedent) by its answer (consequent). The fugue is distinguished from the canon in its greater freedom and development based on the material of the theme.

*Canon cancrizanz* – the "crab" canon; an eccentricity in which the music is read backward.

*Canon oenigmaticus* – the "ænigma" canon; an eccentricity in which the title or some other reference indicates the method of performance.

*Cantilena* – essentially a secular form but transferred to the Church. Distinguished as a flowing melody; used in a generic sense as a "tuneful" song.

*Cantus firmus* – the leading voice or principal voice in polyphonic music; also used to identify the "subject" of a canon or fugue.

*Chant, plain* – applied to that monody peculiar to the Church and written in the ecclesiastical modes. Four principal types of chant are distinguished in the Western Church: Gregorian, Ambrosian, Gallican, and Mozarabic.

*Cheironomy* – the use of the hand by the director to indicate visually the flow of the melody.

*Chorale* – a form in modern music peculiar to Protestant churches but also descriptive of Catholic *organ* music. The form is based on chords supplied to a strophic melody and is hymnlike.

*Conductus* – a polyphonic form in earliest times merely descriptive of singing in processions; as a musical form all the voices usually move in the same rhythm to a metrical text and the *same* text is sung by *all* the voices (the latter quality distinguished it from a *motetus*).

*Counterpoint* – the science of setting one melody against another. Distinguished from harmony (modern music) in that counterpoint directs its attention to the horizontal flow of one voice against another, whereas harmony is concerned with chords (notes sounded simultaneously).

*Cursus* – a metrical scheme employed principally at cadences; transferred from poetry to an application in melody; found only in chant.

*Discant* – the earliest form of polyphony (together with *organum*); distinguished from *organum* in that *organum* does not employ measured (repeated) meter whereas discant employs a repeated rhythmic pattern.

*Dominant* – used in two senses: (1) in chant the note about which the melody weaves; and (2) in modern music the chord built on the fifth tone of the scale.

*Double counterpoint* – the interchange (upon repetition) of a theme in a higher voice with a simultaneous theme in a lower voice.

*Ecphonesis* – the earliest melodic figures used to break up reciting tones.

*Faux bourdon* – a polyphonic form in which the music for three voices was *written* with each voice a third from the other two, but *sung* with the bass (lowest) voice an octave above the way it was written, with the result that the harmony was a series of 6–3 chords; in modern times the term means a harmonized reciting tone with chord changes at the cadences.

*Flexa* – in psalmody, the melodic figure at the middle of both halves of the verse.

*Fugue and Canon* – see Canon and fugue, above.

*Graduale* – the term is used in two senses: (1) to refer to the part of the *Proprium* of the Mass which follows the Epistle and precedes the Gospel, and (2) to distinguish the book of chants for the Mass from the book of chants for the Office (the latter is the *Antiphonale*).

*Ground Bass* – the continuous repetition in the bass voice of a short melodic figure while the upper voices proceed on a different path.

*Gymel* – two-part writing usually at the interval of a third between voices.

*Harmony* – the science of setting accompanying voices to a principal voice. Distinguished from counterpoint (polyphonic music) in that harmony proceeds in chords whereas counterpoint directs the attention to the flow of one voice against another.

*Hoquetus* – an eccentricity in which each voice is alternately silent while the other one sings.

*Isorhythmic* – the repetition of the rhythmic pattern of an entire section of music but with the melody different.

*Jubilus* – an extended melodic figure on a single vowel.

*Leisen* – the early German hymn form which developed from the popular practice of interjected *eleison* with words in the vernacular during processions.

*Mediatio* – in psalmody, the melodic figure at the middle of a verse.

*Melisma* – a chant term to describe elaborate melodies, i.e., many notes sung to each vowel.

*Mensural Music* – music divided into "bars," i.e., following a set rhythmical pattern with arsis and thesis recurring regularly.

*Mode* – two meanings: (1) the ecclesiastical modes which are scales whose character is determined by the location of the half tones and of the tone about which the melody weaves (the dominant) and on which the melody ends (the final); (2) the rhythmic modes which are patterns of rhythm built up before the time when music employed "bars" and "measures."

*Modern music* — the term used in this book to distinguish the third type of music — that based on harmony — from the preceding two types: (1) the chant and (2) polyphony.

*Modulation* — in medieval times shifting from one mode to another in the same composition; in modern times, shifting from one key to another in the same composition.

*Monody* — a single voice (without accompaniment), the generic term used to distinguish chant from polyphony.

*Motetus* — an early polyphonic form in which (1) the several voices sang different texts, and (2) the leading voice sang a melody usually borrowed from some of the well-known tunes and frequently from the chant.

*Musica ficta* (or *falsa*) — the early form of chromatics (the use of a scale composed entirely of half tones); the earliest introduction of "sharps" and "flats" into music.

*Musica mensurata* — the earliest form of music employing *regular* rhythm (i.e., repeated rhythmic patterns).

*Neum* — term used to describe chant notation; the notes singly or combined (ligatures) into groups are called neums.

*Ordinarium* — that part of the Mass text which does not change from day to day as opposed to the *Proprium* of the Mass which varies according to the ecclesiastical feast. The *Ordinarium* consists (for musical purposes) of the *Kyrie, Gloria, Credo, Sanctus, Benedictus,* and *Agnus Dei.*

*Organum* — the earliest form of polyphony with one voice at an interval of a fourth or a fifth from the other voice. Distinguished from discant in that *organum* does not employ different rhythm in each of the two voices.

*Plagal mode* — see Authentic and plagal modes.

*Polyphony* — term used in this book to distinguish the second type of music — that based on counterpoint — from its predecessor, the chant, and its successor, modern music.

*Proprium* — that part of the Mass text which changes from day to day as opposed to the *Ordinarium* which remains constant. The *Proprium* consists of the *Introitus, Graduale, Alleluia, Tractus, Sequentia, Offertorium,* and *Communio.*

*Psalmody* — generic term describing music in the style of the psalm tone.

*Psalm Tone* — the chant form in which the music consists of an opening melodic figure, a reciting tone, a middle cadence figure, another reciting tone and a final cadence figure.

*Responsory* – a form involving the singing of alternate verses by a soloist and a choir. *Cf. Antiphon.*

*Sequence* – a melodic pattern in which a figure is repeated usually beginning on a different tone each time.

*Sequentia* – part of the *Proprium* of the Mass.

*Solmization* – system revived by Guido D'Arezzo in the twelfth century whereby the different tones of the hexachordal system are assigned syllables (*do, re, mi, fa, sol, la, ti, do* although originally there were only six syllables, *ut, re, mi, fa, sol, la*).

*Sonata* – in church music a form of organ composition borrowed from the piano. The form involves a harmonized principal theme and a contrasting subordinate theme. Usually there are three or four sections related to each other by the keys used.

*Stretto* – a device developed for the fugue in which the repetitions of the subject overlap (i.e., are telescoped).

*Syncopation* – a device introduced in polyphonic music but usually associated with modern music in which the accent of the rhythm is placed at a point where it would not normally occur.

*Terminatio* – in psalmody, the melodic figure at the end of a verse.

*Tetrachord* – the Greek system of treating four tones as a unit. The four tones could have a half tone between steps 1–2, 2–3, and 3–4 (the other intervals being whole tones), yielding respectively the Dorian, Phrygian, and Lydian tetrachords.

*Tonalia* – medieval books containing chant melodies grouped by modes.

*Tonus in directum* – the psalm tone beginning immediately on the dominant without a melodic figure.

*Tonus peregrinus* – in psalmody, the only psalm tone which changes dominants (at the *mediatio*).

*Triplum* – the term applied to voices above the *cantus firmus* (leading voice) of a *motetus.*

*Trope* – the interspersion of miscellaneous texts in an elaborate melody to cause more syllables to be sung to the melody (thus the number of notes per syllable was greatly reduced).

*Vox organalis* – the accompanying voice in *organum* or *discant.*

*Vox principalis* – the leading voice in *organum* or *discant.*

An extensive glossary of terms will be found in Hughes, Anselm, *Liturgical Terms for Music Students* (Boston: McLaughlin & Reilly, 1940).

# APPENDIX II

## *BIBLIOGRAPHY OF BIBLIOGRAPHIES*


Baumker, Wilhelm, *Das Katholische Deutsche Kirchenlied* (Freiburg: Herder, 1883–1891), 4 vols. Bibliographies in Vol. I at pp. 40–124; Vol. II at pp. 20–43; Vol. III at pp. 19–118; and Vol. IV at pp. 16–287.

Casimiri, Raffaele C., *Cantantibus Organis, Raccolta di Scritti per la Cultura della "Scholae Cantorum"* (Rome: Edizione del Psalterium, 1924). Bibliography at pp. 499–536.

Plainsong and Mediaeval Music Society of London, *Catalog of The Society's Library* (Nashdom Abbey: Burnham, Bucks, 1928), 39 pp.

Sunol, Gregorio Maria, *Introduction á la Paléographie Musicale Gregorienne* (Paris: Desclee, 1935). Bibliography at pp. 511–565.

Reese, Gustave, *Music in the Middle Ages* (New York: Norton, 1940). Bibliographies at pp. 425–464.

Weissenbach, Andreas, *Sacra Musica* (Vienna: Augustinus-Druckerei, 1937).

# APPENDIX III

## *LEADING CATHOLIC CHURCH MUSIC PERIODICALS*

### AMERICAN

*The Catholic Choirmaster* (Official Bulletin of Society of St. Gregory of America), from 1915, New York, N. Y.

*The Caecilia,* from 1874 (J. Fischer & Bro.), Dayton, Ohio; from 1875 (J. Fischer & Bro.), New York; from 1877 (Pustet), New York; from 1885 (J. Singenberger), St. Francis, Wis.; from 1925 (O. Singenberger), Mundelein, Ill.; from 1930 (McLaughlin & Reilly), Boston; from 1944 (McLaughlin & Reilly), St. Louis, Mo.

*Church Music,* from Dec., 1905, Philadelphia, Pa. Discontinued 1909.

*The White List* (official publication of Society of St. Gregory of America), 1 ed., 1928; 2 ed., 1932; 3 ed., 1939; 4 ed., 1947.

### MEXICAN

*Schola Cantorum,* from 1938, Morelia.

### GERMAN, AUSTRIAN, AND SWISS

*Caecilienkalendar,* from 1876, Regensburg; combined with *Kirchenmusikalisches Jahrbuch,* 1886.

*Caecilienvereins-organ,* from 1866, Regensburg.

*Der Alpenländische Kirchenchor,* from 1947, Innsbruck.

*Der Chorwächter,* from 1886, Einsiedeln.

*Der Kirchensänger,* from 1877, Freiburg; from 1910, Beuron.

*Die Kirchenmusik,* from 1938, Düsseldorf.

*Gregorianische Rundschau,* from 1902, Graz, Styria; combined with *Musica Divina,* 1913.

*Gregoriusblatt* (and its supplement *Gregoriusbote*), from 1876, Düsseldorf.

*Kirchenmusikalisches Jahrbuch,* from 1886, Regensburg. No volumes 1912 to 1929.

*Kirchenmusikalische Vierteljahrsschrift,* from 1866 to 1905, Salzburg.
*Liturgie und Kirchenmusik,* from 1929, Dülmen.
*Musica Divina,* from 1913, Vienna, Austria; combined with *Die Kirchenmusik* in 1938.
*Musica Sacra,* from 1877 to 1896, Berlin.
*Musica Sacra,* from 1868, Regensburg; combined with *Caecilienvereins-organ,* 1928.

### FRENCH

*La Petit Maitrise,* Paris.
*Musica Sacra,* from 1874 to 1883, Toulouse.
*Revue du Chant Gregorien,* from 1892, Grenoble.
*Revue Gregorienne,* from 1911, Tournai, Belgium.
*Revue Liturgique et Musicale,* from 1917, Lille.
*Tribune de Saint Gervais* (Organ of Schola Cantorum), from 1895 to 1922, Paris.

### ITALIAN

*Bolletino Ceciliano* (Official Bulletin of St. Cecilia Society), from 1905, Rome.
*Musica Sacra,* from 1874, Milan.
*Rassegna Gregoriana,* from 1911, Rome.
*Santa Cecilia* (Official Bulletin of National Society of St. Cecilia), from 1898, Turin.

### DUTCH

*St. Gregorius Blad* (Official Organ of Dutch Society of St. Gregory), from 1875, Tilburg.

### BELGIAN

*Musica Sacra* (Official Organ of Society of St. Gregory of Belgium), from 1881, Brussels (interrupted 1914–1927).

### ENGLISH

*Liturgy,* formerly *Music and Liturgy.* (Official Bulletin of Society of St. Gregory of Great Britain and Ireland), from 1930, London.

### CZECHOSLOVAKIAN

*Cyril* (Official Bulletin of St. Cyril Society of Czechoslovakia), from 1873, Prague.

HUNGARIAN

*Magyar Körnes,* from 1931, Budapest.

JUGOSLAVIAN

*Sveta Cecilija,* from 1906, Zagreb.

SPANISH

*Espana Sacro Musical,* from 1930, Barcelona.
*Musica Sacra Hispana,* from 1908 to 1923, Bilbao.
*Revista Parroqual de Musica Sagrada,* from 1924, Barcelona.
*Tesoro Sacro Musical,* from 1930, Madrid.

POLISH

*Hosanna,* from 1925, Warsaw.
*Musyka Koscielna,* from 1925, Poznan.

# APPENDIX IV

## *MOTU PROPRIO OF POPE PIUS X ON SACRED MUSIC*

(NOVEMBER 22, 1903)

AMONG the cares of the pastoral office, not only of this Supreme Chair, which We, though unworthy, occupy through the inscrutable disposition of Providence, but of every local church, a leading one is without question that of maintaining and promoting the decorum of the House of God in which the august mysteries of religion are celebrated, and where the Christian people assemble to receive the grace of the Sacraments, to assist at the Holy Sacrifice of the Altar, to adore the most august Sacrament of the Lord's Body and to unite in the common prayer of the Church in the public and solemn liturgical offices. Nothing should have place, therefore, in the temple calculated to disturb or even merely to diminish the piety and devotion of the faithful, nothing that may give reasonable cause for disgust or scandal, nothing, above all, which directly offends the decorum and sanctity of the sacred functions and is thus unworthy of the House of Prayer and of the Majesty of God. We do not touch separately on the abuses in this matter which may arise. Today Our attention is directed to one of the most common of them, one of the most difficult to eradicate, and the existence of which is sometimes to be deplored in places where everything else is deserving of the highest praise – the beauty and sumptuousness of the temple, the splendour and the accurate performance of the ceremonies, the attendance of the clergy, the gravity and piety of the officiating ministers. Such is the abuse affecting sacred chant and music. And indeed, whether it is owing to the very nature of this art, fluctuating and variable as it is in itself, or to the succeeding changes in tastes and habits with the course of time, or to the fatal influence exercised on sacred art by profane and theatrical art, or to the pleasure that music directly produces, and that is not always easily contained within the right limits, or finally to the many prejudices on the matter, so lightly introduced and so tenaciously maintained even among responsible and pious persons, the fact remains that there is a general tendency to deviate from the right rule, prescribed by the end for which art is admitted to the service of public worship and which is set forth very clearly in the ecclesiastical Canons, in the Ordinances of the General and Provincial Councils, in the prescriptions which have at various times emanated from the Sacred Roman Congregations, and from Our Predecessors the Sovereign Pontiffs.

It is with real satisfaction that We acknowledge the large amount of good that has been effected in this respect during the last decade in this Our fostering city of Rome, and in many churches in Our country, but in a more especial way among some nations in which illustrious men, full of zeal for the worship of God, have, with the approval of the Holy See and under the direction of the Bishops, united in flourishing Societies and restored sacred music to the fullest honour in all their churches and chapels. Still the good work that has been done is very far indeed from being common to all, and when We consult Our own personal experience and take into account the great number of complaints that have reached Us during the short time that has elapsed since it pleased the Lord to elevate Our humility to the supreme summit of the Roman Pontificate, We consider it Our first duty, without further delay, to raise Our voice at once in reproof and condemnation of all that is seen to be out of harmony with the right rule above indicated, in the functions of public worship and in the performance of the ecclesiastical offices. Filled as We are with a most ardent desire to see the true Christian spirit flourish in every respect and be preserved by all the faithful, We deem it necessary to provide before aught else for the sanctity and dignity of the temple, in which the faithful assemble for no other object than that of acquiring this spirit from its foremost and indispensable fount, which is the active participation in the most holy mysteries and in the public and solemn prayer of the Church. And it is vain to hope that the blessing of heaven will descend abundantly upon us, when our homage to the Most High, instead of ascending in the odor of sweetness, puts into the hand of the Lord the scourges wherewith of old the Divine Redeemer drove the unworthy profaners from the Temple.

Hence, in order that no one for the future may be able to plead in excuse that he did not clearly understand his duty and that all vagueness may be eliminated from the interpretation of matters which have already been commanded, We have deemed it expedient to point out briefly the principles regulating sacred music in the functions of public worship, and to gather together in a general survey the principal prescriptions of the Church against the more common abuses in this subject. We do therefore publish, *motu proprio* and with certain knowledge, Our present *Instruction* to which, as to a *juridical code of sacred music* (*quasi a codice giuridice della musica sacra*), We will with the fullness of Our Apostolic Authority that the force of law be given, and We do by Our present handwriting impose its scrupulous observance on all.

## INSTRUCTION ON SACRED MUSIC

### I

### *General Principles*

§ 1. Sacred music, being a complimentary part of the solemn liturgy, participates in the general scope of the liturgy, which is the glory of God and the sanctification and edification of the faithful. It contributes to the decorum and the splendor of the ecclesiastical ceremonies, and since its principal office is to clothe with suitable melody the liturgical text proposed for the understanding of the faithful, its proper aim is to add greater efficacy to the text, in order that through it the faithful may be the more easily moved to devotion and better disposed for the reception of the fruits of grace belonging to the celebration of the most holy mysteries.

§ 2. Sacred music should consequently possess, in the highest degree, the qualities proper to the liturgy, and in particular *sanctity* and *goodness of form,* which will spontaneously produce the final quality of *universality.*

It must be *holy,* and must, therefore, exclude all profanity not only in itself, but in the manner in which it is presented by those who execute it.

It must be *true art,* for otherwise it will be impossible for it to exercise on the minds of those who listen to it that efficacy which the Church aims at obtaining in admitting into her liturgy the art of musical sounds.

But it must, at the same time, be *universal* in the sense that while every nation is permitted to admit into its ecclesiastical compositions those special forms which may be said to constitute its native music, still these forms must be subordinated in such a manner to the general characteristics of sacred music that nobody of any nation may receive an impression other than good on hearing them.

## II

### *The Different Kinds of Sacred Music*

§ 3. These qualities are to be found, in the highest degree, in Gregorian Chant, which is, consequently, the Chant proper to the Roman Church, the only chant she has inherited from the ancient fathers, which she has jealously guarded for centuries in her liturgical codices, which she directly proposes to the faithful as her own, which she prescribes exclusively for some parts of the liturgy, and which the most recent studies have so happily restored to their integrity and purity.

On these grounds Gregorian Chant has always been regarded as the supreme model for sacred music, so that it is fully legitimate to lay down the following rule: *the more closely a composition for church approaches in its movement, inspiration and savor the Gregorian form, the more sacred and liturgical it becomes; and the more out of harmony it is with that supreme model, the less worthy it is of the temple.*

The ancient traditional Gregorian Chant must, therefore, in a large measure be restored to the functions of public worship, and the fact must be accepted by all that an ecclesiastical function loses none of its solemnity when accompanied by this music alone.

Special efforts are to be made to restore the use of the Gregorian Chant by the people, so that the faithful may again take a more active part in the ecclesiastical offices, as was the case in ancient times.

§ 4. The above-mentioned qualities are also possessed in an excellent degree by Classic Polyphony, especially of the Roman School, which reached its greatest perfection in the fifteenth century, owing to the works of Pierluigi da Palestrina, and continued subsequently to produce compositions of excellent quality from a liturgical and musical standpoint. Classic Polyphony agrees admirably with Gregorian Chant, the supreme model of all sacred music, and hence it has been found worthy of a place side by side with Gregorian Chant, in the more solemn functions of the Church, such as those of the Pontifical Chapel. This, too, must therefore be restored largely in ecclesiastical functions, especially in the more important basilicas, in cathedrals, and in the churches and chapels of seminaries and other ecclesiastical institutions in which the necessary means are usually not lacking.

§ 5. The Church has always recognized and favored the progress of the arts, admitting to the service of religion everything good and beautiful discovered by genius in the course of ages — always, however, with due regard to the liturgical laws. Consequently modern music is also admitted to the Church, since it, too, furnishes compositions of such excellence, sobriety and gravity, that they are in no way unworthy of the liturgical functions.

Still, since modern music has risen mainly to serve profane uses, greater care must be taken with regard to it, in order that the musical compositions of modern style which are admitted in the Church may contain nothing profane, be free from reminiscences of motifs adopted in the theatres, and be not fashioned even in their external forms after the manner of profane pieces.

§ 6. Among the different kinds of modern music, that which appears less suitable for accompanying the functions of public worship is the theatrical style, which was in the greatest vogue, especially in Italy, during the last century. This of its very nature is diametrically opposed to Gregorian Chant and classic polyphony, and therefore to the most important law of all good sacred music. Besides the intrinsic structure, the rhythm and what is known as the *conventionalism* of this style adapt themselves but badly to the requirements of true liturgical music.

## III

### *The Liturgical Text*

§ 7. The language proper to the Roman Church is Latin. Hence it is forbidden to sing anything whatever in the vernacular in solemn liturgical functions — much more to sing in the vernacular the variable or common parts of the Mass and Office.

§ 8. As the texts that may be rendered in music, and the

order in which they are to be rendered, are determined for every liturgical function, it is not lawful to confuse this order or to change the prescribed texts for others selected at will, or to omit them either entirely or even in part, unless when the rubrics allow that some versicles of the text be supplied with the organ, while these versicles are simply recited in the choir. However, it is permissible, according to the custom of the Roman Church, to sing a motet to the Blessed Sacrament after the *Benedictus* in a Solemn Mass. It is also permitted, after the Offertory prescribed for the Mass has been sung, to execute during the time that remains a brief motet to words approved by the Church.

§ 9. The liturgical text must be sung as it is in the books, without alteration or inversion of the words, without undue repetition, without breaking syllables, and always in a manner intelligible to the faithful who listen.

## IV

### *External Form of the Sacred Compositions*

§ 10. The different parts of the Mass and the Office must retain, even musically, that particular concept and form which ecclesiastical tradition has assigned to them, and which is admirably brought out by Gregorian Chant. The method of composing an *introit,* a *gradual,* an *antiphon,* a *psalm,* a *hymn,* a *Gloria in excelsis, etc.,* must therefore be distinct from one another.

§ 11. In particular the following rules are to be observed:

*a*) The *Kyrie, Gloria, Credo,* etc., of the Mass must preserve the unity of composition proper to their text. It is not lawful, therefore, to compose them in separate movements, in such a way that each of these movements form a complete composition in itself, and be capable of being detached from the rest and substituted by another.

*b*) In the office of Vespers it should be the rule to follow the *Caeremoniale Episcoporum,* which prescribes Gregorian Chant for the psalmody and permits figured music for the versicles of the *Gloria Patri* and the hymn.

It will nevertheless be lawful on greater solemnities to alternate the Gregorian Chant of the choir with the so-called *falsibordoni* or with verses similarly composed in a proper manner.

It is also permissible occasionally to render single psalms in their entirety in music, provided the form proper to psalmody be preserved in such compositions; that is to say, provided the singers seem to be psalmodising among themselves, either with new motifs or with those taken from Gregorian Chant or based upon it.

The psalms known as *di concerto* are therefore forever excluded and prohibited.

*c*) In the hymns of the Church the traditional form of the hymn is preserved. It is not lawful, therefore, to compose, for instance, a *Tantum ergo* in such wise that the first strophe presents a romanza, a cavatina, an adagio and the *Genitori* an allegro.

*d*) The antiphons of the Vespers must be as a rule rendered with the Gregorian melody proper to each. Should they, however, in some special case be sung in figured music, they must never have either the form of a concert melody or the fullness of a motet or a cantata.

## V

### *The Singers*

§ 12. With the exception of the melodies proper to the celebrant at the altar and the ministers, which must be always sung in Gregorian Chant, and without accompaniment of the organ, all the rest of the liturgical chant belongs to the choir of levites, and, therefore, singers in church, even when they are laymen, are really taking the place of the ecclesiastical choir. Hence the music rendered by them must, at least for the greater part, retain the character of choral music.

By this it is not to be understood that solos are entirely excluded. But solo singing should never predominate to such an extent as to have the greater part of the liturgical chant executed in that manner; the solo phrase should have the character or hint of a melodic projection (*spunto*), and be strictly bound up with the rest of the choral composition.

§ 13. On the same principle it follows that singers in church have a real liturgical office, and that therefore women, being incapable of exercising such office, cannot be admitted to form part of the choir. Whenever, then, it is desired to employ the acute voices of sopranos and contraltos, these parts must be taken by boys, according to the most ancient usage of the Church.

§ 14. Finally, only men of known piety and probity of life are to be admitted to form part of the choir of a church, and these men should by their modest and devout bearing during the liturgical functions show that they are worthy of the holy office they exercise. It will also be fitting that singers while singing in church wear the ecclesiastical habit and surplice, and that they be hidden behind gratings when the choir is excessively open to the public gaze.

## VI

### *Organ and Instruments*

§ 15. Although the music proper to the Church is purely vocal music, music with the accompaniment of the organ is also permitted. In some special cases, within due limits and with proper safeguards, other instruments may be allowed, but never without the special permission of the Ordinary, according to prescriptions of the *Caeremoniale Episcoporum.*

§ 16. As the singing should always have the principal place, the organ or other instrument should merely sustain and never oppress it.

§ 17. It is not permitted to have the chant preceded by long preludes or to interrupt it with intermezzo pieces.

§ 18. The sound of the organ as an accompaniment to the chant in preludes, interludes, and the like must be not only governed by the special nature of the instrument, but must participate in all the qualities proper to sacred music as above enumerated.

§ 19. The employment of the piano is forbidden in church, as is also that of noisy or frivolous instruments such as drums, cymbals, bells and the like.

§ 20. It is strictly forbidden to have bands play in church, and only in special cases with the consent of the Ordinary will it be permissible to admit wind instruments, limited in number, judiciously used, and proportioned to the size of the place — provided the composition and accompaniment be written in grave and suitable style, and conform in all respects to that proper to the organ.

§ 21. In processions outside the church the Ordinary may give permission for a band, provided no profane pieces be executed. It would be desirable in such cases that the band confine itself to accompanying some spiritual canticle sung in Latin or in the vernacular by the singers and the pious associations which take part in the procession.

## VII

### *The Length of the Liturgical Chant*

§ 22. It is not lawful to keep the priest at the altar waiting on account of the chant or the music for a length of time not allowed by the liturgy. According to the ecclesiastical prescriptions the *Sanctus* of the Mass should be over before the elevation, and therefore the priest must here have regard for the singers. The *Gloria* and the *Credo* ought, according to the Gregorian tradition, to be relatively short.

§ 23. In general it must be considered a very grave abuse when the liturgy in ecclesiastical functions is made to appear secondary to and in a manner at the service of the music, for the music is merely a part of the liturgy and its humble handmaid.

## VIII

### *Principal Means*

§ 24. For the exact execution of what has been herein laid down, the Bishops, if they have not already done so, are to institute in their dioceses a special Commission composed of persons really competent in sacred music, and to this Commission let them entrust in the manner they find most suitable the task of watching over the music executed in their churches. Nor are they to see merely that the music is good in itself, but also that it is adapted to the powers of the singers and be always well executed.

§ 25. In seminaries of clerics and in ecclesiastical institutions let the above-mentioned traditional Gregorian Chant be cultivated by all with diligence and love, according to the Tridentine prescriptions, and let the superiors be liberal of encouragement and praise toward their young subjects. In like manner let a Schola Cantorum be established, whenever possible, among the clerics for the execution of sacred polyphony and of good liturgical music.

§ 26. In the ordinary lessons of Liturgy, Morals, Canon Law

given to the students of theology, let care be taken to touch on those points which regard more directly the principles and laws of sacred music, and let an attempt be made to complete the doctrine with some particular instruction in the aesthetic side of sacred art, so that the clerics may not leave the seminary ignorant of all those subjects so necessary to a full ecclesiastical education.

§ 27. Let care be taken to restore, at least in the principal churches, the ancient *Scholae Cantorum,* as has been done with excellent fruit in a great many places. It is not difficult for a zealous clergy to institute such *Scholae* even in smaller churches and country parishes — nay, in these last the pastors will find a very easy means of gathering around them both children and adults, to their own profit and the edification of the people.

§ 28. Let efforts be made to support and promote, in the best way possible, the higher schools of sacred music where these already exist, and to help in founding them where they do not. It is of the utmost importance that the Church herself provide for the instruction of her choirmasters, organists, and singers, according to the true principles of sacred art.

## IX

### *Conclusion*

§ 29. Finally, it is recommended to choirmasters, singers, members of the clergy, superiors of seminaries, ecclesiastical institutions, and religious communities, parish priests and rectors of churches, canons of collegiate churches, and cathedrals, and, above all, to the diocesan ordinaries to favor with all zeal these prudent reforms, long desired and demanded with united voice by all; so that the authority of the Church, which herself has repeatedly proposed them, and now inculcates them, may not fall into contempt.

Given from Our Apostolic Palace at the Vatican, on day of the Virgin and Martyr, St. Cecilia, November 22, 1903, in the first year of Our Pontificate. PIUS X, POPE

# INDEX

## INDEX